W9-CHP-115

About Our Kits

The SafeBox Contents
You might have purchased our remarkable product—the SafeBox. It comes completely packaged with information and test equipment to help you prevent your children from trying drugs or to test them to find out if they have been experimenting. We use a variety of different test devices, but the most common are the integrated DrugCheck® (included in the SafeBox), E-Z split cup, and the all-in-one Redicup. Other devices are available, but we find these three types to yield the most comprehensive results.

Our Most Popular Items
Substance Abuse Family Education Book
    "Drugs and Your Teen"

DrugCheck 10-Panel Test Kit
    Please refer to page nos. 208 – 211

Alcohol Swab Test Kit
    Please refer to page nos. xxi – 1

Unity Oath
    Included in the "Drugs and Your Teen" book
    Please refer to page no. 305

One of Our Ten-Panel Drug-Test Kits
Our Ten-Panel drug-test cup is accompanied by an alcohol swab that allows you to detect ten different drugs and alcohol.

This test cup will screen for the following drugs (all our cups are FDA approved and over 99 percent accurate):

Amphetamines	Barbiturates
Benzodiazepines	Cocaine
Marijuana	Oxycodone (Percocet, Percodan, Vicodin)
Methamphetamines	Methadone
PCP	Opiates (heroin, codeine, morphine)

consultants—the information we give you includes good advice on how to cope as well as some useful tools for fighting the problem.

In this book you will find what you need to know about drugs, how to test for them, how to read the test results, and how to get help. At the back is a wealth of reference charts. We even provide a response card, so you can give us feedback on our product and share any stories you may have—which, with your permission, might be a part of our next book on drugs. If, after reading this manual, you have suggestions on items you think we should add or delete, please fill out the Reader Response Card in the back of the book and mail it to us. We're eager to read your feedback. Please refer to the glossary for any unfamiliar words.

About This Book

Substance usage is a major issue and has many angles, from experimentation to severe drug and alcohol abuse, as well as the misuse of prescription medications and inhalants. We realize we could only hit some of the major points with this book. We want you to understand the problem is not hopeless—many drug users and abusers have learned how to control their habits and have gone on to live normal lives. The secret is discovering the problem early enough to stop it while it is still manageable.

This book is a unique and rare product and, coupled with our drug and alcohol instant-test kits, is unlike anything currently available. We provide a self-contained item that offers everything you need to learn about your children's relationships with peers and others who may have a negative influence on them. Along with this book, we offer instant-result kits, which will tell you if your children are doing drugs and then will help guide you through the process of treating the condition. Although we have tried packing all the vital information possible on drugs and alcohol into this book, please know there is much more information out there, and no one source can provide it all. What we've tried to do here is key in on the subject matter most helpful in dealing with the drug issues facing you and your family.

This book is meant solely for parents. In your hands lies the power to keep your children safe and healthy: mentally, physically, emotionally, and spiritually. We want to connect with you and relate to you what we have experienced, what we know to be true, and what we hope to help you avoid. With this in mind we created this book, covering components of alcohol and/or drug abuse. We define terms, we lay out problems for you, and we explain how drugs can ruin not only our children's lives, but our communities, our society, and our country as well. We give you facts and stats. We tell you what to look for—signs and symptoms. We describe the drugs of abuse in detail and attempt to give you a look into how they affect your children's bodies and brains. We provide methods for you to protect your children.

Culled from years of experience—from experts in drug treatment, speaking engagements, endless hours of research, and our time as in-the-field drug-test

Welcome

Congratulations on taking the first step in helping your children cope with the issue of drug and alcohol use and abuse by investing in our book. This book will give you direction in determining if your child is experimenting with or seriously indulging in illicit drug usage—and, yes, alcohol is a drug.

Many parents today either deny a drug/alcohol problem exists or refuse to test their children, for fear they will think they don't trust them. However, addiction worsens if the wheels of motion don't grind to an immediate halt and if parents don't live up to their responsibilities to their children. Their children could be walking the streets searching for drugs—or worse. So, thank you, dear parents, for taking on the bold and much-needed obligation of overseeing your children.

We hear parents say, "I can't test my children. They'll think I don't trust them." The truth is that they'll get over feelings of mistrust—but they won't get over addiction. Rest assured that you are doing the right thing by purchasing this product and that you are being a good, loving parent. If you did nothing, you would be remiss and ultimately responsible for your children's addiction, as well as all the problems that stem from that condition: thievery and other crimes, overdose, personality distortions, poor grades, and much more. And, if your children are minors, you can be held accountable for any crime they commit, even if that crime is an accident. Parents have gone to jail for their children or have paid hefty amounts in compensatory damages to victims. The longer you wait to test your children, the deeper their drug use and abuse could become.

As the authors, we have our own very personal reasons for undertaking this project and wanting to help you. We invite you to read about us and what prompted us to write this book.

Again, we welcome you and praise you for caring so much about your children and our future leaders.

Gianni DeVincenti Hayes, Ph.D.
Michael J. Talley Jr.

Introduction

What It's All About

purpose is to provide you with insight and motivation to make sure they never become *your* children's stories.

I hope you will take the valuable information the authors have provided to heart, because the truth is that, as parents, we are all connected by the world of our children. Every child helped by this book means my own children are that much safer, because their community of peers is safer. I want my children and yours to grow up in a safer, healthier world. They deserve it.

Michael Lotterstein
The Drug Test Consultant

Michael Lotterstein, along with Jerry Lotterstein, are the owners of The Drug Test Consultants (http://www.drugtestconsultants.com), who originated the Parents Package (the architect of the SafeBox). They offer entrepreneurs the opportunity to own a drug-testing company.

Preface

A Letter from Michael Lotterstein,
Founder of The Drug Test Consultant Company

When I became a member of the drug-detection and abuse-prevention industry, I knew an added bonus of my new career would be doing good while making a living. The effects of illicit drug use and trafficking are measured not in the billions, but in the *hundreds* of billions of dollars, and every effort to contain and defeat this epidemic is of benefit to my neighbors, my community, and my nation.

It wasn't until I became a father that the impact of my choice really hit home. These were *my* children I was protecting; the crusade to fight drug abuse began in *my* home. I knew that, like every responsible parent, I owed it to my family to learn everything I could about the enemy we faced and the weapons and tools available to wage the battle.

Helping our children face the issues of drugs and resist the ever-present temptations they present is a daunting challenge for every parent. It means educating ourselves, staying vigilant, and, most importantly, always being "on message" in the ways we communicate with our children.

The authors of this book, Gianni DeVincenti Hayes, Ph.D., and Michael J. Talley Jr., share my commitment to providing the support every parent needs. In these pages, they have given you information on drugs and their effects, drug dealers, signs of abuse, and the means of detecting drug use. More importantly, you will find assistance on how to speak with your children about the issue—a conversation we all find uncomfortable. Knowing how to begin this conversation is the most important step, because open communication with our children is the most powerful weapon we have to protect them. Here you will find vivid, heartbreaking—yet hopeful—stories of the victims of drug abuse; their

Acknowledgments

We owe debts of gratitude to the many people who have assisted us in various ways to make this book happen. We cannot possibly name them all, but of prime importance are:

Michael and Jerry Lotterstein, for their encouragement, and for setting up the model of what a good book on drugs should contain, along with their dedication and spirit in fighting drug and alcohol abuse through their company, The Drug Test Consultant. This serves as the benchmark in drug- and alcohol-testing products and education, and it was the originator of the Parents' Package, a drug prevention kit—our SafeBox.

James R. Hayes, for all his hours spent photocopying, gathering information, critiquing, and making this book a reality. His computer assistance has been immeasurable.

Lisa Fratoni-Talley, for her patience, understanding, and extensive time in proofreading, as well as for her loving support.

Mike Talley's daughter: Melaina Talley, for her input and proofreading skills, as well as her strength of character in dealing with the trials and tribulations of her recovery. She serves as my inspiration in writing this book. Mike Talley's other daughters, Tara and Nichole, for the difficulties and hardships they went through with Melaina, acting as a buffer between her and me, as well as the maturity they showed in dealing with this long road of recovery while still being sisters in every sense of the word. I never would have made it without them.

Contents

Dedication

To our spouses, James R. Hayes and Lisa Fratoni-Talley for their assistance, patience, and understanding throughout all these long months of working on this book.

To our daughters, for their acceptance of our limited time with them while we focused on this book and for their assistance in proofreading and research, but, more importantly, for their inspiration and input.

Thomas Nega Drug Free Lifestyle 7/7/11 Grant 2011

Omni Publishing House
Philadelphia, PA

A subsidiary of Omni Drug Screening, LLC.

Published by OMNI Corporation
Newtown Square, PA 19073

In conjunction with

AuthorHouse™
1663 Liberty Drive
Bloomington, IN 47403
www.authorhouse.com
Phone: 1-800-839-8640

First published by AuthorHouse 2/17/2011

ISBN: 978-1-4520-9846-3 (e)
ISBN: 978-1-4520-9845-6 (sc)
ISBN: 978-1-4520-9844-9 (hc)

Library of Congress Control Number: 2011901802

Printed in the United States of America

This book is printed on acid-free paper.

DRUGS AND YOUR TEEN

All You Need to Know about Drugs to Protect Your Loved Ones

The *Substance Abuse Family Education* Book

Gianni DeVincenti Hayes, Ph.D. and Michael J. Talley Jr.

authorHOUSE®

DRUGS AND YOUR TEEN

I have reviewed Dr. Gianni DeVincenti Hayes, Ph.D. and Michael J. Talley Jr.'s new book, Drugs and Your Teen – All You Need to Know about Drugs to Protect Your Loved Ones. *It's a well organized manual for parents to use while working with their medical and other professionals to help keep their children safe from drug use. It is written in language parents will understand and has sections on the wide variety of questions a parent might face in dealing with this difficult topic. The book covers the background of drug use, detection, drug information, adolescence, the Internet, testing, home issues, and resources*

The authors took a path of writing for a parent who might have specific questions at different stages of parenting and needed to learn about specific concerns quickly and conveniently. They also included reference points, helping direct families to sources of information that are likely to be updated regularly in the future.

One useful feature is the way that the authors wrote the book for three different audiences at seemingly the same time – parents who are working to prevent drug use before it starts, parents who are dealing with a child in the middle of use/abuse, and parents who are trying to intervene at the addiction stage. Information is readily available using the thorough table of contents and the accessible language of the authors. The short topical chapters will be very useful for parents who are pressed for clear information, time to act, and other resources.

This book can serve as a useful reference tool for a parent to use as they work to protect their child from drug use and abuse.

John E. Fredericksen, Ph.D., Superintendent of Schools
Wicomico County Public Schools

The Salisbury Area Chamber of Commerce has done several projects with Gianni DeVincenti Hayes, Ph.D. She has provided excellent, historical accurate depictions of our community in previous joint projects. This latest book uses Dr. Hayes and Mike Talley's expertise in drug testing, and in the programs needed to identify and fight youth drug abuse. Their book will be a great asset to concerned parents.

Bradley A. Bellacicco, Executive Director
Salisbury Area Chamber of Commerce

Detailed information on this follows in chapters 6 and 7. This is a simple test that gives instant results, based on a urine sample.

Information on our Alcohol Swab Kit

Image courtesy of Chematics, Incorporated; N. Webster, IN

Our alcohol test swab has a twelve- to eighteen-month shelf life and will detect the following levels of alcohol in your child's system:

None, 0.02%, 0.04%, 0.08%, 0.30%

This test is fast, convenient, sensitive, and will not give a false positive. Detailed instructions are given in chapter 7. This test is a rapid, highly sensitive, and noninvasive method for determining the level (if any) of alcohol ingestion.

Consider the following chart as an illustration of alcohol usage and age of first use.

Primary Alcohol Admissions Aged 21 or Older, by Age of First Use of Alcohol (by percent)

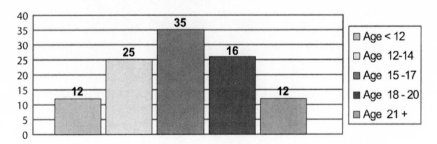

Age of First Use of Alcohol

Chart date taken from 4/2005 DASIS report (Drug and Alcohol Services Information System)

Of the 683,000 primary admissions (those patients admitted for alcohol abuse as the primary diagnosis) aged twenty-one or older in 2002, 88 percent reported their age of first use of alcohol at younger than twenty-one years. One-fourth reported their age of first use of alcohol as between twelve and fourteen years; 12 percent reported their age of first use as younger than twelve; and another 12 percent reported their age of first use as twenty-one or older.

Our products are designed to give you every opportunity to test your children and loved ones to learn whether they are engaging in substance abuse. Besides this manual, you may have purchased a highly rated drug-test kit to detect ten different drugs, along with a test that helps you determine the level of alcohol your child may have consumed.

Chapter One

Who's Who

The Authors' Stories

Dr. Gianni DeVincenti Hayes's Story

I'm Gianni, and I'm a victim of a drunk driver.

When I was in college, I did something stupid. I went to a party with the fellow I had been dating for about five months. Had I not also been drinking—a guilt that took me a long time to admit—I would have known he was too drunk to drive. I got into the passenger's seat and turned around to talk to the couple in the backseat. My life changed in those few seconds. My date passed out at the wheel, hitting a telephone pole and then a school building. I went flying into the windshield at the same time as the engine came up through the floorboards, so part of me was splattered in the windshield, while half of me was pinned by the engine. Recently, I had my fifteenth facial reconstructive surgery, and there are more planned. I have many plates and wires in the right side of my face, some loss of vision and damaged mouth nerves, and I have suffered for years with aching joints and muscles.

I will never look the way God originally intended me to appear. Daily, when I wake and look in the mirror, I am reminded of that fateful day many years ago. I live a life of self-consciousness and seldom get my picture taken; I usually only do so if I can digitally fix it. As I age, I lose more bone mass in areas that received the most trauma: my face, my arm, and my hip. There is little more any surgeon can do to undo what the driver—and I—did that warm, starlit night a week before graduation. I never saw the driver again.

I wanted to do something to help parents, as well as people whose businesses could be lost as a result of employee alcohol and drug use. Hence, I started my company, American Drug Testing Consultants, to help fight our addiction problem.

Several years ago, I decided to share my story with students, to let them know that mistakes can happen and that we are all vulnerable, even when we are young and think we are immortal. I spoke to schools and MADD (Mothers Against Drunk Driving) groups. I compensated for my scars by spending years studying, earning four degrees, and becoming an author, international speaker, and professor. In this capacity, I saw students in my classrooms stoned from drugs and reeking of alcohol; often they would nod off in class because of drug use.

Combine all this with two car accidents I witnessed where all the passengers in one car (all drunk or high) died, and another accident in which the teenage driver (also under the influence of drugs) was killed right in front of my home, and you have some insight into why I have taken on this project.

I believe our young people need to be made aware of the serious consequences of alcohol and drug use and abuse. And I believe it all starts with the parents. We must keep tomorrow's leaders drug free. Together, you and I can make this happen.

Dr. Gianni DeVincenti Hayes

Michael J. Talley's Story

I own a company called Drug Test Consultants of PA. I was part of the corporate world for most of my career. That was necessary for me to provide for my three daughters. As my girls grew into their teenage years, they all developed in different directions. The youngest was always busy, and that led me to believe she was doing well. It was not until December 23 of her senior year that the truth came out. I was called in to her high school by the guidance counselor and principal, and they told me that they had found ten packets of heroin in her locker. One of her friends had reported her to the principal. The police were notified. She was expelled from school, only five months away from graduating. When I realized that my daughter was doing drugs, I felt as if I'd been hit with a shovel. Knowing nothing of rehab/detox centers, I just went to the phone book and checked her into a local rehab center for five days of detox for heroin. This was December 24. This world of drugs and rehabilitation was new to me, and I thought she would be "cured" after five days in detox. That was eleven years ago, and it marked the start of our experiences with relapses, detox centers, rehab institutions, halfway houses, police problems, auto accidents, and, finally, a transitional house. Recently she started methadone treatments. This minimizes her drug cravings, while it levels off her highs and lows and her personality and mood swings. We finally had time to work on the real reason she had started using drugs. When a teenager uses drugs, their maturation process is delayed. If they become addicted at an early age, their priorities become distorted, and, instead of concentrating on the normal sequence of life, they only think of how to procure their next high.

I have seen several of my daughter's friends die from overdoses. These teens get their drugs in places that would scare most adults. While my daughter was in her five-day detox, I went to the place in Philadelphia where she bought her drugs: an open-air market where all kinds of people came to get their "drug of choice." The buyers ranged from young teenagers to adults in expensive cars. Drug addiction is definitely the great equalizer. All these people had been reduced to a common level due to their addiction. That was my first trip to the depths of that particular netherworld. You can't imagine my level of hate and disgust for the people who introduced my daughter to that life. Once your child enters that world, it becomes a part of your life forever. It is a constant battle for sanity and sobriety.

I started this business to try to educate parents on the signs of drug use, as well as teach them what to do if they find out their child is a user. Unfortunately, children get involved in alcohol/drug use at ages as young as eleven and twelve—even younger, in some cases. Parents need to understand that the drug world is very real, and they really need to discuss drugs and drinking with their children. Children whose parents talk to them about alcohol/drug use are five times *less* likely to use. Parents also need to keep their children busy with good activities and get to know their friends. This is crucial!

Today, many parents are afraid of their children. I don't mean they fear violence from their children (which also happens), but they fear confronting them with discussions concerning use of mind-altering substances and questions about what they do when they are away from home. I believe that if I can help one family avoid the hardships, disappointments, and pain that my family has endured, this venture will be 100 percent worthwhile. Parents need to know the warning signs, so they can step in and take control of their children's lifestyles before it is too late.

Michael J. Talley Jr.

The Drug Dealer

Can you picture him? He's a guy with a wide-brimmed straw hat; a funky, neon-colored suit; sunglasses; and a gold chain hanging around his neck, or a gold fob falling off his pants. He's the big-time dealer, right? He tempts your children to try illicit drugs, gets them hooked, and then makes them rely on him for their future supplies while he collects all the money. Right?

Drug Money

Source: www.dreamstime.com

Wrong.

Drug dealers come in all sizes and shapes: individuals, big drug cartels, strangers, and the kid next door. They are of all races, genders, religions, nationalities, education levels, and income levels, and they are everywhere. Your child's first drug contact could be with a schoolmate who encourages him to take that first drag on a reefer (marijuana) or that first sip of beer or liquor.

When children are confronted by drug dealers who are classmates, friends, acquaintances, or friends of friends, they don't feel threatened, because the dealer doesn't look like a dealer. Some of their friends may be dealers who do not stand out, because they are in the same school activities as your children. The traditional, old image of a drug dealer is incongruous with the image of the kid down the block your children play with. It is such an inconsistent picture that your child is deceived into thinking this kid offering him a sip of beer, a hit on a joint, or a half of a Darvon pill can't be so bad. So, your child may take the offer. What your children don't learn at home, they learn in the streets. It is crucial to discuss drugs with your children at home.

It is important to know that there are guys in suits out there selling drugs, and there are major drug groups (cartels) who deal in the big business of buying, selling, and smuggling drugs. There are also gangs who would love to get your children hooked. The average drug dealer is a kid who goes to school with your children. You need to teach your children to refuse any offer of illicit drugs, alcohol, and prescription medications in any form. This includes over-the-counter drugs that can be toyed with and manipulated and household solvents that can be inhaled. Selling drugs to children is big business. It is not a random act of irrational stupidity; drug dealers have a "business" plan—just like any other successful organization.

Seldom do dealers sell any pure drug. They may start a new user with pure substances, but, once their victim is hooked, they begin to mix the drug with other substances. Then, when your child becomes a user, he or she will rely on the dealer (and others) for a ready supply—but the dealer wants to make money from your child, so the price goes up, while the drug is being diluted with other substances. Some of these mixtures can be deadly, such as heroin cut with fentanyl. Your child ends up not only hooked but also in poverty, because he or she can no longer support the habit. Your addicted child resorts to stealing, usually starting with family members, followed by friends and strangers, graduating to shoplifting and robbery, murder and/or suicide. None of it is a pretty picture, but all of it can be prevented simply by testing your children periodically, to let them know you're watching what they do and that you are not going to let them get sucked into the wormhole of substance abuse. Testing has the capability of deterring your children from even trying substances; simply having the drug-test kit in your home can be a deterrent in itself.

You, the parent, may actually be an unknowing drug dealer by having prescription and over-the-counter (OTC) medications somewhere in your home easily accessible to your children. You may be contributing to your children's problem without even realizing it. This is merely one way parents can actually enable their children. If you are taking prescribed medications, lock them up; the same goes for over-the-counter drugs and alcohol. Children may start sneaking pills and alcohol if they know where you keep them and how much is available to them—without you knowing they have done so. Lead by example. Don't do drugs or drink recklessly in front of your children. Illicit drugs are illegal for everyone. Don't abuse your prescription medications, either. Take them as prescribed; do not self-medicate. And teach your children to respect prescription medications, as well. Your children are much, much more inclined to do what they see you do than what you tell them to do.

Your children do not want a "cool" friend for a parent. They yearn for discipline; otherwise, they feel as if you don't care. A lack of boundaries makes them think they can do whatever they want, disregarding right and wrong.

You have to learn who your children's friends are and what kind of homes and families they have. Investigate their school lives, grades, and activities, and keep tabs on the money they spend, where it comes from, and what they buy. Give your time generously to them, just talking and enjoying one another's company. Discuss rules and consequences, be consistent in enforcing them, and provide discipline when it is needed.

Consider this image (via an anonymous poem as offered on the Internet) of what a drug dealer does. This graphically describes what an addicted person goes through, no matter what the drug, but particularly with meth. Read this closely. Close your eyes and picture this person as your son or daughter; you'll understand why it's important for you to take control now.

He swaggers and is full of it
Overjoyed your kid will take a hit.

He'll suck him in, ruining your love for he who you gave birth,
Knowing he is stealing your child's worth, destroying your mirth.

Your child will run after that dealer,
Even if he turns him into a killer.

Your kid needs that supply,
Steal, cheat, live, or die.

Your child will fade right before your eyes,
His mouth will utter only ugly lies.

He'll distort into someone you don't know,
Yelling, screaming, fighting blow by blow.

His teeth will rot and decay,
His mind will wither, go astray.

His eyes will sink into his skull,
His body will shrink and fall.

This poem gives you insight into a child doing drugs or alcohol. It is a quick, transitory glimpse into what the future holds for families whose children are doing chemicals. Drug use is devastating—it destroys every shred of decency, severs any bonds of love, pierces each beating heart, and eats the bodies of users and abusers inside out.

A Recovering Addict's Poem

The following poem is by Melaina, Mike Talley's daughter, who became addicted to marijuana at the age of twelve and eventually was introduced to heroin by her "boyfriend" (who ran back to Mexico). Some say marijuana is not a "gateway" drug—but *it is*! The poem shows the level of despair an addict feels.

Where Do We Go Now
by Melaina Talley

If I could be anything besides me
I would be a butterfly, beautiful and free
I'd spread my wings, fly through the sky
I wouldn't have to pick up a needle and get high
I remember the feeling of being numb inside
Friends dying all around me, and I couldn't even cry

You would ask me how my day was
And I would say, "fine"
Yeah, screwed up, insecure, neurotic, and emotionless
That was me all the time
But I would follow up with these words
In the back of my mind
For if you knew the real me
I'd be scared you might hide
I reminisce about the things I have seen
Like the old lady pushing a cart

And washing in a public restroom
Just to get clean
How we lowered our standards, our morals—no freedom
And got shot at or stabbed, searched or beaten
And all for what?
For a euphoric feeling

But wait, it's not over yet
The game has just begun
This is hell
Welcome

For you have entered the jungle
Need a ride down the way?
There's no turning back now
At least that's what I thought
On those hopeless, empty days
Think about my past?
No freaking way

I'm gonna kick tomorrow
Screw that; another opportunity
To run away for another day
But things have changed now
I'm gonna give this recovery thing a try
For once in my life, it's a good shot I'm taking
One to give me a different high
Cause if it doesn't work out
I can always go back to die.

And you might say,
"It could be your last high, Melaina
You just might die"
And I think to myself
As I ponder that thought
For my fear is all the suffering
That goes along with getting high
I wouldn't be one of the "lucky" ones
Who go out and die

What's the solution? Prevention! If you prevent the problem, you won't have to worry about your child ever starting the cycle of hellish addiction.

Source: www.dreamstime.com

Chapter Two

Understanding the Problem

The Awful Facts

Statistics are often thrown at us, but do we really pay attention? If we did, we would probably all be out protesting the availability of drugs and alcohol. Statistics don't always show the whole truth. By the time numbers are taken, recorded, verified, and published, they are already outdated—and meanwhile the problem has grown worse. Drug abuse numbers never get better over the years. Dealers have just gotten more devious. Take a good look at these stats.

Statistics on Youth and Substance Abuse
(Some of these statistics appeared in the original manual by *The Drug Test Consultant*; refer to the Preface). Nearly *every* child, of any age and income level, is offered drugs. Consider the following:

- America accounts for approximately 6% of the world's population, yet consumes approximately 67% of the world's illicit drugs.

- Over 35 million Americans are addicted to legal and nonlegal medications.

- 18 million Americans are alcoholics. [*National Household Survey*, NIDA—the National Institute on Drug Abuse].

- Nearly 20 million Americans regularly use hashish or marijuana.

- Over 5 million people regularly use cocaine or crack.

- Every day 5,000 people use cocaine or crack for the *first time*.

- Today's marijuana is at least 5–20 times stronger than that of the 1960s and 1970s. Kids have a wide choice of powerful, mind-altering drugs (such as ecstasy, Ketamine, and GHB).

- 88.5% of school-aged children say it is easy to get drugs.

+ More than 60% of youth who use marijuana before the age of 15 go on to cocaine.

+ Over 54% of high-school students will have used an illegal drug by the time they are seniors. Age 13 is the average for first use.

+ 1 out of every 2 kids has tried drugs.

+ 2 out of 10 kids regularly use illegal drugs, prescription drugs, or alcohol.

+ 82% of those of working age have used cocaine.

+ "Club drugs" are often available at raves (parties) where supervision is lacking and secrecy, unsafe sex, and impaired judgment are common.

+ Before parents suspect it, their kids have used drugs/alcohol for about 2 years.

+ Medical insurance policies can have clauses allowing them to refuse medical claims if an illegal substance is present in the body at the time of treatment, so parents could be forced to pay as much as $20,000–$30,000 *per month per child* to rehabilitate.

+ NIDA encapsulated info indicated the number of offenders under age eighteen admitted to prison for drug offenses increased twelve-fold (from 70 to 840). (*Source:* http://www.thercg.org/trends/ttoda.pdf [*US Department of Justice, Bureau of Justice Statistics, Profile of State Prisoners Under Age 18, 1985–1997*].)

+ Parents are generally held legally responsible for their children's actions, and several states have enacted the Parental Responsibility Law or Liability (PRL); see http://www.sciencedirect.com/science?_ob=ArticleURL&_udi=B6W64-3YRVR2D-6&_user=10&_rdoc=1&_fmt=&_orig=search&_sort=d&view=c&_acct=C000050221&_version=1&_urlVersion=0&_userid=10&md5=ea7a6cb0d7681eb1675d52f59be32368.

Even if a state doesn't have a PRL, damages done by a child are usually paid for by parents, even if they don't know their child is using drugs. The problem is big; the solution is powerful. Test your children, your employees, sports teams, youth in camps, students, and church groups. Just knowing they can be randomly tested serves as a deterrent for youth to trying drugs/alcohol. Testing can easily be accomplished using our small kit in the privacy of your home; children can even be tested without their knowing it. Instantly you can know the results, which lets you help your children before they are so deep into abuse that they can't be saved. There is hope, so test your children. The kits are legal, safe, reliable, easy to use, and private.

True Stories

Some parents believe every word that comes out of their children's mouths, even when they know in their hearts that their children's words are lies. Here are several examples that will illustrate the illusions parents force themselves to believe.

Source: www.thinkstock.com

How Privacy Can Kill

A sixteen-year-old boy had been behaving strangely for the last year. He would come home from school and lock himself in his room. The parents didn't believe in violating his domain and never searched his room. One morning, the boy didn't come down for school. They finally had to break down his bedroom door. What they found totally shocked them. There was their son, lying on the floor with a needle in his arm. He was dead, a victim of heroin overdose or heroin that was cut with a poison. You see, drug dealers don't care about the users. They cut drugs (heroin and cocaine, to name a few) with strychnine, fentanyl, and other substances. All they want to do is extend their profits by diluting the drugs with anything they can get their hands on. They know if the user dies, there will be more lining up to buy their product. The parents finally searched the boy's room and found all of his drug paraphernalia in the top drawer of his dresser. They are partially responsible for his death. All they had to do was check their son's room, just once, before he overdosed, and they might have prevented his death. This is not a matter of violating a child's privacy; it is a matter of protecting them from themselves. As a parent, you're responsible for your children, ad infinitum. Remember, too, that addicts are in denial, and that they lie. Never trust an addict's words.

Bobby's Story

Bobby was in the heartbreaking position of having to live with elderly grand-parents, as his parents had divorced and neither had really wanted to take responsibility for him. Not only were his "foster parents" many years older than he, but they were too old to be an integral part of his life and attend the frenetic activities that most young children get involved in. Bobby turned to drugs. Instantly he liked the sensations. As his body craved more and more, he resorted to stealing from his grandparents, then from friends, and, lastly, from department stores. Each time he was caught his grandparents punished him, but the energy and effort needed to effectively discipline him and remain consistent were too hard on them. Bobby gradually went his own way, until he had little interaction with his grandparents. At eighteen, he was arrested for drug use, dealing, and trafficking, and he ended up serving a ten-year prison sentence.

Correta's Story

Correta was a willful, independent child, always rebelling and irritating others, especially her struggling, single mother—who was trying to raise four chil-dren, three of whom were younger than nine-year-old Coretta. Every day her mother had to contend with calls from Coretta's principal: "Correta sassed the teacher in fifth period today," or, "Jane's mother called the school, asking that Correta not hang around her daughter anymore," or "Your daughter kicked a girl this morning in gym class." Her mother did her best to teach Correta right from wrong, but she was working two jobs, taking care of four children, had no transportation, and still had to cook, clean, and do laundry. She felt that Correta was slipping through her hands. And slip away Correta did, starting by hanging around the wrong kind of kids, trying alcohol, moving on to marijuana and then harder drugs, and, finally, succumbing to total addiction to crack cocaine and methamphetamine. Her mother watched her once beautiful child fall to decay, with her teeth rotting, her body thinning and beyond pain, and her hair falling out. The child was seriously *addicted*, and her mother realized that she had lost her baby.

Eric's Story

Eric came from a solid family, a good home life, and indulging parents. When his mother was very busy, often the housekeeper doubled as his nanny. And when Dad had to work late, he always brought something home for Eric, like video games. The stone house was large enough for all his friends to play in when it was cold outside, or they could swim in the outdoor pool when it was hot. Many times Eric found himself eating dinner alone, because Mom was busy and Dad was working. When he dined alone, he watched television or played games with his silverware. Sometimes he upturned his plate full of food and just walked away. But no one called him back to clean up the mess he had made. On those rare occasions when his parents were home and had dinner with him, the table was completely silent. No one talked. No one asked him how his day had gone, what he had done at school, if he had gotten any grades back, or if he needed help with his homework. Eric started hanging out with older kids, who introduced him to marijuana. Within a year, Eric had moved on to narcotics. At the end of two years, he was hooked on crack. By the time he was thirteen, he had his own meth lab set up in his home, right under his parents' unwatchful eyes. He traveled the road to addiction all alone.

Micah's Story

Ten-year-old Micah was placed in a position that's becoming all too common today. He was being raised by a single parent. His mother was overwhelmed with all the roles that parents have to fulfill and had little money to help overcome the situation. Micah's mother worked two jobs, trying to feed and clothe her five children, pay the monthly rental on her low-income apartment, along with utilities, and cover a host of other expenses. One day, Micah and his friends went to a convenience store. Micah thought they were going to shoplift some items to pawn later for drug money. However, Tiger, the leader of the gang, pulled out a revolver and demanded that the store clerk empty the cash register. The clerk hit the silent alarm, but his fear made him slow to move to the cash register. Tiger shot the clerk and then ordered Micah to pull the money from the cash register. Just as he did, the police whisked in and arrested all of them. By the time his mother realized this, Micah had been arrested for shoplifting, along with crimes he had not committed but was associated with because of the type of people he was hanging around with. Micah went to a juvenile detention center, his future already set while he awaited sentencing. His mother had to pay restitution for her son's thefts, as well as face court charges for deficient supervision of her son's school attendance. Micah's mother saw her once vital and handsome son turn into a pale, thin little boy with ragged hair and decaying teeth. He would spend a long time in detention and have a police record for the rest of his life. Not only was Micah's life ruined, but so were the lives of his mother and siblings, as well as the clerk and his family—and all of it can be traced back to that first hit of marijuana.

Denial When Confronted

Mike Talley participated in a large flea market at a local community college. The purpose was to provide funds for a high-school post-prom party. This seemed to be a perfect time to show the public what in-home instant testing devices were available for drugs and alcohol. It was a full-day show, and he wasn't surprised to see everyone walking around his table instead of talking to him. People didn't even want to be seen close to the table. The prevalent attitude was exemplified by one mother who walked by with her teenage son. Mike was out of sight but could hear their conversation. She looked at the drug-testing devices on the table and made this comment to her son, "If you can't believe your sixteen-year-old son, who can you believe?" That comment, in all its ignorance, proves that it is easy to have a baby but very difficult to be a parent. Mike made the false assumption that most parents with children attending proms would be concerned about their children drinking and doing drugs. In this case, most were not.

My Plan to Steal

I'm an addict. Using drugs for more than half my life made me see things that, as a child, I probably wouldn't have been exposed to. When you're sick, really dope-sick, you will do pretty much anything to get well. I've known people who would go get a gun, pull up real quick in their cars to the corners where the dealers were working, and pretend they were undercover cops. They did this a couple of times and pulled it off—stole their whole supply. Addicts pull crazy stunts, and they get into some really scary predicaments. I had a good thing going for a while at a gas station. I was young, and the loser who introduced me to heroin used to work at this particular gas station. I thought he would never bring me any harm or put me in danger, so when he told me how to steal money from this place, I listened like a lovesick puppy. Because he worked there, he knew there weren't any cameras and that between certain times only one person was working. So I was to walk in (alone, of course, and he wanted me to do all the dirty work; I just wanted to reap the benefits) and I would politely ask to use the bathroom. I would take the key, go inside, and return about two minutes later. I would come out a little frazzled and I would behave very prissy, telling the attendant, "My ring slipped right off my finger into the toilet. Do you have anything I could get it out with?" Sure enough, they would grab a tool and go outside where the bathroom was to try to get the ring. Meanwhile, I would grab the key, open the cash drawer, and skim from the top, so they wouldn't notice anything was missing till the end of the day. I made a quick eighty to one hundred dollars each time. I was able to pull this off four times before they started to catch on, or so I thought. I even did it without him. At first, it was for him, and then it started to be less about him and more about the drugs. This is just one example of the many schemes I've pulled off for dope. I should be doing life in jail right now.

Ella's Story

I have seen so many people struggle to stay clean. They're in and out of AA as if it's a revolving door. They take "breaks"—going into detox and/or rehab for "three hots and a cot" (regular meals and a place to sleep), especially if it is wintertime. Sleeping on the streets is much more deterring in the freezing cold. Ella had a bad habit; she was too far gone in the game. If people were overdosing from a particular "bag" of heroin, she would be the one running to the corner where that bag of heroin was sold. She had a theory (like most junkies) that if someone overdosed from it, that bag must be strong enough for her to feel a good high. It is called "chasing the dragon." A junkie can never get the same feeling they had from their first high.

The Wrong Truth

A young man of eighteen went to the "rooms," a place (AA or NA) for meetings throughout the day where you can play cards and just get to know recovering people. He was on antidepressants. Several people in the room said he was still using, which was *not* true. If you have a chemical imbalance and are depressed for no reason, and a doctor prescribes the antidepressant, you should take it. Unfortunately, this boy listened to these people (and not the doctor) and stopped taking his meds. He killed himself three days later. I am a heroin addict, but I got clean in AA. A bottle doesn't tempt me, but don't be confused—alcohol *is* a drug.

Miscellaneous Remarks

I know of or have met—unbelievably—a lot of kids whose parents leave them money every day so they won't go out and steal or do something worse. They would rather have them in the house and using there. When the kids go out, the parents pace back and forth in the house. It becomes 1:00 or 2:00 AM before their kid gets home. The parents are so mad they can't wait to punish the kid, but as soon as their son or daughter walks into the room, no matter how late it is, they're so relieved he or she is home and safe that they don't impose any punishment. This sends mixed messages.

Anonymous Friend

My one friend, Kip, struggled with getting clean. He couldn't figure out why he couldn't. Well, we were in rehab together at one time. Two weeks later, he hanged himself. He had been on the phone with a friend at 2:30 AM and crying from being dope-sick and fed up and tired of living like that. He had a check in his hand but couldn't cash it until morning, and he needed it to get "well." He really didn't want to get high, but the craving was horrendous! I call this stage purgatory. He didn't want to get high anymore, but he felt he couldn't stop. He thought the only way out was to end it.

Threat Sources

There are many reasons why young people get involved in drugs. Studies indicate that there are several areas that affect their behavior. Adolescence is a tough time for children, as they are trying to manage all the changes in and around them, as well as to form relationships. If you, as their parents, can help cut back on their stress, you may prevent them from becoming users. The following are the major risk factors that contribute to drug and alcohol abuse.

Socioeconomic

Problem:

Research shows both family income level and status are major factors in whether a child will try any illicit substances or medications. The research indicates that children of all economic classes are at risk, and family members may be the ones leading them to use, by allowing their children to drink alcohol, smoke grass, or take prescription medications, or by doing nothing to address suspicions of drug use. Young people from deprived socioeconomic classes, however, do appear to be more vulnerable to substance abuse. Unfortunately, many teens see selling drugs as an easy way to make money. Additionally, a population may be situated in an area where drugs are readily available to children, which tempts them to try using the drugs. Supporting this is a lackadaisical attitude on the part of neighborhood enforcement groups and parents' unwillingness to prevent the problem in the first place. It is important that the entire community fight a neighborhood's drug problem. This starts at home, with testing.

Solution:

If your community doesn't have a drug awareness program, initiate one yourself. Call a meeting of families around you, and have a police officer talk about drug and alcohol addiction and ways to prevent abuse in your neighborhood. Many neighborhoods and schools employ officers whose sole job is to operate drug prevention programs. In many places this is the DARE (Drug Abuse Resistance Education) program, though there are many similar programs. Try to clean up your neighborhood, if drugs are readily available. And though you may have to work two jobs to pay your bills, don't overlook your children in doing so. Get involved in your Parent-Teacher Association or similar organization. Make sure everyone is informed about the damage drugs and alcohol can do and what can be done to prevent it in your children.

The Home
Problem:
The family element plays a big role in youth substance abuse. Children may turn to drugs and alcohol to escape problems, such as a death in the family, divorce, illness, relocation, physical and verbal abuse, and tension between parents. Other home factors include a high crime rate in your area, poor role modeling, a lack of involvement by parents in their children's lives, a one-parent family, a lack of communication, absence of rules and consequences for violation of the rules, and parental use of drugs and alcohol. How children are disciplined from early childhood years determines in part whether they will become aggressive or rebellious and turn to drugs in later years. If children see their parents drink, use illegal drugs, or misuse prescription drugs, they will think that behavior is acceptable.

Solution:
The most important thing you can do is parent your children's behavior. Put yourself in their shoes, and ask yourself what you would do if your parents argued a lot, if they constantly moved, if you lost a parent early in your life or had a seriously ill one, or if you were a product of divorce or a victim of your parents' anger. Once you've done this, you will have a sense of what your child might be going through. It is a good idea to encourage your child to have a close relationship with an adult who has a positive influence on him or her; this may or may not be a relative. It is important to discipline your children and to be consistent in imposing penalties for rule violations. Your children will come to appreciate the structure and realize that you discipline because you love them. According to your own religious beliefs, make spiritual activities part of your family life, thus giving your children a foundation of love for a higher being and a sense of a moral contract. Get

your children involved in wholesome activities, which may be found in school extracurricular programs. Pay attention to your children, praise and reward them for doing the right things, and get to know your children's friends. We can't stress this enough. It is crucial that you serve as a good role model.

Peers/Self-Image

Problem:

Friends and fear are chief causes of drug use. Friends can pressure your children to try substances in order to become accepted or become a part of an inner circle, or to avoid being mocked or ridiculed. Fear of consequences for refusing to experiment with drugs is part of the equation. Children may feel intimidated or afraid of being physically harmed if they don't try them. They may be led to believe drugs aren't harmful and that they'll feel better and perform better in school by indulging in substances. A child's self-image may be a negative one, causing them to lack self-confidence or become rebellious and turn to drugs and alcohol for what they believe is a personality booster. Coercion and bullying may be peer tactics to get your children to do drugs and drink alcohol.

Solution:

Children gain a degree of self-worth from parents and peers. Children will make mistakes, but it is imperative you do not react hypercritically, so you do not shatter their egos, especially in their formative years. You can still correct them, but you should do so in a loving manner. Ridiculing and yelling at them for everything will have negative effects in their later years. You can discipline without demeaning them. Criticize the *act*, not the *child*. It is also essential that you know your children's friends and have your children bring them home, so you can learn about them. If you do not approve of their friends, demand they not hang out with those who might have negative influences on them. This may require disciplinary action on your part. Start early with your children. The older they get, the harder it becomes to correct them. Instead of just telling your kids, "Say no to drugs" (which is easier said than done), tell them to blame their rejection of drugs on you, the parents. This way they can still look "cool" to their friends. Suggest your children say to those peers pushing drugs or alcohol on them, "I can't do drugs. My parents test me at home. If I test positive, they'll ground me." Your kids probably won't have any problem blaming you, so provide them with this "out" as a tool to help them extract themselves from bad situations. Check on what your children are doing and if they are where they're supposed to be.

School

Problem:

School is a foremost stressor for young people. This is the place where children are on their own to become successes or failures. If their role models have not emphasized the importance of schooling, children will not discern the importance of commitment to education and may thus find themselves trying other things to get through the day—often drugs. If they lack the self-discipline to study, or have antisocial tendencies or attention deficit, they may also find escape through substance abuse. It is important that you emphasize the importance of education and get involved in their school lives.

Solution:

Knowing what your children are doing away from home requires effort on your part, particularly if you are working, but this is perhaps the single most important step you can undertake. Schools are the first defense against drug problems, but today's overloaded teachers cannot substitute for your involvement. You need to be in touch with your children's teachers and counselors, attend PTA or other types of meetings, and stay informed on how your kids are doing academically and behaviorally inside and outside the classroom. If your children's performance is substandard, investigate whether your school can provide tutors, or perhaps you can work out tutoring with a relative or a friend. Try to get your children involved in healthy extracurricular activities.

The bottom line is to always be involved in your children's lives and let them know you care and love them, even if they act as if they don't want to hear it. As parents, we walk a fine line between loving and disciplining, overseeing and embarrassing, being interested and doting. You have to work at finding the right mix for your children.

Why a Drug Problem

America accounts for approximately 6.0 percent of the world's population yet consumes approximately 67 percent of the world's illicit drugs. Researchers aren't quite sure why this is the case. Many of our children—our future leaders—are walking chemical plants. Not only are they able to obtain illicit substances and street concoctions, but they seem to have no problem getting their hands on prescription medications, a rising crisis in our country.

Why are our children involved in drugs? Here are some insights:

Money

Big bucks are made from drug deals, and drugs are truly a business—a money-making venture. Organized criminals and even members of our country's own intelligence organizations have been involved in making, smuggling, and selling illicit substances. The sale of illegal drugs is a key funding mechanism for terror groups. Three examples of these groups are Hezbollah, the Islamic Movement of Uzbekistan, and Al Qaeda. They all deal in trafficking of illegal drugs. Home labs have been constructed just for the purpose of making such addictive chemicals. Even street junkies pull in a hefty amount of cash, so making money is a major incentive. If dealers themselves are on drugs, they often sell to maintain their own habits.

Peer Pressure

Friends and associates are powerful influences on young people, who often believe they need to take, or at least try, drugs in order to be accepted by a group or looked upon as being cool. For adolescents who feel a strong desire to be accepted by their peers, trying a drug may not seem bad or dangerous. What many don't realize (or want to admit) is that experimenting with addictive substances can cause lifelong problems, many of which lead to criminal behavior. In essence, they feel they can't say no. To many of them, popularity is much more important than physical or mental health. The ready availability of drugs in communities sparks another concern. While indigent neighborhoods tend to have more drug problems, upper-class kids have more access to money to purchase drugs. Many of these kids go into the worst areas of the city to get their drugs, places their parents would be afraid to visit. Another concern is that many youth attend late-night parties where indulging in drugs and alcohol is the norm and sexual promiscuity is common. These parties are sometimes referred to as raves, and, under the influence of alcohol or surrounded by friends who engage in illicit behavior and encourage everyone else to do the same, young people find it difficult to avoid participating in such behavior. It is wise to know exactly where your children are going, whom they will be with, what they will be doing, and if a responsible adult will be present. For parents who are worried about their children making the right decisions, it is best to incur and enforce a curfew. You gave life to that child; he or she is your responsibility—not someone else's.

Media Glamorization
Our media tends to glamorize drugs and create users through television, radio, and print advertising. Along with this, video games show aggressive behavior and advocate substance use. It is easy to see why our children can become targets. Monitor what your children watch, hear, and read, and don't encourage them to play video games that glorify crime and influence them to engage in drug use. There are several excellent shows on TV that show the dirty side of drug abuse. One is Dr. Drew Pinsky's show called *Celebrity Rehab*. This depicts real stories of actual celebrities who are addicted to drugs and what they go through to try to stop. Another is a show called *Intervention*. These stories follow a person who is addicted and show how family and friends try to help. Both are eye-openers to children (and adults).

Boredom
Because of television, radio, movies, and computers, our children are at risk of losing their creativity. The media gives mixed messages to kids who have become dependent on these venues to be entertained. Commercials on various prescription medications instill the idea that drugs can solve all their ills and make them feel better. If your children are using electronics as a crutch for boredom, help them to rediscover their creativity. Almost all users say that boredom is a *big* factor in their addictions. Addiction is typically a symptom, not the disease.

Concern for Physical Appearance
America has a body image obsession. Despite being a country with a growing obesity epidemic, we are also a competitive nation of joggers, bodybuilders, and would-be Olympians. We have an intense drive to look slim, dress smart, and build up our bodies, with everything portrayed in the media as the perfect look. Too many feel compelled to be the strongest, and greatest, and thus have a sense of urgency and immediacy to have perfect reflections in the mirror. Athletes illegally take steroids to construct the "perfect body," but what many

don't realize is how hazardous these prescription drugs are. Do not emphasize an ideal body image to your children. Instead, encourage them to exercise regularly and eat right. Keep your eyes open for steroid or other drug usage. See the sections in chapter 5, "Drugs of Abuse—Part II." These sections provide more detail about steroids, most of which are hormones.

Access to Prescription Drugs

If you have children in your house, you run the risk of them sneaking your medications for themselves or to sell to others. Refrain from popping a pill in front of your children every time you feel a need to "fix" something, even if it is simply a headache. If you need a prescription medication for a true health problem, sit down with your children and explain the situation with them. Children will model themselves after you. Refer to chapter 5 for details.

Mistakes

Though it is uncommon, your children can become addicted to drugs or be taken advantage of sexually because someone put a substance in their drink. This is not a far-fetched occurrence, and the date-rape drug Rohypnol is often used specifically to get someone high without his or her knowing he or she has taken it. Users and dealers also have been known to cut marijuana with cocaine or heroin in order to get the user addicted to harder drugs and thereby up the dealer's chances for future profits. So there *are* those with addiction issues due to someone's deception.

Need for Escape

The feeling of a drug high is a large contributor to our nation's serious drug problem. Our children are under intense stresses, and they often want to make things right. For many of them, drugs seem to be the answer. Escaping problems or the tensions of our fast-paced life is, for many children, a way to handle matters they don't want to confront, or to more easily face the consequences of their actions. School and home life are the two environments placing the most pressure on kids. There is always some degree of tension in any situation or surroundings we're placed in, but most home influences can be controlled, unlike many school situations. Curtail arguing with your spouse in front of your children. Don't yell at them, and be consistent in what you say and do. Open up your home to warmness and love, as these are the conditions under which children thrive. Teach your children to manage stress and to cope with their concerns. Kids who are using are looking to get numb and have a small amount of time where they can forget their problems. They dread the knowledge that this numb feeling, this escape, only lasts a short time and then they will come down and realize their problems are still there, only now they loom bigger. In the end, their using only makes them feel worse. Remember that their problems, although they may seem small to us, are still very large and real to them. The guilt they feel from using usually contributes to them wanting to forget reality and use more.

Desire to Experiment

Kids will often take drugs just to "see what it's like." Consider your teen years and younger when you might have had that first cigarette, or taken that first drag on a joint. Children today are no different than when you were growing up, except they have more pressures and demands placed on them, and more forms of illegal drugs are available to them. Educate them on the dangers of doing drugs and on developing the willpower not to try something just because it is there. Give them examples of how going against the crowd mentality can be beneficial to them. Give them the gift of self-discipline and individuality.

Lack of Parental Guidance

A key reason our society has such an overwhelming drug problem is the number of parents who don't take responsibility seriously. Many don't take the time to teach their children right from wrong, don't want to punish or make the effort to be consistent and stern with their children, or simply can't find time to spend with their kids. Many parents use television as a babysitter, and thus modeling comes from an inanimate object that can deliver a remarkable amount of obscenities, untruths, and immorality. You must invest yourself in your children's life and future—no matter how tired you are. More kids are on drugs when parents are *not* involved than when the parents are an active part of their lives. Statistics show that children whose parents talk to them about drug use and check on their kids' activities and friends are five times *less* likely to use.

Societal Pressures

A society that tacitly approves of drug use—by doing little to prevent or stop it—will deteriorate. Although there are many government and other agencies attempting to prevent abuse, a lackadaisical attitude toward stopping drug abuse can actually promote drug activity. Teachers are too overwhelmed and too restricted in their relationships with students to be allowed to be effective. Instead, they find themselves guarded and unwilling to get involved at all times so they won't be accused of some type of inappropriate action. Churches often don't address the drug problem, because they have such restricted time with youth. After-school activities have a very limited window to teach children to stay away from drugs and alcohol. The solution rests with you, the parents, who are representative of society as a whole. If you don't start at home to thwart abuse, society in general can't support your efforts.

Consequences of a Drug-Problem Society

Many problems in our lives today result from substance-abuse issues. If we take no action, the problems will only worsen. We need to fight drug and alcohol abuse before it gets worse.

Crime

Drug and alcohol users will commit crimes for money to buy more drugs, even at the risk of getting caught and spending their lives in jail. Here are several examples:

Property Damage

Vandalism is often committed to retaliate against someone challenging a user's habit or refusing to help them get their drugs. Vehicles, homes and yards, offices, and businesses have all suffered property damage from addicts.

Theft

Stealing from parents and family is often the first act by a user. Addicts may think nothing of stealing cash or anything else they can get their hands on to pawn to support their drug use. Look for missing money and objects. Make sure no one—not even your children—has access to your money, checkbook, or other investments.

Human Harm

Murder, maiming, assault, and rape are some of the more violent crimes committed against others by abusers craving drugs and needing to find ways to get them. Often, offenders are already high on drugs when they commit crimes and may have no recognition of the severity of their crimes, although this makes them no less guilty.

Impaired Judgment

Because drugs and alcohol greatly affect the functions of the brain (discerning right from wrong, maintaining coordination, etc), it is no surprise that addicts show bad judgment and little moral integrity. Children may become belligerent, rebellious, and irascible, and adults may become dysfunctional. Even professional fields, such as medicine, may house individuals who rely on drugs to maintain high energy, thus creating serious risk for patient mishaps—even deaths. Driving under the influence of drugs or alcohol is a bad choice and against the law.

Medicare Scamming
Drugs are big business, and some doctors and nurses manipulate the system to get money from welfare, Medicaid, and Medicare in order to support their own drug habits. In the end, taxpayer dollars end up bridging the gaps to compensate for misallocated medical funds.

Cost to Taxpayers
We pay in various ways to prevent and/or stop drug abuse in our society. This includes money used by the government (taxpayers' money) to create drug-free agencies, produce educational materials, and fund antidrug organizations. Insurance companies raise consumers' premiums to compensate for claims from accidents, overdoses, and damages to others due to drug addiction. They also collect more from consumers to pay for lab testing of these individuals. The funding for the fight against drug abuse is coming out of our pockets.

Physical Impairment/Permanent Damage
Users only want to satisfy their cravings. They ignore how much physical and mental impairment the substances cause. Much of the damage is permanent. The millions of brain cells killed each time they take a drink of alcohol and/or use a drug are staggering, and those cells do not regenerate. Not only do drugs damage the brain, but their effects are often much worse than those of alcohol.

Spiritual Disconnectedness
When alcohol and/or drugs become central to a user's life, the user no longer has room for spirituality. Spiritual emptiness is as demoralizing as the actual drug habit, but, with the lack of a connection to faith, the user sees little hope for going on, and thus suicide looms as a feasible option for escape. While rejection of faith can contribute to an addict's downward spiral, connectedness to a higher power is often the turning point in an addict's recovery, offering sanctuary, hope, and comfort.

Presence of Drug Rings

It is frightening to think you or your children could be attacked by someone on PCP or other drugs or those in gangs. Drug rings are a nightmare to innocent people and death to a neighborhood.

Societal Problems

Our parents and society are failing our children. Everywhere drugs have their grip on us, and we see this daily in our home lives, on our jobs, in our health, in crimes committed against humanity, and in our attitudes. To fix our societal woes, we must stop drug abuse, and to do this, we must first prevent it. Testing and education are the solutions.

A Discussion with Your Children about Drugs

It can be difficult to approach your children about drugs and alcohol. Parents have different relationships with their children than the ones they had with their parents. Many parents shy away from talking about serious issues with their children, for whatever reasons: fear, a lack of knowledge, the attitude of their children, time, and so on. But if you don't have a discussion with them and they get caught up in world of drugs, you will blame yourself forever, and the damage will be done. It is your job as a parent to talk with your children about these things.

Here are some pointers to help you get the dialogue going:

1. **Start early.**
    Preventing your children from indulging in drugs and alcohol isn't something you can do one night when they're teenagers and expect that the next day everything will be hunky-dory. You have to start talking to them when they're young, and let them know you have rules they *must* follow. Build from there, all through their growing years, to repeatedly teach them about the dangers of drugs. As they grow older, encourage dialogue. Education about drugs and alcohol is an ongoing process.

2. **Do your homework.**
    Before you sit down with your kids to discuss drugs and alcohol, educate yourself. Read this book to understand what's going on in the drug scene, the names and effects of various drugs, how today's youth get drugs over the Internet, and much more. You can also check online for more information. In the appendix of this book is an extensive list of resources. You should be able to talk with authority to your kids about drugs.

3. **Make a plan and take notes.**

   When you're reading this book, bookmark pages of interest that may help get your point across. Please take notes on what you're going to talk about. Talk to your spouse or significant other about how the two of you will approach the subject matter. Who's going to talk first? Who's going to say what? Who's going to lay out the rules and consequences? If you're a single parent, you can do this yourself. Have the facts and support material to help you stress the dangers of chemicals to your children.

4. **Listen to each other.**

   Talking and listening are critical in prevention. Don't make your talk with your children a preaching session or a lecture. You're sitting together to hear each other's thoughts and concerns. Listen to everything your children say. Study their facial expressions and body language. Are your children presenting a defensive stance? Making faces at everything you say? Feeding you lines that you know are lies? Be aware of your child's voice inflexion as well. Discuss friends, cliques, and peer pressure. Maintain open communication throughout, and be honest.

5. **Lay out the rules.**

   You need to make it clear where you stand on the drug and alcohol issue and what you expect from your children's behavior regarding drugs and alcohol. These rules might include the following, though you could certainly have others:

   + No drugs or alcohol in the house.

   + No drugs or alcohol outside the house, including the car or friends' homes.

   + No getting into a vehicle with anyone under the influence of drugs or alcohol.

   + No passing drugs or alcohol to others, even if you don't indulge in them.

   + No purchasing drugs or alcohol for others.

- A curfew on school nights of 9:00 PM; bedtime at 10:00 PM; weekend curfew at 11:00 PM (or whatever you, as parents, decide).

- No sexual relationships until marriage (whatever you, the parents, decide).

- No computer after _____ (whatever time you, the parents, choose). The computer should also be in a common area, not in their rooms.

- No TV, computer games, phone calls, etc., until homework is done.

- Homework reviews will be conducted by an authority figure.

- No smoking inside the house or with friends, anywhere, anytime.

- Grade reviews will be conducted by home authority figures (parents, guardian).

- No extracurricular activities if grades fall below a B or a C

- Family dinner will be eaten and conversation about the day's events will take place.

- A zero tolerance policy will be enforced for drug and alcohol use and smoking.

Any rules you lay out for your children must be realistic and achievable. If your child plays soccer after school every day until 7:00 PM, you'll want to adjust homework time and maybe even dinnertime together. Don't impose rules you can't uphold. When you lay out the rules, explain to your children why you have created them.

6. **Set consequences and be consistent.**
Enforcing the rules you have created and imposing consequences can be difficult. It will be harder on you than it is on

your children, but you must do it. What consequences you'll impose is a function of your children's ages, your financial status, and your strength to stand up to your children. You need to decide what punishment to set, but, whatever you do, it must be effective, and you must be consistent. Even if you are tired, you still have to discipline. Here are some suggestions for consequences of rule-breaking:

- Take away cell phones.

- Deny driving privileges.

- Forbid socializing with friends or others.

- Forbid any interaction with girlfriend or boyfriend.

- Stop allowance.

- Remove TV, DVDs, videotapes, radios, computer games, Wiis, iPods, Twitter access, and MP3 players.

- Cut out extracurricular and co-curricular activities.

- Increase chore load.

- Impose additional homework on your children.

- Arrange a visit with police on drug patrol (if possible).

- Arrange for the child to volunteer hours at a community charity organization.

- Assign an extensive written report on how drugs/alcohol work, the damage they do, and how they've ruined users and their families' lives.

7. **Emphasize responsibility.**
A continual game of crime and punishment won't yield progress if your children fight you and make your life miserable. Even if your children follow your rules and are punished when they don't, there is no guarantee they won't do drugs when

you're not looking or they won't break your rules. Make them accountable for their actions. Don't allow them to scapegoat or fall into self-pity.

8. **Role-play and teach your children to say no.**
This can really be shaped into a fun family event. After the discussion period, assign roles to your children. One might be a friend pushing drugs; another might be a bully who is applying peer pressure; another might be the role of a parent at wit's end over one of their children doing drugs (let your children play the parents); and so on. You and your children should discuss the importance of role-playing by assigning roles to each member of the family. Teach them how to say no. Our drug kits are great assets in this department.

9. **Build self-esteem.**
Don't go on the attack. If anything, reassure your children that you do trust them—and you should, unless they prove you wrong. Let them know you believe in them and they're great kids who can make age-appropriate, sound decisions. Praise them for the things they do right, such as hanging out with good kids, following your rules, working on their grades, and so on. Only censure their negative acts, not them personally. Be affectionate with your children. Don't kill their dreams, but do guide them to a realistic outlook. Most children are sensitive—even if they don't show it—and internalize your words, voice inflection, and expressions differently than do adults. That doesn't mean you can't tease them. If you do need to chastise them, do so with love and tenderness.

10. **Teach them how to cope with stress and worry.**
Studies have shown that kids turn to drugs and alcohol for several reasons:

+ They know their parents engage in drugs.

+ They are threatened or pressured by friends.

+ They want to be accepted by peers.

+ They're under a lot of stress.

KidsHealth (http://www.kidshealth.org/parent/emotions/feelings/kids_
stress.html) offers the following information in their article, "What Kids
Say about Handling Stress."

A poll of kids shows that their stress was created from school (36%), from
family (32%), and from their social peers (21%). Many went on to say they
used some coping techniques to relieve that stress. The highest percentage
answer (52%) used an activity to cope and another 42% coped by [using] the
electronic media.

Ref: http://www.education.com/reference/article/Ref_What_Kids_
Say_About/

About 25% of the kids we surveyed said that when they are upset, they take
it out on themselves, either by hurting themselves or doing something else
that is harmful to them. These kids also were more likely to have other unhealthy coping strategies, such as eating, losing their tempers, and keeping
problems to themselves. The idea that kids would do things to try to harm
themselves may be shocking to parents. But for some kids, feelings of stress,
frustration, helplessness, hurt, or anger can be overwhelming. And without
a way to express or release the feelings, a kid may feel like a volcano ready to
erupt--or at least let off steam.

Sometimes, kids blame themselves when things go wrong. They might feel
ashamed, embarrassed, or angry at themselves for the role they played in
the situation. Hurting themselves may be a way to express the stress and
blame themselves at the same time. The poll also revealed important news
for parents. Though talking to parents ranked eighth on the list of most
popular coping methods, 75% of the kids surveyed said they want and need
their parents' help in times of trouble. When they're stressed, they'd like
their parents to talk with them, help them solve the problem, try to cheer
them up, or just spend time together.
(http://www.kidshealth.org/parent/emotions/feelings/kids_stress.html)

These are just some suggestions. You know your children best, and you know
their capabilities, strengths, and weaknesses, so you'll be the one to decide
what's best for you and your children. Make sure the punishment fits the offense. Your children must understand the seriousness of what they did wrong
and why they are being punished.

The above reasons give insight into how stress arises from a disruptive home life, illnesses or deaths of loved ones, pressures to get good grades, tensions from too many extracurricular activities, pressure from friends, and/or awareness of a poor financial situation in the home.

Be patient with your children when they are under stress, but, most importantly, get your children to talk about it. Teens are reluctant to share their feelings. Help them with their emotions by asking how they feel about something, such as, "I know you wanted the lead role in the school play, but you got the understudy part—how do you feel about that?" Ask open-ended questions, those questions that require explanation and not just a yes or no answer. Be ready to listen. Give subtle advice, but don't shy away from giving it. And don't put on airs of perfection in front of your children or be rigid. You want to relieve their stress, not compound it.

The best solution is to teach your children how to handle stress. This is something that we, as parents, don't always do well, because we're handling our own set of stressors on a daily basis. Most parents, however, can put stress into perspective, even at the worst times. Children, on the other hand, see everything in terms of immediacy. If something upsetting is going on in their lives at one moment, they tend to lose sight of the fact that in a week or a few months things will have worked their way through. Hence, they internalize stress and pressure more than an adult might.

You can help them with this advice:

- Maintain logic and rationale when confronted with a problem.

- Analyze the problem rather than having a knee-jerk reaction to it.

- Understand the old adage that "tomorrow is another day." The world will not permanently stop at this moment when things look gloomiest. Instead, matters have a way of working out, even if it means trade-offs.

- Don't expect or demand perfection in everything. It is okay to fail if one has tried one's best.

+ Talk about worries with parents, family members, friends, parents of friends, teachers, school or professional counselors.

+ Find outlets for stress other than substance usage, such as sports, or writing in a journal, taking a walk, cutting grass—anything that releases that pent-up pressure and allows some time to gain perspective.

+ Refrain from screaming and yelling and throwing temper tantrums, as that only increases ire, while often hurting others in the process.

+ Walk away from agitators. Count to ten, listen to soothing music, and use energy to find solutions.

+ Don't use the car as an escape. This usually results in speeding and potentially fatal accidents for the driver, passengers, and others on the road.

+ Be willing to find a compromise and settle for something different. Though you want to support your children in their efforts to reach the loftiest goals, you also want them to realize that sometimes it is okay to settle for less.

11. **Serve as a good role model.**
It is a scientific fact that, immediately after hatching, a baby duck knows how to waddle simply by observing its mother. This is called imprinting. Humans do it, too. If children see their parents doing drugs, indulging excessively in alcohol, lying, and so on, they often follow suit. And the younger they are, the more likely they are to fall into this trap, because they aren't yet sure of the difference between right and wrong behavior. They have only their parents setting examples.

12. **Read, discuss, and sign the Unity Oath. (See appendix)**
The Unity Oath was designed to establish a contract between you and your children, with each party being responsible for upholding his or her end of the deal. Be sure each party understands what he or she is signing, and discuss each line in depth. If your children willingly sign the Oath, be sure to thank them and encourage future conversations about drugs

and alcohol. If your children refuse to sign the Unity Oath, you may have bigger problems than you realize. Refusal may indicate they are already indulging in substance abuse. They may claim that having them sign means you don't trust them. Let them know you have tenets to uphold in that contract as well. If they don't want to sign, you need to determine why. If your children continue to refuse to sign, you may have to take extreme measures.

What to Do If ...
Before you have this discussion with your children, "condition" them. While you're doing your research and reading this manual, begin light discussions about drugs, such as:

> While you're making dinner: "You know, Morgan, today I heard on the news that many kids get hooked on drugs without even realizing it. They may have thought trying it wasn't dangerous, but then they ended up addicted. Did you know that?"

Or:

> "I read about a high-school girl who had a scholarship to the University of Pittsburgh, but she went out with her friends, did binge drinking, and is now in a coma. What a loss. Have you heard of binge drinking?"

Bring up whatever topic you feel will cut through the thick silence and emotionally prepare your children for your discussion on drugs. By foretelling them of your desire to have regular family meetings that include discussions on drugs and alcohol, you are preparing them for the moment when you announce the meeting. Thus, they'll be more likely to expect and accept this change in your family dynamics. Don't be afraid to call family meetings" to discuss substance abuse, and other family-related matters. You can make this a regular event, such as a monthly family meeting *plus* whenever you feel the need to have additional ones. If any of your children want to call a family meeting, let them do so, as long as it is not over a frivolous matter. During these meetings, and at other times, it is imperative that each family member shows respect for the others.

The following may be of help if your children balk at signing the Unity Oath after you've had the discussion with them. Maybe they even seem open throughout the discussion, but when you get to the Unity Oath, they object. Here are some helpful hints:

1. **If your child walks out:**
   Wait at the discussion table for your child to return. If after a reasonable amount of time he still has not returned, call him again. If that fails, then simply tell him that his behavior is uncalled for and that by his actions you can only assume he has some reason for not signing. Tell him you're willing to discuss his concerns. If that still doesn't get him to sign the oath, then you'll need to test him for drug/alcohol use.

2. **If your child denies any involvement:**
   You may suspect your child of using drugs. Inform her of your concerns, and present your reasoning in a cool, controlled manner. Your child will either admit your suspicions are true or deny it. You can decide to have her tested right away, or you can wait a few more days before following through on testing. The delay helps you to keep track of your concerns. (Write them down: what you see your child do, what you hear your child say, how her grades are; what you sense about her friends, and so on.) After a little time has passed, again present your concerns. If your child still refuses to sign the oath, test her for drugs.

3. **If your child gives you the silent treatment:**
   This is always hard. You feel as though you're talking to a brick wall. In one sense, you think you'd rather have him yell and carry on, because at least you'd be hearing him say something, but, in another, his temper tantrums drain too much energy from you. Be creative in this department to get him to talk. You can tell him that if he continues to refuse to discuss or sign the pledge that he, and the family, will have to talk with a professional psychologist, and payment will come out of his allowance or chore money. Determine the best fair and consistent punishment for you and your child, and carry it through.

4. **If your child gets angry:**
   This is likely to happen. It is a way for your child to unburden everything that's on her, especially any drug usage. But anger is never the solution, and you must stress that to your child. Just say you'll be glad to listen to her comments when she presents them in a calm, straightforward, respectful, and calm manner. If not, she can go to her room until you call her. The cooling-off period often brings different insight and a better attitude.

Keep in mind that if your child carries on about having to sign a unity oath, or makes a big deal out of it with the you-don't-trust-me defense, there is something more to the issue, and it is possible she is already doing drugs. On the other hand, if she willingly and happily signs the oath, don't be fooled into thinking everything is all right and your child is *not* doing drugs or alcohol. Users deny, lie, and defy. No parent wants to hear that his or her child is lying, but if your child is on drugs and alcohol, she is now a different kid than the one you raised.

For other conversational clues and age-specific discussions, visit the KidsHealth Web site (http://www.kidshealth.org/parent/positive/talk/talk_about_drugs.html), and look under "KidsHealth for Parents." There is a wealth of information and sample conversations.

Have a look at this example of how to have a conversation with your teen about drugs and alcohol, taken from The Anti-Drug Web site ("Having the Conversation—With Your Teen": http://www.theantidrug.com/ei/conversations_teen_points.asp):

Key Talking Points

We are here to make it clear that we will not tolerate any drug or alcohol use by you.

We have rules in the family. The rules do not permit teen drug and alcohol use.

Even though you think everyone is using drugs or alcohol, it is illegal and not allowable.

You can endanger your life and the lives of others. We don't want anything bad to happen to you. I don't know what I'd do if I lost you. We count on you as a family member. Your siblings respect you and care about you. What would they do if you were gone?

Drug and alcohol use can ruin your future and your chances to graduate, go to college, get a job, and keep your driver's license.

We are here to support you. What can I do to help you not use?

Sometimes kids use drugs and alcohol because there are other issues going on, like stress, unhappiness and social issues. Have you thought about this?

Are there other problems you want to talk about?

Are your friends using? How are you handling that? Is it hard to not use in that environment?

We won't give up on you, because we love you. We're going to be on your case until you stop completely. If you need professional help, we will be there to support you and help make it happen.

Taken from "Having the Conversation ... with Your Teen"

http://www.theantidrug.com/ei/conversations_teen_points.asp

Information here is age specific and gathered from the KidsHealth Web site.

What Should I Say to My Children?
From KidsHealth
http://www.kidshealth.org/parent/positive/talk/talk_about_drugs.html
Reviewed by: Barbara P. Homeier, MD

Here is a brief summary of the article points by age.

Preschool to Age 7
Take every opportunity to teach your children about drugs, their implications, their effects, and danger. Give them specific information, so they can be aware of how much they can be hurt by using drugs not prescribed for them specifically.

Ages 8 to 12
At this age, you can actually discuss your children's view of drugs. They are able and anxious to discuss their views on drugs and still willing to have an open conversation. You will always be able to find current events to discuss as applicable to illegal drug usage.

Ages 13 to 17
By this time, they might have friends who are using drugs, alcohol, or pills. They might even be driving. This greatly increases the danger, by drinking or using drugs while in charge of an automobile. They are now exposed to true dangers, life/death decisions, and threat of getting in trouble with the law. This is a good time to develop a contract between you and your children. You might tell them you will pick them up if they can't drive (because of drugs and/or alcohol) and not ask questions until the next day.

You can gauge what's best in approaching your child to discuss the issue of drugs. Take into consideration all aspects of his or her personality, maturity, and interests, along with how you view your relationship with your son or daughter. Most important is to open the conversation and, over time, keep it going.

Actions to Take

You've discovered your child is doing drugs or drinking. What do you do next?

Ask. Say to your child, "John, there's proof in this cup that your urine tests positive for one or several different drugs. Are you doing drugs?" John may or may not choose this minute to be honest with you. If the test is positive, there is a 99.9 percent chance those drugs are in his system. Something you should be aware of is that John may know how to adulterate the results to show a false negative, but it is unlikely he knows how to make the results positive, other than through drug use. Adulteration occurs when a person being tested applies different techniques to the sample to make it come out negative or invalid. There are many ways to do this, and there are instructions available online. Some sites exist simply to help people fool urine testing. Most of these methods do not work, but understand that your child may be aware of them. Most of the online solutions make the user drink an excessive amount of water. Their intent is to dilute the specimen so the drug content will be under the drug cutoff level in the instant test kit.

Confirm. If John insists he's not doing drugs, even after testing positive, have him take a confirmation drug test to validate the results. This is a good way to find out if John is telling the truth, not doing drugs, yet still testing positive. A confirmation can be done by having him urinate into a new, sterile, unused cup, with someone in the bathroom with him to ensure he does not attempt to dilute the sample. And, as in the first test, you'll know within five minutes what drugs are in his system. Here are other possible options for confirmation testing:

> a). Call us for information and the cost of providing a "Custody and Control" form and information on local collection centers. These samples will be analyzed in a lab and you will be provided the confidential results.

> b). Contact us about arrangements to spray or wipe down your child's room to determine if there has been drug use or trafficking on the site.

Don't waste too much time trying to prove to your child you know he or she is on drugs. You want to act fast once you know. After confirmation of drugs, or if your child confesses to experimentation or regular drug use, you must take action!

Intervene. Once you're sure your child is experimenting with or addicted to drugs and/or alcohol, you must step in and get treatment. You can check the Yellow Pages of your phone book or go to http://dasis3.samhsa.gov/ online to find a nearby treatment center. Always check out references on any treatment center you consider. Many are capable of providing an assessment of your child's situation. There may even be state or county resources available to help with the financial arrangements.

Stay in tune with your child. Even as your child gets treatment and has begun the road to recovery, you *must* stay on top of his life to make sure he doesn't stumble. If he does, help him pick himself up and start over. If your eyes aren't trained on your child before, during, and after treatment, you could lose him physically, emotionally, spiritually, and/or mentally. As is true with alcoholics, once you're a drug addict, you're always one. A "recovered" addict still feels temptation all the time. Always try to talk with your child. Even if you don't think he's paying attention to what you have to say, he is—but it is important to have an ongoing open line of communication with him.

Remain calm. No matter how worried or upset you are, keep calm. Yelling, screaming, hitting, and making idle threats will just worsen the situation. The calmer you are, the more clearly you can think. Know what you're talking about when you sit down and chat with your child. Above all, let your child know you love him and that no matter what he is into, you're there to help him, from beginning to end.

Restate your position. Remain calm, and let your child know that under no circumstances will you tolerate alcohol or drug use. Be very clear about this. Let him know that if he is experimenting or using drugs, perhaps even addicted, you are there to work with him to get help. The Anti-Drug Web site (http://www.theantidrug.com/ei/advice_parents.asp), offers an article titled "Tips for Parents—What To Do and When: When you have a suspicion that your teen is 'experimenting' with drugs, what do you do?" The following is their advice:[1]

Here are some suggested things to tell your son or daughter:
(from http://www.theantidrug.com/ei/advice_parents.asp)

- You LOVE him/her, and you are worried that he/she might be using drugs or alcohol;

- You KNOW that drugs may seem like the thing to do, but doing drugs can have serious consequences;

- It makes you FEEL worried and concerned about him/her when he/she does drugs;

- You are there to LISTEN to him/her;

- You WANT him/her to be a part of the solution;

- You tell him/her what you WILL do to help him/her.

- Know that you will have this discussion many, many times. Talking to your kid about drugs and alcohol is not a one-time event.

Chapter Three

The Keys to Detection

Abuse

According to the Oxford English Dictionary, one of several meanings of *abuse* is "to use improperly or to excess." There are several different types of abuse, some of which are physical abuse, verbal abuse, self-abuse, solvent abuse, and, of course, there is drug and alcohol abuse. Abuse can cover a wide range, from hurting oneself to hurting others.

Unfortunately, abuse can affect everyone. Drug and alcohol use can result in some dreadful abuses by the users to others, and to the users themselves. Below are types of abuse often witnessed in this destructive situation. Many of these types of abuse overlap, and we've included some online resources where you can learn more about them.

Physical Abuse
http://www.preventchildabuse.com/abuse.shtml
Physical abuse is any act that results in bodily injury. Usually physical abuse occurs when corporal punishment is inflicted to the point where a person displays physical evidence (bruising, cuts, scratches, etc.). It should be noted that not every bruise on a child is a sign of physical abuse; it could be that the child was injured while playing. Physical abuse often happens while a person is under the influence of drugs or alcohol. This may result from falls, accidents, or injuries inflicted by others.

Verbal Abuse
http://www.healthguidance.org/entry/12798/1/Verbal-Abuse-Signs-and-Help.html
Verbal abuse is any statement that is undeserved and causes lasting emotional scars. "Verbal abuse in relationships is a serious matter that can leave an individual feeling worthless and stressed indefinitely. However the situations do vary in severity, and in some cases can even be two way."[2] While verbal abuse may be hidden, it can cause stress, which, over time, can result in lasting effects, such as depression. Despair, a lack of self-confidence, gloominess, or depression can affect not only the afflicted person, but also everyone with whom he or she comes in contact. Substance users/abusers often resort to verbal ill-treatment and violence, which is as damaging as physical abuse. Users exploit profanity and hurtful words because they are inconsiderate of feelings of others. Most

important to them is obtaining a supply of drugs or alcohol. They are out of control, and their minds don't think rationally, so anyone who stands in the way of their indulgent lifestyle is a threat to their usage, and thus becomes the target of their anger and verbal abuse.

Emotional Abuse
http://www.preventchildabuse.com/
Emotional abuse is similar to verbal abuse, except that with emotional abuse people are systematically torn down emotionally. They are constantly reminded they will never amount to anything. Eventually this could affect them psychologically, as well as warping their self-concept. Children may show signs of low self-esteem and low self-worth through disruptive acts. Signs of emotional abuse, like those of verbal abuse, are hidden and may not manifest until after considerable damage has occurred. Parents often experience extreme emotional abuse when their child or teen is on drugs. Likewise, users can be affected emotionally, not only from the drugs and alcohol indulged in, but from others as well. Users suffer from the worst form of self-inflicted emotional abuse. They use, and they feel they have disappointed themselves and their loved ones. Then they feel so bad—and they use again to forget. This self-perpetuating cycle makes addicts feel worse and worse about themselves. Serious help is needed.

Psychological Abuse
http://www.ncbi.nlm.nih.gov/pubmed/12787841
Similar to emotional abuse is psychological addiction, whereby the person believes he needs to have something in order to function on a daily basis. This type of addiction results in abuse. The addict's cravings are not healthy for the individual and cause conflicting thoughts and wants. He beats himself up for wanting something that isn't good, and yet he fights to satisfy the desire to have it. The psychological addict is constantly at odds with himself. An example is a person dependent on pornographic material. This is not healthy or moral, and the person berates himself for wanting it, but the need in his mind to have it causes great internal battles.

Self-Abuse
http://www.focusas.com/SelfInjury.html
Self-abuse is defined as "behavior that causes damage or harm to oneself." It can therefore take several forms, such as cutting oneself, attempting suicide, driving recklessly, intentionally overdosing, and so on. Self-abuse is often inflicted to escape strong emotions. When inflicted, it usually causes bodily injury to the person and has little to no physical effect on other people who come into

contact with the user or abuser. However, the emotional effect on loved ones can be devastating. Often, self-abuse is a subconscious cry for help. Suicide threats by users should be taken very seriously. The use of hallucinogenic drugs often results in unintentional self-harm.

Sexual Abuse
http://www.sexualrecovery.com/resources/articles/recognizesigns.doc
Users may resort to sex to release stresses resulting from drugs. Sexual abuse may also occur when they are intoxicated and can no longer discern right from wrong or good from bad. Frequently, youth who have not indulged in sexual activities prior to trying drugs do so after experimenting, because they are easily influenced. Peer pressure is powerful while they are under the influence of substances, and good kids can turn bad. Raves—unsupervised parties by teens where drugs, sex, and secrecy are common—can open the gates to sexual trials. It is not uncommon for youth with less conviction to become victims of sexual abuse by drug and alcohol users. Sexual abuses are part and parcel of usage. Some users resort to prostitution to get money for their habits. This takes an already bad self-image and makes it worse—and leaves the user vulnerable to a wide range of diseases that can be contracted from careless sex.

Financial Abuse
http://jop.sagepub.com/cgi/content/abstract/12/1/3
Bankruptcy can also confront parents and spouses of drug/alcohol users. If abuse is not caught early, a vicious cycle ensues in which loved ones are spending a lot of money to try to help an addict, while the addict can only think about getting and taking drugs. Unless a user gets help quickly, everyone close to them can sink into financial loss. Cars, jewelry, homes, antiques, stocks, and anything else marketable are sold to help users. If one's insurance doesn't cover treatment, families could end up paying twenty to thirty thousand dollars *per month* out of their own pockets to rehabilitate the loved one who is addicted. Addicts may also steal money or pawn goods. Add this element to the picture, and you can see how loved ones trying to help an addicted family member can drown financially and be taken advantage of to the point of abuse. Many addicts lose their homes, cars, families, and everything of value just to buy their drugs.

Solvent (Inhalant) Abuse
http://www.allwords.com/word-solvent%20abuse.html
Solvent abuse is the inhalation of fumes given off by various solvents (often cleaning substances) commonly found in the home. Solvents have been abused for some time, but this has only gained more attention in the last few years.

"Huffing" or "dusting" (inhaling fumes) is often done to get a quick buzz, and it can seriously affect the brain and lungs. It can cause permanent damage, as inhaling the fumes from chemical cleaners and other solvents causes oxygen deprivation to the brain. If this act is practiced constantly, it can be fatal. Sometimes, the first use can cause instant death. SAMHSA (Substance Abuse and Mental Health Service Administration) tells us that substances such as ink cleaners, paint thinners, aerosols, glue, shoe polish, gasoline, lighter fluid, deodorizers, correction fluid, degreasers, cleaning fluid, ether and other anesthetics, lacquer thinners, paint solvents, butane or propane, nail polish, spray paints, and other sprays can be used by young people to get high. Some will even sniff magic markers (highlighters used in studying) to get a buzz. Another form of inhalant is whippets. These are containers of nitrous oxide that children use to fill up balloons; they then breathe in the nitrous oxide from the balloon. These are very popular among children and very dangerous.

Alcohol Abuse
http://www.healthyplace.com/Communities/addictions/site/alcohol_substance_abuse.htm
Alcohol abuse is a destructive pattern of using alcohol to excess. Signs and symptoms of alcohol abuse can be nausea, anxiety, seizures, sweating, etc. It is often easy to tell someone has been abusing alcohol, as the odor is difficult to remove from the breath, and a distinct smell is emitted as it is eliminated from the body through sweat.

Drug Abuse
http://en.wikipedia.org/wiki/Drug_abuse
Drug abuse is the misuse or overuse of psychoactive or performance-enhancing drugs for a nonmedical (recreational) purpose. Drugs are not necessarily always harmful substances, but, when misused, they can damage one's health. Drug abuse has many signifiers and consequences, and, in the long run, can even cause someone to commit crimes. Drug abuse can seriously affect the lives of those close to the addict in many ways, including emotionally, psychologically, physically, and financially.

Stages of Abuse

Research indicates that users who have become physically or mentally dependent on drugs go through various stages before they are actually hooked. In most cases, users can attempt recovery at any of these stages—providing they are willing to quit and obtain help. Early treatment is valuable, and prevention through periodic testing is best. Experimentation, regular use, risky use, dependence, and addiction are the stages of substance abuse. Related behaviors can be addressed and treated at any stage. Not all users need to hit rock bottom before they can benefit from help. Here are descriptions of the basic stages of abuse:

1. **Trying/Experimenting**
   In this stage, the user voluntarily tries tobacco, alcohol, or drugs to see what kind of effect it has on him or her. Seldom does someone try substances with the goal of becoming addicted. Addiction can be an unfortunate by-product of experimentation. Most of the substances tried are usually obtained from, and used with, friends. Risks can be high, even in simple experimentation. A first hit can be a person's last. How drugs affect each individual is dependent on many factors, such as potency of the substance, size of the person, the nature of other substances ingested before and/or after the drug, the location of the experimentation, and much more. In experimentation, the user learns that he or she can produce a good feeling (euphoria) by using substances, so the desire grows. This can grow into using substances at parties, under peer pressure, or on weekends. In short order, the user discovers a lack of tolerance for the substance and soon discovers he or she can easily get drunk or high. In this stage, however, the user can still moderate his or her use via quantity to control mood swings or other noticeable side effects. The user has no sense of the danger he or she might be in at this stage. Often, people experimenting are trying to escape a problem. An older person might self-medicate by drinking to cope with depression after losing a spouse. A teenager, angry about his parents' divorce, could start smoking marijuana or huffing inhalants. Experimentation may even include a husband taking his wife's

prescription painkillers to cope with his back problem. Binge drinking is another example of experimentation that soon develops into serious addiction. In all of these cases, the substance seems to solve the problem—while, in reality, it only deepens it. Peer pressure is often a major factor in youth trying marijuana and alcohol for the first time. Alcohol and marijuana are gateways to harder drugs: cocaine, opiates, crack, prescription medications, amphetamines and methamphetamine, heroin, and many other drugs, such as club drugs and designer drugs. New drug mixtures are created every day by users and dealers searching for more bang for the buck. None of them is safe.

2. **Social Use**

The user, having learned that some substances can produce good feelings, starts to actively seek those feelings by planning a strategy as to when, where, and how much of the substance she will take. She will also strategize as to how to get the substance and how to pay for it. Tolerance develops, making the user need more of the substance to get the same level of feeling experienced when she first tried it. Still, the social user rationalizes the decision to use and often formulates basic rules to follow, such as: "I won't have a drink, or smoke a joint, until after I get home from work." She will not risk her job at this point, but she walks a fine line of wanting more of the drug or alcohol during inappropriate times and trying to not give herself away. She lives under self-deception. Too much social use begins to create problems: physical (i.e. hangovers), emotional, and social.

3. **Regular Use**

The user indulges in alcohol or drugs on a regular basis—maybe every weekend at fraternity parties, or every time he goes to a certain friend's home, or after every football game. Social drinking in adolescents often involves binge drinking, which can lead to death within hours, because of the high and quick alcohol toxicity in the blood. Regular use is also very serious, because it leads to the next step of abuse (below).

4. **Problem/Risky Use or Dependency**

This is the stage wherein the youth engages in ongoing drug/alcohol use, despite the harm. Users lose good judgment, self-control, and discernment of what is appropriate and what isn't. Behavior changes. and abuse manifests in failing grades, school disciplinary action, car accidents, physical or sexual assaults, and illegal acts. Users may start to encounter problems with the law, as well as withdrawal and alienation from their families. If, when, and how the transition from regular to risky use happens will differ with every individual. And while it doesn't happen to everyone, the National Institute on Alcohol Abuse and Alcoholism (NIAAA) estimates that nearly one-third of Americans engage in risky drinking patterns.

A study was completed by:
Reference: Partnership for a Drug Free America: Web site address: http://www.drugfree.org/intervention/wherestart/stages_of_substance_abuse

Percent of U.S. adults aged eighteen or older

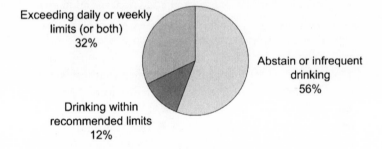

Exceeding daily or weekly limits (or both) 32%

Abstain or infrequent drinking 56%

Drinking within recommended limits 12%

5. **Chronic Use**

Individuals undergo mood swings and worry about their increasing tolerance to the drug along with the decreasing euphoria achieved. They try more of the drug, along with other drugs and alcohol. There is no control over the drug usage. Fainting spells and blackouts are common, emotions run high and wild, and rationalization and projection of the problem onto others is common. Sneakiness and deception are also common, illegal and desperate behavior increases, and the user's personality changes. Denial rules, and the family values fade. The user encounters problems at home, school, work, and with finances. His or her interest in good hygiene, self-esteem, and overall physical appearance deteriorate.

6. **Addiction**

   In this phase, the user is preoccupied with use and develops a higher tolerance—and withdrawal symptoms. Because of cravings for the substance, the user gives little regard to risk-taking or engaging in dangerous drug-related behaviors. The goal is to attain the euphoria and avoid physical and emotional pain. Criminal activities, prostitution, lying, and other antisocial behavior are common. Paranoia and psychosis occur. The user may attempt suicide. Blackouts are longer and more frequent. The user spins out of control, desperate for the next high. Despite dangers to herself or her family, job, or education (or any type of negative consequence), the addict will persist in using. Addiction is a rapid downhill run. Without treatment, the user will move toward a life-threatening existence.

7. **Denial**

   This accompanies the end stage of addiction, the addict now having run the full spectrum from trying, to social use, on to regular use, then risky use, followed by chronic consumption, and, ultimately, addiction. In this stage, the user refuses to admit there is a serious addiction problem that needs to be treated. Instead, the user comes up with dozens of excuses for poor performance, physical dishevelment, poor grades or loss of work, withdrawal from and loss of friends, alienation from family, and the ever-demanding state of addiction itself. If an intervention has not occurred before this stage, the user will likely see little means of redemption. At this stage, recovery takes a lot of commitment, a lot of time, and many deep pockets, along with the positive influences of faith and family.

8. **Treatment**

   As hopeless and disheartening as addiction may be, the disease is still treatable. Recovery rates for addiction are comparable to those found in such diseases as asthma, but they vary greatly depending on the drug the individual is addicted to. The key is to intercede as soon as possible to get help for the user. The longer the wait, the harder it becomes for the user to sustain recovery, and the more desperate the addict becomes—and the lower your bank account balance can drop. Recovery takes money, and lots of it. Before taking money out of your own pocket to finance the battle to save your loved one, check with your insurance companies to find out if your child is covered. Some communities may offer low-debt care facilities through special state or grant funding. Check out all the resources in your area, starting at the local level and moving up to the possibility of federal assistance, if need be. Sometimes private organizations offer funding for treatment or provide treatment through some type of community center (clinic, hospital, foundation). Addiction can be treated through programs and twelve-step groups. Treatment takes many forms, so be sure to check out the nature of the place where you will be sending your child for help. Learn about the therapy being used and what types of methodologies the therapists employ to help the user reach recovery. The addict may need to undergo repeated rehab programs. To learn more about understanding addiction, go to http://www.drugfree.org/Intervention/WhereStart/Understanding_Addiction

Substance use can be addressed *before* the person becomes addicted or dependent. When you check your loved one in to a treatment program, you have committed yourself as well as your family to the process, as all of you will serve as her support, her encouragement. You will need to know everything you can about drugs, alcohol, and other substances, as well as what you should expect in this long process of treatment—such as relapses.

Addiction is a cycle. Users become physiologically and psychologically addicted to chemicals. At some point, if they are lucky, they realize their lives are on a path of total destruction. They may try to quit drugs themselves—and they usually fail. If they don't get professional help, an intervention staged by concerned family or friends might lead them to get help. Users then go to a rehabilitation center, undergo detoxification, receive counseling, and then are expected to be responsible for their ongoing recovery. Often, users return to their old drug/alcohol habits (or relapse) and then must go into a rehab facility once more. This can happen several times, so please do not give up. The addict will be the one who determines when he or she has had enough.
(*Source: Mary Ann Amodeo/Join Together. Mary Ann is, Director of Alcohol and Drug Institute for Policy, Training, and Research and Associate Professor of Clinical Practice, Boston.*)

Determining Risky Behavior

What constitutes risky behavior by another person can be difficult to gauge, unless the issue is obvious. If others' behavior worries you, you owe it to yourself and them to say something. The slope from risky behavior to dependence is slippery and steep, and there are interventions for such users that can reduce the risk of harm to them and others. Alcohol or drug dependence follows risky behavior. According to Mary Ann Amodeo, Director of the Alcohol and Drug Institute for Policy, Training and Research at Boston University, the characteristics of dependence include:

+ Repeated use of alcohol or other drugs, leading to failure to fulfill major responsibilities related to work, family, school, or other roles.

+ Repeatedly drinking or using drugs in situations that are physically hazardous, such as driving or using heavy machinery while intoxicated.

+ Repeated legal problems.

At this stage, alcohol or other drug use may not yet be out of control. Many dependent people are able to work, maintain family relationships and friendships, and limit their use of alcohol or other drugs to certain time periods, such as evenings or weekends. But it is also difficult for them and for others to see the effect their substance use may be having on themselves, friends, and family members. And, again, there are appropriate interventions for substance users in this stage and for those close to them. Bright Futures offers tips on ways to be in tune with your children and to prevent experimenting that might turn into addiction:

<u>**Preemptive Precautions**</u> (from http://www.brightfutures.org)

+ Be aware of children and adolescents at risk for substance abuse.

+ Consider these factors:
    + Family history of alcohol or drug abuse
    + Early onset of conduct disorders or aggressive behavior

- History of ADD, school difficulties, mood and anxiety disorders
- History of poor supervision, trauma, or abuse

- Encourage and support continued abstinence. Users who want to get off drugs will find themselves swinging in and out of recovery. Enable them to not try drugs at all, but if they have, help them stay in recovery.

- Build your youths' self-esteem and allow them to try activities that will propel them to victory and not failure, such as art or music, band, sports, community volunteer events, or church-related involvement.

- Talk with your child or adolescent on how to handle peer pressure regarding drugs or alcohol. Also, discuss the dangers of tobacco use, stressing how substance (drugs, alcohol, tobacco) abuse indulgence can damage their social, academic, and family lives, as well as their pleasures in life, such as playing sports at school.

- Emphasize the hazards of riding with someone who is under the influence of substances. Tell your child it is fine if she calls you, no matter where she is, if she needs a ride home or feels threatened in any way. Also tell her that if she's been drinking or is under substance influence that you prefer she call you, even in the early hours of the morning, rather than ride or drive. Let your child know you will not chastise her when you pick her up from wherever she is but that the next day you will confront her on the matter.

- Discuss the Unity Oath and have everyone sign it. Make sure it is periodically discussed and that you check that your children are being faithful to it. You can photocopy the Oath, so all members of your family can sign it and have their own copy.

To customize the Oath to meet your family needs, feel free to add to or delete aspects of it. What is presented in the Oath are basic promises guaranteed by parent and child.

Before either party signs an oath, be sure to hash out the rules ahead of time. Along with this should be an agreement of what the punishment will be for violation of those rules. Once that aspect is agreed upon, you should move on to the oath where both parties will sign.

General Signs and Symptoms

Substance abuse is an extensive, excessive use of alcohol and/or drugs. So, how can you tell if someone you know is abusing a substance? It is not simple to tell if someone has gone above their limit, or even to know when you yourself have exceeded safe consumption. Signs and symptoms of substance abuse can be divided into short-term and long-term observations. Not everyone exhibits the same signs as the next person. There are many variables that influence how a person behaves under chemical influences. Some of these variables consist of the following:

+ The potency and purity of the substance

+ The quantity of substance ingested

+ The environment where use is taking place

+ The height/weight of a person doing drugs or drinking

+ An individual's level of tolerance to the substance

+ The nature of other substances (drugs/alcohol) the person may have taken

+ How much a person ate before and after indulging in drugs and/or alcohol

+ Type of food or beverage consumed prior to or after taking drugs/alcohol

+ The mental and emotional state of the person before indulging

Although there is no average drug user, there are some basic signs and symptoms displayed by users, especially habitual users, that can be more or less classified according to the person's performance or behavior, family environment, peers and/or school life, race, gender, and upbringing. We've compiled a list of some of the recognizable signs and symptoms.

Some signs of substance abuse by children or adolescents:

+ Their breath smells of alcohol or marijuana.

+ Their pupils may be dilated or constricted.

+ They experience abrupt attitude changes. If they previously enjoyed activities with the family, users may start refusing to interact with family members and friends.

+ Their school grades drop, and they have a lack of interest in homework.

+ They show emotion differently than what would be considered normal for them.

+ They're always arguing with siblings, even after being together for only a short time.

+ Their mood swings become more volatile, and they express unnecessary outbursts of temper and uncharacteristic withdrawal and self-isolation.

+ They refuse to do any chores.

+ They display a lack of interest in their appearance and/or diminished interest in their looks, hygiene, and social and presentation skills.

+ They attempt to hide red or dilated/constricted eyes by wearing sunglasses and/or using eye drops to make their eyes look normal.

+ They hang out with friends who are known users or sellers of illegal drugs.

+ They suddenly exhibit school discipline problems and poor attendance.

+ Their friends are always getting into trouble at home and/or in school.

- They constantly borrow money from family or friends and never pay anyone back.

- They steal, shoplift, and/or have costly things they can't afford, which they obtained illegally.

- They talk secretively to their friends, often in lingo or coded language.

- They show changes in their conversations with friends and become more secretive.

- There's evidence of drug paraphernalia (rolling papers, pipes, nitrous oxide canisters, balloons etc.) in their possession, their rooms, hidden throughout the house, in their cars, or elsewhere.

- Signs of inhalant usage (nail polish, correction fluid, etc.) are found; rags and bags, which can be used to sniff chemical fumes, may also be found.

- Gum, breath mints, mouthwash, or other breath-freshening substances to mask the smell of alcohol are found around the house.

- Prescription medications may go missing, or your pills may seem reduced in number. The same could be true for cough syrups.

- They spend an inordinate amount of time in their rooms, the bathroom, isolated in a rec room, or anywhere that they won't call attention to themselves. This allows them to conceal their drug use and stay out of the family mainstream.

- You smell incense, air deodorizers, or perfume in the house, perhaps especially in your children's rooms. They may use such items to hide smoke or chemical odors.

Always be on the lookout. Don't be lulled into complacency, thinking your child would never use drugs or drink. Think again. Keep the above list in mind, and key into your child, his actions, and his environment.

Drug Addiction Information:
An Overview

Overview

Even though we refer throughout this manual to *drug abuse*, we are also including alcohol and inhalants as substances that are abused and are also drugs.

Many people view drug abuse and addiction as strictly social problems. Parents, teens, older adults, and other members of the community tend to characterize people who take drugs as morally weak or having criminal tendencies. They believe drug abusers and addicts should be able to stop taking drugs if they are willing to change their behavior. These myths have not only pigeonholed those with drug-related problems, but they also have generalized the users' families, communities, and the health care professionals who work with them. Drug abuse and addiction make up a public health problem that affects many people and has wide-ranging social consequences. It is our goal to help the public replace myths and long-held mistaken beliefs about drug abuse and addiction with the scientific understanding that addiction is a chronic and relapsing, but treatable, disease. It is also our objective to stop children from becoming addicts. Testing and education can deter usage.

Addiction can begin with drug experimentation, followed by use and abuse, usually as a result of an individual making a conscious choice to use drugs. Innocent people have become addicted through trickery, deceit, and someone deliberately placing addictive substances in their systems through food or beverages. Addiction is not just a lot of drug use. Recent scientific research provides overwhelming evidence that drug addiction interferes with normal brain functioning, resulting in long-term metabolic damage and permanent impairment of brain activity. Changes that turn drug abuse into addiction can occur in the brain. It is a chronic, relapsing illness. Addicts suffer from obsessive drug cravings and usage, and they need help to stop using. Drug addicts need treatment for drug addiction to control this compulsive behavior. Many approaches are used in treatment programs to help patients deal with these cravings and possibly avoid drug-use relapse. Research by NIDA (National Institute on Drug Abuse) indicates that addiction is treatable but, most importantly, preventable, even if there is a family history of substance-abuse addiction. Treatment is tailored to individual needs. Users can learn to control their conditions and live relatively normal lives. Treatment can have a profound effect not only on drug abusers but also on society as a whole, because it significantly improves social and psychological behavior, decreases related criminal acts and violence, and reduces the spread of HIV and hepatitis. It can also dramatically reduce the costs to society of drug abuse.

Understanding drug addiction also helps us understand how to prevent use in the first place. Results from NIDA-funded prevention research have shown that comprehensive prevention programs that involve the family, schools, communities, and the media are effective in reducing drug abuse. It is necessary to keep sending the message that it is better to not start at all—and that is our hope for our children.

(Portions reprinted from the National Institute on Drug Abuse [NIDA], http://www.drugabuse.gov/)

Drug Dependency Characteristics

Treatment counselors and research show that although each client may display a unique pattern of addiction, he or she will probably manifest three or more of the symptoms listed below. Check to see if someone you know (your child?) is exhibiting any of these symptoms.

1. **Excessive or inappropriate use of drugs or alcohol**
   For example, getting high or drunk and not being able to fulfill obligations at home, at work, or with others; feeling as if cocaine or other substances are needed for inclusion in a group, to fit in with others, or to function at work or at home; or driving under the influence of substances.

2. **Preoccupation with drugs or alcohol**
   Some examples are: obsession with getting high or drunk; making substance use a high priority in life.

3. **Change in one's tolerance for addictive substances**
   For example, needing increasingly large amounts of substances to get high, or, conversely, getting high much more easily and by using less of the substance than was used in the past. This is typical.

4. **Having trouble reducing or abstaining from substance use**
   This includes not being able to control how much or how often one uses drugs or alcohol.

5. **Exhibiting withdrawal symptoms**
   Being physically sick, having the shakes, feeling nauseous, having gooseflesh, having a runny nose, or experiencing mental symptoms, such as depression, anxiety, or agitation.

6. **Using substances to avoid or stop withdrawal symptoms**
   Utilizing drugs or alcohol to prevent withdrawal sickness or to stop such symptoms once they've started.

7. **Using substances even though they cause problems in one's life**
   For example, not taking a doctor's, therapist's, or other professional's advice to stop using despite the ongoing problems these substances have caused in the user's life.

8. **Giving up previously important activities or losing friendships as a result of substance use**
   Discontinuing participation in activities once considered important, giving up friends who don't get high, losing friends because of substance abuse-related tendencies.

9. **Repeatedly returning to drugs or alcohol**
   Stopping substance use for a period of time (days, weeks, or months), only to relapse.

10. **Getting into trouble because of substance use**
    Losing jobs or being unable to find a job, getting arrested or having other legal problems, sabotaging relationships or having trouble with family or friends, or having serious money problems.

Because addiction is a disease that involves losing control, addicted individuals often enter treatment feeling demoralized and helpless. They get help to regain control of their lives. Thus, treatment must provide a safe, structured environment and regular, frequent contact with supportive treatment staff.

Drug Categories

(Please see charts in the appendix.)

Drugs are divided into major groups, and each group has its own subdivisions. Below are the main categories. Each specific drug type is discussed in detail in the following pages. Keep in mind that drugs *do* affect individuals differently.

Stimulants/Uppers
This group of drugs causes feelings of euphoria. The central nervous system (CNS) is stimulated, speeding up circulatory and other systems, which may result in heart failure. This category includes (but is not limited to) Ecstasy, amphetamines, methamphetamine, cocaine, and LSD.

Relaxants/Downers
These drugs act as tranquilizing agents, slowing down heart rate, breathing, and mental processes. The user feels calm, tranquil, and stress-free. With high doses, metabolic activity can slow to the point of stopping altogether, resulting in death. Depressants include alcohol, barbiturates, opiates, Ketamines, marijuana, methadone, GHB or Rohypnol (date-rape drug), and PCP, among others.

Inhalants
Depending on the substance inhaled, these chemicals may cause either stimulation or tranquilization. Often they can put a user in a state referred to as "on the nod," meaning euphoria alternating with sluggishness. There are over fourteen hundred different chemicals documented as being abused as inhalants; abusers (usually kids) seek out easy-to-obtain substances for the fumes to get high. This is most dangerous, because they are not meant for human consumption, and thus their effects on the body can be violent and deadly. Examples include correction fluid (such as Wite-Out®), airplane glue, nail polish remover, cooking spray, and many more. Currently, there is no test available to detect the type or amount of inhalants a user might be indulging in. If you

believe your child is engaging in this type of behavior, educate yourself more fully on inhalants, and lock up every type of substance in your home that may lend itself to being inhaled. Be sure to talk to your children, and detail in depth the harm these substances can do to their brains and other organs. Cite examples reported in newspapers and magazines, as well as on the Internet and other places you might find information. Remove or hide these household supplies. It is possible that the first abuse of inhalants will cause death.

Prescription Medications

Prescription medications can cause a vast array of effects, from stimulating to depressing and tranquilizing. Some of the most commonly abused prescription medications are morphine, Darvon, oxycodone, fentanyl, codeine, Talwin, Valium, and many more. All of these have derivatives, such as Darvocet in the Darvon group.

Over-the-Counter (OTC)

These drugs can be purchased without a prescription; some (Sudafed®, as an example) have limitations and restrictions on their purchase.

Steroids

These drugs are in a group by themselves, because they are not taken to achieve euphoria. Rather, they are ingested to increase muscle mass by increasing testosterone levels. They are prescription drugs, and they are banned in athletics.

Controlled Substances

These drugs are discussed in detail in succeeding pages in this book.

Controlled substances are heavily regulated, categorized, and catalogued so as to limit the opportunity for abuse.

Subject to the Controlled Substances Act of 1970:

CII: High Potential for Abuse

Use of these drugs may lead to severe physical and/ or psychological dependence. Written prescriptions are required. If not written, they must be confirmed in writing by a medical professional. No renewals are permitted.

CIII: Some Potential for Abuse

Use may lead to low-to-moderate physical dependence or high psychological dependence. Prescriptions may be oral or written and may have up to five renewals within a six-month period of time.

CIV: Low Potential for Abuse

Their use may lead to minor physical or psychological dependence. These prescriptions can be written or dictated orally, with up to five renewals permitted within a six-month period of time.

V: Subject to State and Local Regulation

Abuse of these drugs is low. These may be available without a prescription.

Club Drugs

Drugs in any of the above groups that are used illicitly at parties are referred to as club drugs. The use of them at such gatherings often prompts secretive behavior, sexual activity, and other unusual problems. This book discusses club drugs throughout.

Painkillers

Addiction from these can be deliberate or accidental. "Deliberate" are those people who desire the free feeling, high, or euphoria they get from taking Oxycontin, Vicodin, Percocet, Darvon, and a host of other pain-killing, hypnotic, or tranquilizing drugs. People who are addicted to these drugs will do anything to get their hands on them, as their bodies really crave the chemicals and their minds are entranced with the pleasing feeling and pain relief they get from ingesting these drugs. "Accidental" are those who have had to be on painkillers post-surgery or because of chronic, unforgiving pain, such as that with back injuries. In either case, these are truly addictive, life-changing, mind-affecting drugs. The authors have seen many people who ended up addicted to these medications after they had been legally prescribed by a physician. If you think your loved one is addicted to such medications—whether intentionally or accidentally—you need to get them help. Read our section on these drugs to get a better understanding of their effects, the signs and symptoms, and resolutions. An intervention might be needed.

Chapter Four

Drugs of Abuse, Part I

Alcohol

Common Terms for Alcohol: booze, sauce, juice, spirits, and hooch.

What It Is

Most people don't think of alcohol as a drug, but it is, and it's just as potent as cocaine, crystal meth, or any other substance that can be abused. Many think that because alcohol is legal:

+ it isn't dangerous;

+ you can't get addicted.

But, because alcohol is not classified as an illicit drug, it is easy for drinkers to overuse, and many people use alcohol with the sole intention of getting high (drunk). Alcoholics often accompany their drinking with pills (amphetamines, benzodiazepines) and/or cocaine.

Because alcohol is easy to get, it is dangerous, so when you consider the drugs your children are at risk of using, don't overlook alcohol. Often, if they are drinking, they are trying—or are addicted to—other substances.

Alcoholism is a condition of dependence that includes the following four symptoms:

+ **Craving:** A strong need or urge to drink.

+ **Loss of control:** Not being able to stop drinking once drinking has begun. Binge drinking is often a part of this scenario, especially in young people (i.e., college students).

+ **Physical dependence:** Withdrawal symptoms, such as nausea, sweating, the shakes, and anxiety after drinking is stopped.

- **Tolerance:** The need to drink greater amounts of alcohol to achieve a high. Many alcoholics need to drink daily to attain a level of functional normality. Alcoholics drink because their bodies crave the substance, not necessarily to get high. Many will drink before going to work, sometimes while at work, and then after work.

Diagnostic Criteria

It is sometimes easy to tell when someone is drunk simply by the strong smell of alcohol about them, as well as their uncoordinated actions, slurred speech, and social blunders. Often parents are able to sense something is wrong with their child but are unable to determine whether the problem is alcohol, drugs, or teenage angst.

It is surprisingly easy to drink beyond the legal alcohol limits and not seem impaired or show the classic obvious signs of drunkenness. Clinical and research studies have issued formal diagnostic criteria for alcoholism, including in the *Diagnostic and Statistical Manual of Mental Disorders, Fourth Edition*, published by the American Psychiatric Association, as well as in the *International Classification of Diseases*, published by the World Health Organization. These formal criteria come from the National Institute of Health:

> Diagnosis is the process of identifying and labeling specific conditions such as alcohol abuse or dependence (1). Diagnostic criteria for alcohol abuse and dependence reflect

the consensus of researchers as to precisely which patterns of behavior or physiological characteristics constitute symptoms of these conditions (1). Diagnostic criteria allow clinicians to plan treatment and monitor treatment progress; make communication possible between clinicians and researchers; enable public health planners to ensure the availability of treatment facilities; help health care insurers decide whether treatment will be reimbursed; and allow patients access to medical insurance coverage (1–3).

Diagnostic criteria for alcohol abuse and dependence have evolved over time. As new data becomes available, researchers revise the criteria to improve their reliability, validity, and precision (4, 5). This Alcohol Alert traces the evolution of diagnostic criteria for alcohol abuse and dependence through current standards of the American Psychiatric Association.[3] Please refer to Web site link for balance of study.

(Note: Information was excerpted from http://www.moderation. org/faq/alcoholism.shtml)

Effects

Alcoholism is a disease. Alcoholics feel a craving that can be as strong as the need for food or water. An alcoholic will continue to drink despite serious family, health, or legal problems. As is true with substance-abuse diseases, alcoholism is chronic, meaning that 1) it lasts a person's lifetime, 2) it usually follows a predictable course, and 3) it has symptoms. The risk for developing alcoholism is influenced by both a person's genes and lifestyle.

Many people believe alcoholism isn't inherited, but research shows the risk for developing alcoholism is genetically inclined. The University of California, San Francisco (UCSF) Family Alcoholism Study offers insight on this characteristic (http://web.pdx.edu/~hue/alcoholism_and_genetics.htm). Researchers now are working to discover the specific genes that put people at risk for alcoholism. Your friends, the amount of your stress, and the availability of alcohol are also factors that may increase the risk for alcoholism. These sites—as examples—reference alcoholism and genetics: http://alcoholism.about.com/ od/genetics/Genetics_of_Alcoholism.htm , http://pubs.niaaa.nih.gov/publications/aa60.htm and http://www.washingtonpost.com/wp-dyn/content/ article/2008/11/20/AR2008112002654.html.

But, remember—risk is not destiny. Just because alcoholism tends to run in families (genetic or familial) doesn't mean a child of an alcoholic parent will automatically become an addict. Some people develop alcoholism even though no family members have a drinking problem. By the same token, not all children of alcoholic families get into trouble with alcohol. Knowing you are at risk is important, though, because then you can take steps to protect yourself from developing problems with alcohol. Each person must learn whether he or she is at risk of developing addictions. Alcoholism cannot be cured. Even if an alcoholic hasn't been drinking for a long time, he or she can still suffer a relapse. To guard against relapse, an alcoholic must continue to avoid all alcoholic beverages throughout life. This is why former alcoholics refer to themselves as "recovering" alcoholics. Most treatment programs use a combination of counseling and medications to help a person stop drinking. Most alcoholics need help to recover from their disease. With support and treatment, many people are able to stop drinking and rebuild their lives. An alcoholic cannot risk having even one drink during recovery. One drink can lead to a relapse.

Alcoholism treatment can work, but, as with any chronic disease, there are levels of success. Even occasional drinkers can experience as many problems as addicts. Abuse can be just as harmful as full-blown addiction. A person can abuse alcohol without actually being an alcoholic. He or she might drink too much and too often but still not be fully dependent on alcohol. Some problems and effects linked to alcohol abuse include:

- Inability to fulfill work duties.

- Neglect of school or family responsibilities.

- Drunk-driving arrests (DUIs) and/or vehicular accidents

- Drinking-related medical conditions.

- Work-related problems and accidents.

Under some circumstances, even social or moderate drinking is dangerous, such as when driving, during pregnancy, or while taking certain medications. Alcoholics who try to cut down on drinking rarely succeed. Eliminating alcohol is usually the best course for recovering alcoholics. People who are not suffering from alcoholism but have experienced alcohol-related problems may be able to limit the amount they drink. If they can't stay within those limits, they need to stop drinking altogether. Less—or none—is always better.

(Note: *The above information has been extracted from an article by and reprinted with the permission of the National Institute on Alcohol Abuse and Alcoholism.*)

Source: *wwwdreamstime.com*

Alcohol Self-Test

To take this quiz, pretend you are your child and answer these questions honestly the way he or she would respond. You do not have to show this to anyone. (Note: These categories in no way constitute clinical diagnoses. As always, when seeking diagnosis and treatment for any health or mental condition, please see your doctor.)

+ Do you lose time from work or school because of your drinking?

+ Is drinking making your home life unhappy?

+ Is drinking affecting your reputation?

+ Have you ever felt remorse after drinking?

+ Have you gotten into financial difficulties as a result of your drinking?

+ Do you turn to those of questionable reputation for companionship?

+ Do you drink alone?

+ Does your drinking make you careless of your family's welfare?

+ Has your ambition decreased since drinking?

+ Do you crave a drink at a definite time daily?

+ Do you need a drink in the morning?

+ Does drinking cause you difficulty in sleeping?

+ Has your efficiency decreased with drinking?

- Is drinking jeopardizing your schoolwork, career, job, or business?

- Do you drink to escape from worries or troubles?

- Have you ever had a complete loss of memory as a result of your drinking?

- Has your physician ever treated you for drinking?

- Do you drink to build up your self-confidence?

- Have you ever been in a hospital or institution on account of drinking?

- Do you take a drink when you wake up to start your day?

If you have answered **"yes"** to any one of the questions, there is a strong likelihood you are an alcoholic or an abuser of alcohol.

If you have answered **"yes"** to any two, the chances are high you are an alcoholic.

If you have answered **"yes"** to three or more, you are likely an alcoholic.

Amphetamines

Common Terms for Amphetamines: bennies, uppers, and dexies.

What They Are

Amphetamines are stimulant drugs. They were first issued to combat troops in WWII to keep soldiers aggressive and ready to fight in the absence of food. They were once prescribed by doctors to reduce depression and suppress appetite. Prescriptions were stopped because of their harmful long-term side effects. This resulted in the prohibition of sales. Amphetamines are prescribed as treatment for the rare sleeping disorder narcolepsy and for hyperactive children. Amphetamines are man-made drugs that are not naturally produced by the body. Amphetamine sulphate (street-sold) is illegally manufactured in powder form and produced in varying strengths. The low quality of street amphetamine sulphate (5–20% purity) encourages users to inject or "mainline" the drug to increase the "rush" effect. The term "speed" is often used for amphetamines and methamphetamine.

Amphetamines were also found to be effective against head injuries, epilepsy, schizophrenia, alcoholism, opiate addiction, ADD/ADDH, chronic fatigue syndrome, and the common cold. They became popular as appetite suppressants to help with weight reduction, as a means of getting high (euphoria), and for the ease with which they could be obtained. However, they dangerously increase blood pressure, cause rapid heartbeat, and over-stimulate the central nervous system.

Well-known figures, such as Judy Garland, Elvis Presley, and even Adolf Hitler (among countless others), routinely took amphetamines. To date, this category of drugs has been taken widely as an alertness booster. Truck drivers, soldiers, and medical residents have been known to take amphetamines in order to keep alert and awake. College students take them during long study sessions, and athletes take them to increase their endurance levels. As a result of such widespread abuse, their use has become restricted as a controlled substance.

Amphetamines' crystalline powder form makes them popular as an injectable drug, which has turned this substance into a hot item in black market trading. Many doctors prescribed amphetamines until they came under scrutiny for overprescribing. Since then, amphetamines have become harder to obtain and thus have lost some of their popularity. They are often overlooked in favor of other stimulants, such as PCP, methamphetamine, and Ecstasy.

Legal Penalties
Although doctors can still prescribe them and patients may possess them by prescription, they are not frequently used because of the long-term dangers they pose to the body's internal systems. If the medication is not obtained by prescription, then it is illegal—illegal to produce, supply or possess. If amphetamines are prepared for injection, the increased penalties of Class A drugs apply. Amphetamine sulphate is an off-white or pale pink powder, though amphetamines in general can be synthesized into pill forms. Many street amphetamines are sniffed (inhaled), but they also can be prepared for injection, swallowed in a drink or as a pill, or smoked when mixed with tobacco and/or marijuana.

Effects

Physical
Amphetamines arouse and activate the body in a similar manner to the body's natural adrenaline. It takes some time and/or large doses to get high, and, once the high is achieved, the individual "crashes" quickly or plummets in feelings and body metabolism. Amphetamines postpone tiredness and hunger but do not satisfy the need for rest or food. The body's energy stores are depleted through the increased demands on it. A battle between the stimulating effects of the drug and the body trying to relax becomes evident when feelings change to anxiety, irritability, and restlessness.

Breathing and heart rate speed up, the pupils widen, and appetite is suppressed. Other effects include dry mouth, talkativeness, sweating, and increased blood pressure. Initially, sex drive can increase, but the long-term use of amphetamines can lead to a reduction in sex drive. Heavy amphetamine users risk damaging blood vessels or experiencing heart failure, particularly those people with existing high blood pressure or high heart rates and those who undertake strenuous exercise while using the drug. Many women who ingest amphetamines regularly find their periods become irregular or cease altogether, a condition that may be linked to the drug itself or the weight loss associated with it. Many amphetamine users refer to the feeling of being "wired" while using the drug. Every system in their bodies has quickened and is overstimulated.

Psychological
Increased confidence, exhilaration, alertness, increased aggression, irritability, and feelings of paranoia are the major psychological effects of amphetamines. Frequent high doses can produce delirium, panic, hallucinations, and overwhelming feelings of persecution and paranoia. Impatience, erratic behavior, and a frazzled mind-set are all characteristic of amphetamine use.

Dependence
To maintain the desired effects, regular users have to take increasing doses. Profound psychological dependence is common. Persons attempting withdrawal experience a deep craving for the drugs. Hunger, tiredness, irritability, disturbed sleep, and acute depression are characteristics of amphetamine dependence.

Health Hazards
Heavy amphetamine use can cause mental illness in which people report seeing, feeling, or hearing things that aren't really there. These drugs can also induce or heighten suicidal tendencies. Injectors run the risk of thrombosis, blood poisoning, and abscesses. Those who share their injection equipment are at risk of infection with blood-borne diseases, such as HIV and hepatitis C. Because irrational feelings of power, strength, and euphoria overtake abusers, they're a danger to themselves and those around them. Amphetamine users who want to stop should seek advice from local drug assistance sources. Counselors and medical workers in the field can help abusers manage their withdrawal and offer supportive relaxation techniques and information on managing cravings.

Rates per 100,000 population of amphetamine and methamphetamine Emergency Department visits by metropolitan area 1995-2002

	1995	1996	1997	1998	1999	2000	2001	2002	% change 1995-2002*
Total Coterminous U.S.	11	9	12	10	9	12	13	15	39.9
Northeast									
Boston	...	4	...	5	6	10	11	15	†
Buffalo	3	3	2	2	4	3	2	4	†
New York	1	1	1	1	1	1	1	2	81.8
Newark	1	1	1	2	2	4	6	9	573.8
Philadelphia	7	7	11	9	10	11	10	8	†
South **									
Atlanta	8	10	17	16	13	15	14	23	170.0
Baltimore	2	2	4	5	7	8	12	10	500.4
Dallas	14	10	17	21	16	19	16	12	†
Miami	1	...	2	4	3	5	4	4	232.9
New Orleans	3	4	6	6	5	10	11	16	506.9
Midwest									
Chicago	3	4	4	4	4	6	7	8	143.8
Detroit	7	11	9	8	4	...	11	11	†
Minneapolis	5	6	12	6	9	14	21	19	270.1
St. Louis	6	5	6	7	12	11	12	24	282.6
West									
Denver	30	13	32	15	21	27	26	29	†
Los Angeles	23	23	23	15	21	28	32	39	71.2
Phoenix	60	51	60	39	41	60	52	65	8.9
San Diego	47	49	78	62	62	67	62	68	43.4
San Francisco	93	75	81	49	50	59	88	91	†
Seattle	26	20	49	29	36	59	51	46	77.1

*This column denotes statistically significant (p < 0.05 increases and decreases between estimates for the periods noted.

**Rates for Washington, DC, were not included as 7 of the 8 years had RSEs greater than 50%

†No statistically significant change was found between rates in 1995 and 2002

NOTE: These estimates are based on a representative sample of non-Federal, short-stay hospitals with 24-hour Eds in the coterminous U.S. Dots (...) indicate that an estimate with the RSE greater than 50% has been suppressed.

SOURCE: Office of Applied Studies, SAMHSA, Drug Abuse Warning Network, 2002 (03/2003 update).

Methamphetamine

Common Terms for Methamphetamine:
Street methamphetamine is called speed, meth, or chalk. Methamphetamine hydrochloride—clear, chunky, icelike crystals that can be smoked—is referred to as ice, crystal, glass, and tina.

What It Is
Methamphetamine is an addictive stimulant drug that strongly activates certain systems in the brain. It's chemically related to amphetamines but has a greater effect on the central nervous system. Both drug types have some limited therapeutic uses, one of which is the treatment of obesity. Methamphetamines are made in illegal laboratories, often in home meth labs, and has a high potential for abuse and addiction. Methamphetamine, an enhanced form of amphetamine, was synthesized in Japan, laying the groundwork for severe methamphetamine abuse and addiction in that country.

From: http://www.amphetamines.com/ice.html

> "Ice is a very dangerous form of methamphetamine and is in much more demand for its deep sense of euphoria, and for its ability to make the user think he can do anything, and the world is a wonderful place to live. But ice is a highly addictive drug, and expensive. It also deteriorates and disfigures your teeth and face tremendously.
>
> Ice is re-crystallized methamphetamine. Characteristic of the highs and lows of drug use, meth users often experience the crash after the high (euphoria), which leads to prolonged depression and fatigue. If meth is smoked in its base form, it is known as SNOT because of its unappetizing smell and appearance. Smoking this substance is similar to smoking crack cocaine."

The effects of using methamphetamines (ice, too) may include:

+ Extreme elation

- Self-empowerment
- Wakefulness and alertness
- Overconfidence
- Lack of good judgment
- Frequent displays of aggression
- Chattiness
- Preference of drug over food; weight loss
- Daredevil attitude
- Increased physical activity, especially in a sports player

But all of these effects have down sides, which include the user suffering the following:

- Loss of mental focus
- Severe cravings for the drug and an obsession with getting a fix
- Profound despair
- Exhaustion, sometimes resulting in the user sleeping for days
- Apathy and lack of interest in what's going on around the user
- Paranoia—trusting no one—and inflicting danger on others
- Deep-seated neuroses

Meth can enslave users, bankrupt them, ruin their looks, and waste them to the point of death. Meth labs in homes, basements, garages, sheds, and other places regularly explode, burning or killing the people in the lab; as well, people nearby may be injured. Meth users are often perpetrators of crimes, particularly theft, robbery, rape, assault, and even murder.

Health Hazards

Methamphetamine initially releases high levels of the chemical dopamine, which stimulates brain cells, enhancing mood and body movement. It also damages brain cells that contain dopamine as well as serotonin, another chemical that boosts energy. Over time, meth-amphetamine appears to cause reduced levels of naturally produced dopamine, which can result in symptoms of depression and those of Parkinson's disease, a severe motor function disorder.

Effects

Methamphetamines can be taken orally, snorted, injected, and/or smoked. Immediately after smoking or intravenous injection, the meth user experiences an intense sensation that lasts a few minutes and is extremely pleasurable. It is a euphoric high, but not a rush. Users may become addicted quickly and use it with increasing frequency and in increasing doses. Taking even small amounts of meth can increase alertness, respiration, body temperature, heart rate, blood pressure, and physical activity, while it decreases appetite. Other CNS effects include irritability, insomnia, confusion, tremors, convulsions, anxiety, paranoia, and aggressiveness. Hyperthermia and convulsions can result in death. It can cause irreversible damage to blood vessels in the brain, producing strokes. Other effects of methamphetamine are respiratory problems, irregular heartbeat, and extreme anorexia. It can result in cardiovascular death.

Extent of Use

Monitoring the Future Study (MTF: National Survey of Drug Use), in 2007, assessed approximately fifty thousand students in eighth, tenth, and twelfth grades in over four hundred secondary schools nationwide regarding their extent of drug use across the country. Recent data from the survey indicates the following: (*Lifetime* means at least one use during the lifetime)

+ In 2008, 2.8% of high-school seniors reported lifetime use of meth.

+ Eighth-graders reported 2.3% lifetime, 1.2% annual, and .7% 30-day use.

+ In the first six months, nearly 59% of substance-abuse treatment admissions (excluding alcohol) in many states were for meth.

+ The numbers of clandestine meth labs increased in various states.

+ Many MDMA (Ecstasy) and cocaine users were found to be switching to methamphetamines, ignorant of its severe toxicity, although cocaine use had remained at a constant level.

+ In alternative-lifestyle clubs, meth is often taken by injection, placing users and their partners at risk for transmission of HIV, hepatitis C, and other STDs.

Methamphetamine versus Amphetamines

Methamphetamines are addictive stimulant drugs that activates certain physiological systems in the brain. Methamphetamine is chemically related to amphetamine, but the central nervous system effects of methamphetamine are more expansive. Both drugs have some limited therapeutic uses, primarily in the treatment of obesity. *(Note: Material excerpted from the National Institute on Drug Abuse, InfoFacts: Methamphetamine [Rockville, MD: US Department of Health and Human Services]),* http://www.nida.nih.gov/infofacts/methamphetamine.html, January 9, 2006.

Your Amphetamine Doped-Up Brain

Brain cells don't regenerate. Some organs try to repair themselves to a certain degree if assaulted by chemicals, but brain cells do not possess this ability.

Thus, consider the graphic representation of your brain on meth, as provided in http://www.nida.nih.gov/infofacts/methamphetamine.html and http://amphetamines.com/braindamage.html. *(Note: Information gathered from National Institute on Drug Abuse, InfoFacts: Methamphetamine; Rockville, MD: US Department of Health and Human Services; from the Web at New York Times, 20 July 2004, January 9, 2006.)*

The *New York Times* (20 July 2004: http://www.dare.com/home/DrugInformation/Story3a64.asp?N=DrugInformation&M=11&S=25 article offers (in part):

> "The brain's region to make memories—called hippocampus—lost 8% of its tissue, which is similar to the loss seen in Alzheimer's patients. Addicts on meth did worse on memory tests than their peers of good health.

> "In the *New York Times* article, Dr. Thompson said, "The study held one other surprise. 'White matter, composed of nerve fibers that connect different areas, was severely inflamed, making the addicts' brains 10% larger than normal. This was shocking,' he said ..."

Marijuana

Common Terms for Marijuana: weed, grass, herb, pot, Mary Jane, joint, ganga, reefer, and hemp.

What It Is

Marijuana is the most commonly used illegal drug in the US. It is made up of dried and shredded leaves, stems, seeds, and flowers of the hemp plant (*Cannabis sativa[active ingredient* 9-tetrahydrocannabinol, or THC.[4] Today's marijuana is many times stronger than that of the 1960s and 1970s. This *is* the most abused drug in the United States and does lead to the use of harder and more deadly drugs. Marijuana *is* a gateway drug! Use consists of joints (rolled cigarettes), blunts (hollowed-out cigars filled with marijuana), and bongs (water pipes where smoke is drawn through water to add a cooling effect). When smoked, its effects begin almost immediately. THC rapidly passes from the lungs into the bloodstream, which carries the chemical to organs throughout the body, including the brain.[5]

Effects

Marijuana (THC) acts upon specific sites in the brain, called cannabinoid receptors, kicking off a series of cellular reactions that ultimately lead to the "high" that users experience when they smoke marijuana. Short-term effects of marijuana use include euphoria, distorted perceptions, memory impairment, and difficulty thinking and solving problems. Additional short-term effects are bloodshot eyes, dry mouth and throat, and a faster heartbeat and higher pulse. Long-term effects include deteriorating physical and mental health, declining cognitive abilities, loss of career advancement due to at-work accidents and other problems, along with increased lateness/absences and workers' compensation claims. The ability to hold on to a job for the long term is minimized because of marijuana usage. Adverse reactions to marijuana are acute panic/anxiety reaction and a feeling of being out of control. Long-term use will lead to addiction as well as a desire for stronger drugs. Someone who smokes marijuana every day may be functioning at a suboptimal intellectual level all the time. Research on the long-term effects of marijuana abuse indicates some changes in the brain similar to those seen after long-term abuse of other major drugs. For example, cannabinoid withdrawal in chronically exposed animals leads to an increase in the activation of the stress-response system and to changes in the activity of nerve cells containing dopamine.[6]

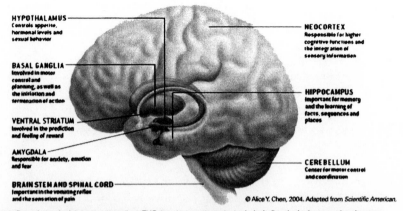

HYPOTHALAMUS
Controls appetite,
hormonal levels and
sexual behavior

NEOCORTEX
Responsible for higher
cognitive functions and
the integration of
sensory information

BASAL GANGLIA
Involved in motor
control and
planning, as well as
the initiation and
termination of action

HIPPOCAMPUS
Important for memory
and the learning of
facts, sequences and
places

VENTRAL STRIATUM
Involved in the prediction
and feeling of reward

AMYGDALA
Responsible for anxiety, emotion
and fear

CEREBELLUM
Center for motor control
and coordination

BRAIN STEM AND SPINAL CORD
Important in the vomiting reflex
and the sensation of pain

© Alice Y. Chen, 2004. Adapted from *Scientific American.*

When marijuana is smoked, its active ingredient, THC, travels throughout the body, including the brain, to produce its many effects. THC attaches to sites called cannabinoid receptors on nerve cells in the brain, affecting the way those cells work. Cannabinoid receptors are abundant in parts of the brain that regulate movement, coordination, learning and memory, higher cognitive functions such as judgment, and pleasure.

Source: *http://www.nida.nih.gov/ResearchReports/Marijuana/default.html*

Background

Marijuana is indigenous to Central America and South America, although it has spread to many other regions and is illegally grown for personal and distributive use. Marijuana consists of the flowers, subtending leaves, and stalks of mature pistillate female plants. Historically, it has been used as long ago as the third millennium B.C.[7]

Effects on Pregnancy

It is conceivable that even low concentrations of THC, when administered during the perinatal period, could have profound and long-lasting consequences for both brain and behavior. Research has shown that some babies born to women who used marijuana during their pregnancies display altered responses to visual stimuli, increased tremulousness, and a high-pitched cry, which could indicate problems with neurological development.[8]

Marijuana, memory, and the hippocampus

The hippocampus is an area of the brain responsible for memory formation. As people age, they lose neurons in the hippocampus, which decreases their ability to learn new information. Chronic THC exposure may hasten age-related loss of hippocampal neurons.[9]

Marijuana's effect on schoolwork and social life

Research has shown that marijuana's negative effects on attention, memory, and learning can last for days or weeks after the acute effects of the drug wear off. Daily use causes students to function at a reduced intellectual level most or all of the time. This daily use can result in lower grades and dropping out of school.[10]

Effect on Driving
Because marijuana impairs judgment and motor coordination, and slows reaction time, an intoxicated person has an increased chance of being in involved in and being responsible for an accident. A recent survey found that 6.8% of drivers, mostly under thirty-five, who were involved in accidents tested positive for THC.[11]

Treatment options (at the printing of this book)
Behavioral interventions, including cognitive behavioral therapy and motivational incentives (e.g., providing vouchers for goods or services to patients who remain abstinent), have shown efficacy in treating marijuana dependence. Although no medications are currently available, recent discoveries about the workings of the cannabinoid system offer promise for the development of medications to ease withdrawal, block the intoxicating effects of marijuana, and prevent relapse.[12]

Source: www.thinkstock.com

Medical Marijuana

Medical marijuana had its start as far back as 1990. Dronabinol (Marinol®) and nabilone (Cesamet®) were the only FDA-approved marijuana-based medications that doctors could prescribe. They were used for the treatment of nausea in cancer chemotherapy patients and for appetite stimulation for patients with AIDS. They were in pill form and contained a synthetic form of THC. Recently, Sativex has been made available in the United Kingdom and Canada. This is a chemically pure mixture of plant-derived THC and cannabidiol. It is available in a mouth spray and has been approved for the relief of cancer-associated pain as well as spasticity and neuropathic pain in multiple sclerosis.

Source: www.dreamstime.com

Source: www.dreamstime.com

Because of the liberal nature of many of our state congresses, marijuana is now available in fourteen states:

Alaska	California	Colorado
Hawaii	Maine	Michigan
Montana	Nevada	New Jersey
New Mexico	Oregon	Rhode Island
Vermont	Washington	Washington D.C.[13]

Interestingly enough, in Washington DC, they have passed a law that allows residents to legally obtain the drug for medical reasons, and it also includes a provision that the drug is to be provided at a discount to poor residents who qualify. At the writing of this book, medical marijuana won't be available in D.C. until 2011.

It is approved for use in the treatment of the following ailments:

Arthritis	Cancer/Chemotherapy	
Chronic Pain	Fibromyalgia	
Multiple Sclerosis	Glaucoma	Nausea

(Collected from many opinion sources.)

Nabilone (Cesamet®) comes in a capsule form. It is also a Schedule II drug, which means it has a high potential for abuse. Dronabinol (Marinol®) also comes in pill form. Sativex marks the arrival of the second generation of cannabis-based medications. This new product (currently available in the United Kingdom and Canada) is a chemically pure mixture of plant-derived THC and cannabidiol, formulated as a mouth spray and approved for the relief of cancer-associated pain as well as spasticity and neuropathic pain in multiple sclerosis.[14]

Authors' Remarks:

As parents, the authors of this book see many problems created by medical marijuana. The individual states are trying to make marijuana legal so they can collect taxes. If they are going to distribute marijuana and call it "for medical use only," they should do the same thing they do with prescription medications. It should be put in a form that can be prescribed only by specially licensed medical doctors treating patients with marijuana, the same as they do for the treatment of opiate addiction with Suboxone. And all of the medical doctors that are able to prescribe marijuana, should be licensed, as are doctors who can legally prescribe Suboxone. Distributing marijuana through dispensaries and not pharmacies opens the whole system to corruption. Marijuana is way too easy to obtain at this time, regardless of medical need. This is a drug that doesn't scare the public, because people think of it as a peaceful drug, a mellow drug, a love drug, a harmless drug. Now that the government is putting out a message that marijuana has medical benefits, parents are supposed to tell their children that marijuana use is bad, knowing that their child will come back saying, "If it's prescribed for various medical problems, how can it hurt me?" How, then, can parents tell their kids not to use it, when their kids have a high chance of coming in contact with so-called medical users? People who use marijuana do not consider themselves drug addicts like those using heroin or cocaine.

Additionally, medical marijuana is distributed in the same form as street marijuana, except is it typically stronger. It doesn't give the appearance of a medication, but rather that of "legal" use of an illegal and damaging drug. Parents who look this up on the Internet will see users trying nabilone and dronabinol to achieve the same high as marijuana. These same people will try (and probably succeed) to get approved for medical marijuana. This is opening up the use of marijuana to rampant abuse. Our nation cannot afford to have this illegal drug spread around and endangering our youth. We need to take this drug more seriously and stop glorifying its use.

Synthetic Marijuana

Common Terms for Synthetic Marijuana: K2, spice, herbal incense, genie, Yucatan fire, and zohai.

What It Is

Synthetic marijuana is non-marijuana plant material (not containing marijuana or other psychoactive plants) that has been sprayed with chemicals. These chemicals target the same receptors that marijuana (THC) targets. They are compounds that don't occur in nature and are basically stronger than their true marijuana counterpart.[15]

Effects

Since synthetic marijuana is stronger than natural marijuana (THC), these products can lead to a potential for high dependency and dangers of overdosing, as well as additional negative physiological effects.

Background

Synthetic marijuana is sold in head shops as incense and is typically produced in China and Korea. Since this is not a controlled, FDA-approved manufacturing process, many users get sick. As usual, the people using these substances are young. This is the age at which drug addiction starts. One study performed by Dr. Anthony Scalzo, a toxicologist at Saint Louis University, said the use of synthetic marijuana has caused hallucinations, severe agitation, elevated heart rates, vomiting, seizures, and other adverse reactions. He goes on to say that these drugs affect the users' cardiovascular and central nervous systems. These are not the areas affected by marijuana. They don't provide the "mellow" that users expect. A CBS news report stated that synthetic marijuana can give the user a high up to fifteen times more powerful than that produced by marijuana. The Georgia Poison Center has received more than fifty calls about synthetic marijuana within a sixty-day period.[16]

Crystal Meth

Common Terms for Crystal Meth: crank, tweak, go-fast, ice

What It Is

Crystal methamphetamine, better known as crystal meth, comes in many forms and can be smoked, snorted, orally ingested, or injected. The smokable form is called ice (see previous page) and is often a powdery substance. The drug alters moods in different ways, depending on how it is taken. Immediately after smoking or injecting it intravenously, the user experiences an intense rush, or "flash," that lasts only a few minutes and is described as extremely pleasurable. Snorting or oral ingestion produces a euphoric high but not an intense rush. Snorting produces effects within three to five minutes, and oral ingestion produces effects within fifteen to twenty minutes. As with similar stimulants, crystal methamphetamine most often is used in a binge-and-crash pattern. Because tolerance for crystal meth concentration in the blood falls significantly—users try to maintain the high by bingeing on the drug. In the 1980s, ice came into widespread use. It's a large, usually clear crystal of high purity that is smoked in a glass pipe like crack cocaine. The smoke is odorless, but it leaves a residue that can be inhaled; this produces effects that may continue for twelve hours or more.

The drug can be sprinkled in with foods; thus, some people ingest the drug without realizing that it was mixed with a common substance. Reports exist of a new form of crystal meth that smells and looks like strawberry pop rocks (a candy) and is deceiving young children into thinking they're just eating candy. The drug also comes in other flavors, such as chocolate, peanut butter, cola, cherry, grape, and orange. Ingestion is dangerous, with speedy effects putting many kids in the ER. Whether this report is accurate or not, you should constantly advise your children to never, ever accept candy or other foods from people, especially those they don't know. Even well-meaning adults can be tricked into thinking they're giving candy to a child when the substance may have been mixed with lethal chemicals.

Crystal meth users often use the drug for days at a time, sometimes for over a week, not allowing their bodies to rest in between usage. Instead, every nerve in the system is energized and agitated. While on speed runs, users don't eat, and their bodies remain tense and taut, their hearts working overtime. Jim Parker, author of *Crystal Meth: Maximum Speed* (Do It Now Foundation, February 2007), offers, "For needle users, add in the hazards that come with injecting any drug. And for ice smokers, multiply it all by the still largely unknown risk factor of exposing lung tissue to vaporized meth crystals. That's why it's not a big mystery that you don't run into many old speed freaks in the real world. They don't live long enough to get old."

Death in a needle

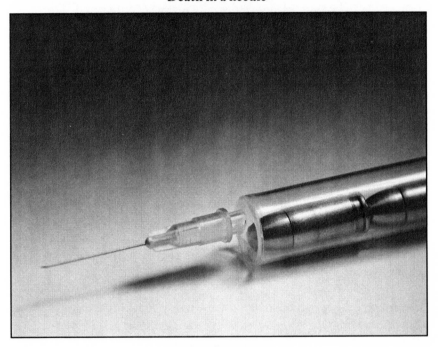

Source: *www.dreamstime.com*

Effects
Crystal meth revs up the body's systems, producing a sort of hyperdrive, and causes neurons to move from synapse to synapse at rapid speeds.

Crystal meth, a powerful stimulant, even in small doses, can increase wakefulness and decrease appetite. It provides a brief, intense sensation, or rush, when smoked or injected. Oral ingestion or snorting produces a long-lasting high, which reportedly can continue for as long as half a day, instead of a rush. Both the rush and the high are believed to result from the release of very high levels of dopamine into areas of the brain that regulate feelings of pleasure.

Long-term crystal meth abuse results in many damaging effects, including addiction characterized by compulsive drug-seeking and drug abuse, accompanied by changes in the brain. In addition to being addicted to crystal meth, chronic users exhibit symptoms that include violent behavior, anxiety, confusion, and insomnia. They also can display a number of psychotic features, such as paranoia, auditory hallucinations, and mood disturbances that can result in homicidal and suicidal thoughts.

With chronic use, tolerance for the drug can develop, resulting in users taking higher doses more frequently. In some cases, abusers forego food and sleep while indulging in a form of bingeing known as a "speed run," injecting as much as a gram of the drug every two to three hours over several days until the user runs out of the drug or is too disoriented to continue. Chronic abuse can lead to psychotic behavior, characterized by intense mistrust and obsessive behavior, hallucinations, and rages.

(Note: Excerpts reprinted from The National Institute on Drug Abuse [NIDA].)

MDMA (Ecstasy)

Common Terms for MDMA: Ecstasy, Adam, XTC, X, hug, beans, M, roll, love drug, and snowbird.

What It Is

MDMA is a synthetic psychoactive drug chemically similar to the hallucinogens mescaline and methamphetamine. MDMA is available in pill form—it's a common party or club drug.

Background

The German pharmaceutical company, Merck, invented MDMA (or Ecstasy or 3,4-methylenedioxymethamphetamine) in 1912. It called attention to itself in the 1950s when government groups, the CIA (http://www.cia.gov), experimented with MDMA on Americans under project MK-ULTRA to brainwash them and manipulate their minds for espionage and assassinations. John Grisham's book and the movie titled *Conspiracy Theory* show this type of attempt at mind control. The United States Army intended to use Ecstasy, as well as LSD and scopolamine, for mind control and as truth serums; their initial studies were limited to dogs and monkeys. The government and military have abandoned their trials using these drugs. Through time, however, MDMA has popped up in the black market and is now used illegally as a recreational drug.

Effects

The purity of MDMA is always an issue, because it is produced in illegal labs. Hence, its perils are extreme, particularly to brain chemistry, where MDMA exerts its primary effects. The brain needs the chemical serotonin for neurotransmission. Serotonin plays an important role in regulating mood, aggression, sexual activity, sleep, and sensitivity to pain, so MDMA's effects on it can cause memory loss, major mood swings, and other psychoses. MDMA interferes with the body's ability to regulate temperature, resulting in an increase in body temperature, as well as possible liver, kidney, and cardiovascular system failure. Abusers face many of the same risks as those who indulge in other stimulants, such as cocaine and amphetamines. There is a rise in heart rate and blood pressure, muscle tension, involuntary teeth clenching, nausea, blurred vision, faintness, chills or sweating, along with confusion, depression, sleep problems, drug craving, and severe anxiety. These problems can occur while taking the drug and sometimes can recur days or weeks after taking MDMA.

Cocaine

Common Terms for Cocaine: As a fine, white crystalline powder, cocaine is also referred to as coke, C, snow, flake, blow, crack, candy, and snowbird, among other terms.

What It Is
Cocaine is a powerfully addictive stimulant that directly affects the brain. It has been labeled the drug of the 1980s and 1990s because of its extensive popularity and use during those decades. However, cocaine is one of the oldest known drugs. The pure chemical, cocaine hydrochloride, has been an abused substance for more than a hundred years, and people have ingested coca leaves, the source of cocaine, for thousands of years.

Snorting cocaine

Source: www.dreamstime.com

How It's Used
Cocaine is a Schedule II drug and has a high potential for abuse. A doctor can administer it for legitimate medical uses: for local anesthesia or for pain regulation in some eye, ear, nose, and throat surgeries. It's usually ingested in powdered form; it easily dissolves in water, can be taken intravenously, rubbed

into mucosal tissues, or taken intranasaly. (through the nose). Freebase is smokable cocaine. The fumes are inhaled and have the same potency as injected cocaine.

Cocaine Apparatus

Source: www.dreamstime.com

The principal routes of cocaine administration are oral, intranasal, intravenous, and inhalation. The slang terms for these routes are, respectively, chewing, snorting, mainlining, injecting, and smoking (including freebase and crack cocaine). Snorting is the process of inhaling cocaine powder through the nostrils. Injecting releases the drug directly into the bloodstream and heightens the intensity of its effects. Smoking involves the inhalation of cocaine vapor or smoke into the lungs, where absorption is rapid. Abusers may experience rotting of the septum and other parts of the nose. The drug can also be rubbed onto mucosal tissues. Some users combine cocaine powder or crack with heroin in a "speedball." The quicker the drug is absorbed into the bloodstream, the more extreme the high. Repeated doses give a prolonged high. The drug is generally sold on the street and may be diluted with cornstarch, talcum powder and/or sugar, or with such active drugs as procaine (a chemically related local anesthetic) or other stimulants, like amphetamines. Its ease of dilution puts its purity in question.

Effects

Through the use of sophisticated technology, scientists can actually see the dynamic changes that occur in the brain as an individual takes the drug: the rush, the high, and, finally, the craving. They can also identify parts of the brain that become active when a cocaine addict sees or hears environmental stimuli that trigger the craving for cocaine. Because these types of studies pinpoint specific brain regions, they are critical to identifying targets for developing medications to treat cocaine addiction. Hallmark symptoms of use include a rise in heart rate and blood pressure, irritability, and sleeplessness. Appetite is reduced, and users show signs of aggravation and other symptoms of drug abuse. Withdrawal results in depression or a crash, extreme fatigue, and sleepiness.

Source: www.thinkstock.com

Crack Cocaine

Common Terms for Cocaine: ice cube, uzi, crack, white tornado, ball, and blowout

What It Is

Crack cocaine is a strong central nervous system (CNS) stimulant and the freebase form of cocaine. The United States and other countries face a serious drug problem because of this—one of the most powerfully addictive drugs of all. The term *crack* refers to the crackling sound heard when the substance is heated. It is almost always smoked, though there are reports of users injecting it. Sometimes users can't find powdered cocaine to inject, so they'll use crack instead. Crack "rocks" tend to be sold in sizes of approximately 0.1 to 0.2 grams that sell for about $10 and $20 respectively (at the printing of this book). Abusers may go into debt trying to maintain or intensify their long-term habits.

Crack rocks are white or off-white and vary in size and shape. This substance produces an immediate high and is easy and inexpensive to produce. Smoking crack cocaine delivers large quantities of the drug to the lungs, producing an immediate and intense euphoric effect, comparable to intravenous injection, but it does not last long. When crack is smoked, the user experiences a high in less than ten seconds. The effects of smoking crack are felt almost immediately and are very intense. For example, the high from smoking cocaine may last from five to ten minutes, while the high from snorting the drug can last for fifteen to twenty minutes.

Compulsive cocaine use seems to develop more rapidly when the substance is smoked rather than snorted. A tolerance to the cocaine high may be developed, and many addicts report that they fail to achieve as much pleasure as they did from their first cocaine exposure. There is no safe way to use cocaine. Any route of administration can lead to absorption of toxic amounts of cocaine, leading to acute cardiovascular or cerebrovascular (brain-blood) emergencies that could result in sudden death. Repeated cocaine use by any route of administration can produce addiction and other serious health consequences. An added threat of cocaine use occurs when cocaine and alcohol are consumed at the same time. When these substances are mixed, the human liver combines cocaine and alcohol and manufactures a third substance, cocaethylene, which intensifies euphoria while also increasing the risk of sudden death. Most cocaine-related deaths are a result of cardiac arrest or seizures followed by respiratory arrest.

(Source: Excerpts reprinted from The National Institute on Drug Abuse [NIDA].)

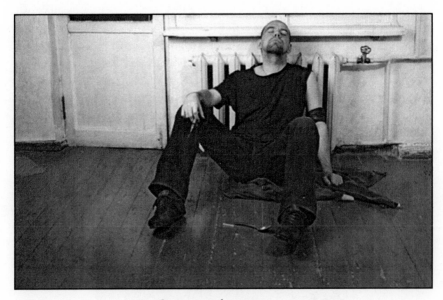

Source: www.dreamstime.com

Effects

Smoking crack cocaine can cause aggressive paranoid behavior. Physical effects include constricted blood vessels and increased temperature, heart rate, and blood pressure. Users may also experience feelings of restlessness, irritability, and anxiety. Evidence suggests that users who smoke cocaine may be at even greater risk of causing harm to themselves than those who snort the substance, and they may suffer from acute respiratory problems, including coughing, shortness of breath, and severe chest pains with lung trauma and bleeding.

(Source: Excerpts are reprinted from The National Institute on Drug Abuse [NIDA].)

Background

Crack cocaine is highly potent and lethal, especially when mixed with substances for freebasing. It's often cut with baking soda for increased profits for dealers. Crack is very inconsistent, presenting between 10% and 90% pure cocaine. The balance can be made up of any substance the maker decides to put in it, such as acetone of bicarbonate, rat poison, or other substances. Ether is sometimes used, though few home chemists choose it because of its flammability when freebasing.

Crack cocaine is not a one-hit drug. The intense euphoria, or highly pleasant feeling, caused by the release of the natural brain chemical dopamine instantly causes the brain to crave more, resulting in a continual desire for the drug, and, thus, addiction. A typical response among users is to have another hit of the drug. However, the levels of dopamine in the brain take a long time to replenish themselves, and each hit taken in rapid succession leads to increasingly less intense highs. It is the compelling desire to recapture the initial high that is so addictive for many users. When they consume the drug, large amounts of dopamine are used up; thus, depression happens in addition to the physiological effects of revved-up body systems. Users may experience "crack lip," which results when the smoked drug blisters the lips and mouth. The inhaled smoke and ash can result in "crack lung." Pregnant women who indulge in crack cocaine risk deformities and even death to their babies.

Source: www.dreamstime.com

PCP and LSD

Common Terms for PCP and LSD: acid, haze, angel dust

What They Are

PCP and LSD are hallucinogens, a term used to describe naturally occurring or synthetic drugs taken primarily for the distorting effects they have on the user's perceptions. Hallucinogens' effects range from mild sensory distortion to full-on hallucinations, paranoia, and delirium

Effects In General

Hallucinogens distort the senses, cloud the mind, and pose grave dangers to users and those around them. LSD may trigger anxiety, panic, depression, paranoia, and psychotic episodes. PCP prompts violence, can induce psychoses, and can cause death by respiratory arrest.

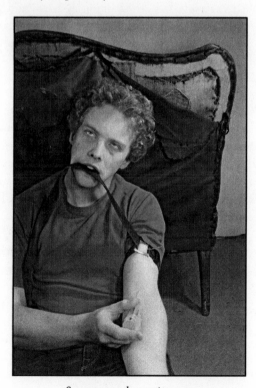

Source: www.dreamstime.com

PCP

Common Terms for PCP: wet, bobbies, dippies, dank, amp, hydro, and purple haze

What It Is
Originally developed in 1959, phencyclidine (also known as PCP or angel dust) is a synthetic dissociate anesthetic. In its pure form, it is a white crystalline powder. Sold as a street drug since the 1960s, PCP is now often produced in home labs and sometimes passed off as mescaline or other hallucinogens. In large quantities, it smells strongly of ammonia. While use of PCP has declined since the 1970s, PCP is experiencing resurgence in the northeastern United States, despite its now-known hazards.

Use
PCP can be smoked, taken orally, snorted, or injected. It is sold in liquid, tablet, capsule, and powder forms. Most often the crystalline powder is sprinkled on a leafy substance—tobacco, parsley, mint, oregano, or marijuana—and then smoked in rolled cigarettes.

PCP's Effects
The effects of PCP can be unpredictable and severe. Moderate doses (five milligrams or less) generally produce initial feelings of relaxation and mild euphoria—but depression, anxiety, or disorientation can also result. Within the normal dosage range, users feel powerful, "spaced out" or detached, and may experience visual distortions. Physical effects include raised heart rate, blood pressure, and body temperature; flushing and sweating; shallow breathing; numbness; and some loss of coordination.

At higher doses, respiration drops, and users may experience nausea, vomiting, loss of balance, and dizziness. They often display dramatic mood swings and are prone to anxiety, paranoia, and aggressiveness. Violence is common. Paranoid delusions and aggressive behavior are sometimes followed by psychoses that may mimic symptoms of schizophrenia. Psychotic episodes can last several days, and it may take as long as two weeks for patients to return to normal. At toxic levels, or when interacting with alcohol or other depressant drugs, PCP can prove fatal, causing convulsions, coma, and respiratory arrest. PCP can also exacerbate preexisting mental disorders.

LSD

Common Terms for LSD: acid

What It Is

LSD (lysergic acid diethylamide) is the best known of the hallucinogens. LSD was used—specifically in the CIA's experiment called Project MK-ULTRA—in the 1950s, as the government searched for ways to develop mind-control techniques. Hallucinogens were popular in the late 1940s through the 1960s as recreational drugs. During these years, many young people took LSD to experience "acid trips." Advocates thought LSD was a mind-expanding aid that helped users achieve mystical states of perception. Though the drug was synthesized in 1938 by Dr. Albert Hoffman in Switzerland, in the hopes of finding a circulation and respiration stimulant for medical use, it was American professor Dr. Timothy Leary who is most often associated with LSD because of his advocacy of LSD as a recreational drug. Leary was highly influential in the drug's widespread popularity in the 1960s. The 1960s and early 1970s became the era of "tripping," with many college kids taking mind-altering drugs like LSD. As a result, many young people lost their lives to the chemical, because of the altered perceptions it gave them.

This hallucinogen can be synthesized in a lab (a chemical process), while other hallucinogens, such as psilocybin (mushrooms), can be found naturally occurring in plants and fungi that are often intentionally cultivated for their hallucinogenic effects.

Use

LSD is generally taken orally and in very small doses. Most often, LSD is found in small squares of paper called blotters. The squares may come in perforated sheets, like postage stamps, sometimes with an eye-catching image on each square. The drug may also come in tiny tablets, called microdots, or in small, thin gelatin squares, known as windowpane. LSD may also be available in a clear liquid solution, which is dispensed with an eyedropper onto sugar cubes or directly onto the tongue. Another variety, blue dot acid, consists of paper slips smeared with a blue solution of the drug.

First introduced as a technique in mind control, this chemical has shown few true benefits from its use. Most effects have been damaging. Some people believe it heightens their sensitivities and awareness to higher creative levels, but this has not been scientifically proven. "Bad trips" are a more likely and frequent result. Though there are no confirmed cases of death resulting directly from LSD overdose, LSD is still common and available as a street drug, and it carries a very real danger of abuse.

LSD's Effects

Physical effects of LSD may include: dilated pupils, high temperature, rapid heartbeat, increased blood pressure, sleeplessness, appetite loss, and muscle tremors or contractions. Psychological effects can last for twelve hours or more. During the first thirty to ninety minutes, changes in visual perception and mood are likely. As the drug reaches its peak (one to two hours after using) the user may experience distorted impressions of time, space, and distance. "Tracers" (the observation of streams of colored light following the path of a moving object) and psychedelic visual patterns may be seen. Judgment and the ability to recognize immediate danger can be impaired, thus increasing the risk of injury.

Acute anxiety, depression, panic, paranoia, or psychotic behavior may accompany a bad trip or may occur even long after most other effects of the drug have worn off. An overdose can result in a longer, more intense, and more frightening trip, and the spontaneous recurring hallucinations known as flashbacks can occur days, weeks, or years after LSD use.

People in rehab facilities will have friends put LSD under the stamp on an envelope. The user gets his mail and knows where the LSD is hidden. Therefore, some of the more cautious rehabs open all of their patients' mail.

Opioids/Opiates

Common Terms for Opiates: morphine, downers, smack, junk, Miss Emma, white stuff, H, horse, and white horse

What They Are

Opioids are prescribed for their analgesic (pain-relieving) properties. Medications in this narcotics class include morphine, codeine, and related drugs. Morphine is often used before or after surgery to alleviate severe pain. Codeine, because it is less effective than morphine, is used for milder pain. Other examples of pain relievers include oxycodone (Oxycontin), propoxyphene (Darvon), hydrocodone (Vicodin), and hydromorphone (Dilaudid), as well as meperidine (Demerol), which is used less often because it is severely habit-forming. In addition to their pain-relieving properties, some of these drugs—for example, codeine and diphenoxylate (Lomotil)—can be used as ingredients to relieve coughs and diarrhea.

Effects

Opioids can produce drowsiness, cause constipation, and can depress respiration. Opioid drugs also can cause euphoria by affecting the brain's pleasure centers. Chronic use of opioids can result in tolerance for the drugs; thus, users must take higher doses to achieve the same initial effects. Long-term use also can lead to physical dependence and addiction, as the body adapts to the presence of the drug, and withdrawal symptoms occur if use is reduced or stopped. Symptoms of withdrawal include restlessness, muscle and bone pain, insomnia, diarrhea, vomiting, cold flashes with goose bumps, and involuntary leg movements. Taking a large single dose of an opioid can cause severe respiratory depression, which can lead to death. Many studies have shown that properly managed, medically supervised use of opioid analgesic drugs can be relatively safe and rarely causes clinical addiction. Taken exactly as prescribed, opioids can be used to effectively manage pain. Users have to take more and more of the drug in order to achieve the same high. This overdose is the main cause of death.

Opioids can be safe to use with other drugs, but only under a physician's supervision. They shouldn't be used with other substances that depress the central nervous system, such as alcohol, antihistamines, barbiturates, benzodiazepines, or general anesthetics. Any combination of opioids with other depressants increases the risk of life-threatening respiratory depression.

(Note: This article was excerpted from The National Institute on Drug Abuse [NIDA].)

Heroin

Common Terms for Heroin: H, horse, or smack.

What It Is

Heroin is an illegal, highly addictive opiate. It is the most abused and the most rapid-acting of the opiates. Heroin is processed from morphine, a naturally occurring substance extracted from the seed pods of certain varieties of poppy plants. It is sold as a white or brownish powder or as the black sticky substance known as black tar heroin. Although purer heroin is becoming more available, most street heroin is cut with other drugs or substances, such as sugar, starch, powdered milk, or quinine. Heroin can also be cut with strychnine or other poisons. Because heroin abusers do not know the actual strength or the contents of the drug, they may overdose or die. Heroin also poses special problems because of the transmission of HIV and other diseases that can occur from sharing needles or the various pieces of injection equipment. Heroin is usually injected, though it can be sniffed/snorted or smoked.

The Nature of the Problem

According to the 2008 National Survey on Drug Use and Health, which may actually underestimate illicit opiate (heroin) use, an estimated 3,788,000 people had used heroin at some time in their lives, and nearly 213,000 of them reported using it within the month preceding the survey. The survey estimated there were 87,000 new heroin users in 2008. A large proportion of these were smoking, snorting, or sniffing heroin, and 108,000 were under age twenty-six. Heroin was mentioned most often as the primary drug of abuse in treatment admissions in Baltimore, Boston, Los Angeles, Newark, New York, and San Francisco.

Effects

Heroin gives a high, a good feeling. It is considered an opiate, and it often gives the user the perception of happiness and being able to do anything, while at the same time providing a feeling of comfortable coziness. Reasoning is impaired on this drug, and often users misjudge the amounts they are taking, resulting in potentially deadly overdoses.

BLTC [originally, this name was derived, tongue-in-cheek, from DuPont's 'Better Living Through Chemistry'Research"]; ("Heroin and the Plague of Walking Dead" http://www.opioids.com/heroin.html) offered this in an article titled "Deadly Short Cuts":

> The consumption of heroin is marked by a euphoric rush, a warm feeling of relaxation, a sense of security and protection, and a dissipation of pain, fear, hunger, tension, and anxiety. When heroin is snorted or smoked, the rush is intense and orgasmic.
>
> Heroin is the most fast-acting of all the opiates—when injected, it reaches the brain in fifteen to thirty seconds; smoked heroin reaches the brain in around seven seconds. A period of tranquility ("on the nod") follows, lasting up to an hour. Experienced users will inject between two to four times per day. After taking heroin, some people feel cocooned and emotionally self-contained. Others feel stimulated and sociable. There is a profound sense of control and well-being. At higher doses still, the user will nod off into a semiconscious state ..."

Heroin is a powerful drug, and it is extremely addictive. The feeling it provides can be deadly for the user. The drug's affordability and availability make it a seriously growing problem for many communities.

Route of Intake
Intravenous injection provides the greatest intensity and most rapid onset of euphoria. Intramuscular injection produces a slower onset. Heroin is also sniffed or smoked All three forms are addictive.

(Source: Parts of this article are reprinted from The National Institute on Drug Abuse [NIDA].)

Methadone and Suboxone

Common Terms for Methadone and Suboxone:
Methadone is also called dollies, linctus, meth, mixture, methadose, amidone, fizzies. Suboxone has no other names.

What It Is
Methadone is a narcotic pain reliever. It is also used in the treatment of opiate dependence. While it has helped manage addiction, it has become a drug desired by addicts.

Purpose
A methadone maintenance program was created to be a viable alternative for recovering opiate addicts—particularly effective in those addicted to heroin. Methadone maintenance clinics are available for drug addicts as an alternative form of detox and treatment, whereby a person dependent on heroin or some other opiate can conceivably withdraw gradually and more comfortably, using methadone to wean themselves off the drug. In some cases, this has been successful. In other cases, the addict has become overly tolerant and utterly dependent upon methadone; in essence, the user has simply traded one addiction for another.

Effects
Some people have become very addicted to methadone, either while using it as a pain reliever or by participating in methadone maintenance programs. In either case, they are faced with the dilemma of how to detoxify. Most detox facilities will not accept patients who are on more than a minimal daily dosage (may vary by facility) of methadone.

Background
According to the Office of National Drug Control Policy (ONDCP) "Fact Sheet": http://www.whitehousedrugpolicy.gov/publications/factsht/methadone/index.html,

> Taken orally once a day, methadone suppresses narcotic withdrawal for between twenty-four and thirty-six hours. Because methadone is effective in eliminating withdrawal symptoms,

it is used in detoxifying opiate addicts. It is, however, only effective in cases of addiction to heroin, morphine, and other opioid drugs, and it is not an effective treatment for other drugs of abuse. Methadone reduces the cravings associated with heroin use and blocks the high from heroin, but it does not provide the euphoric rush. Consequently, methadone patients do not experience the extreme highs and lows that result from the waxing and waning of heroin in blood levels. Ultimately, the patient remains physically dependent on the opioid but is freed from the uncontrolled, compulsive, and disruptive behavior seen in heroin addicts. "Withdrawal from methadone is much slower than that from heroin. As a result, it is possible to maintain an addict on methadone without harsh side effects. Many Methadone Maintenance Patients require continuous treatment, sometimes over a period of years....

A drug that has been found equally effective, and possibly more desirable, is Suboxone. This is the first opioid medication approved—to be used in the treatment of dependence on opiates—that can be used in an office setting. One of the major differences between the traditional opioid treatment (methadone) and the new one is that Suboxone does not relieve pain.

Suboxone comes in pill form, and the patient has to place the pill (or pills) under the tongue to be absorbed into the body. It should not be swallowed or chewed, because the patient won't get the full effect of the medication. Buprenorphine (contained in Suboxone) is a partial opioid agonist that has the ability to block other opioids from attaching to the receptors in the brain. A partial opioid will halt the cravings and mood swings without giving the patient a high. A partial agonist will also block other opioids from entering the receptor sites.

Suboxone contains both buprenorphine and naloxone. It helps to suppress withdrawal symptoms, decrease opioid cravings, and reduce the effects of full opioid agonists (heroin, morphine, etc.). Naloxone is capable of reversing the overdosing of opioids. It can actually displace other opioids at the receptor level. Because naloxone reverses the effects of opiates, the pills are useless to someone wanting to use Suboxone to get high.

Using Suboxone relieves patients from having to go to a methadone clinic every day for their dose. It is much easier to hold down a job while on Suboxone than while on methadone. Suboxone has been studied since 1978, and clinical trials show it can suppress opioid withdrawal symptoms and reduce use of opiates while reducing drug cravings. It has been used for treatment of opiate addiction since 2003.

Getting off Suboxone is similar to getting off methadone. The doctor carefully reduces the dosage level until the patient is able to sustain his recovery on his own. Typically, doctors allow a patient to switch from methadone to Suboxone when the methadone dose is down to 30 mg per day. It's very important that a patient works closely with his or her doctor when on either methadone or Suboxone. Mixing the wrong drugs with either can cause severe reactions, including death.

It's crucial that the patient doesn't take any other medication without clearance from the doctor. He or she should be able to follow the Suboxone regimen in accompaniment with treatment for psychological and behavioral factors just as directed by the physician, and in the assigned dosage and times. You can locate a physician capable of prescribing Suboxone by going to this Web site: http://www.buprenorphine.samhsa.gov/bwns_locator/index.html.

Be sure to examine all aspects of the benefits and disadvantages before enrolling in any new drug regimen. Ask the prescribing doctor for detailed information on the advantages and disadvantages of taking the medication; additionally, request the drug info sheet. Even if you don't understand all the medical and scientific language, you will have a list of side effects and negative interactions with other drugs.

Benzodiazepines

Common Terms for Benzodiazepines: tranqs, downers, and benzos

What Are They?

Benzodiazepines are considered psychoactive drugs. They provide hypnotic, anticonvulsant, sedative, and muscle relaxant sensations. They cause the central nervous system to slow down. They are commonly used by multiple-drug abusers: those who are alcoholics as well as those who primarily use recreational drugs. Abusers of benzodiazepines often take very large doses either orally, by injection, or by snorting. Various intoxicating drug and benzodiazepine combinations, such as "tem-tems" (buprenorphine and temazepam) and temazepam and lager, are very popular. Benzodiazepine abuse is common in alcoholics. Nearly all benzodiazepines have been abused. In general, those that enter the brain rapidly (like diazepam) are preferred to those that are absorbed more slowly (like oxazepam). Flunitrazepam tablets (roaches) have become popular partly because of diversion of supplies across the Mexican border. Potent benzodiazepines such as triazolam, alprazolam (Xanax), clonazepam (Klonopin), and lorazepam (Ativan) have also achieved popularity among abusers. Benzodiazepines can be classified as either tranquilizers (Alprazolam, Clorazepate, lorazepam chlordiazepoxide, prazepam, and diazepam) or hypnotics (lorazepam, nitrazepam, triazolam, temazepam, Flurazepam and Lometazepam). Tranquilizers include: alprazolam, Clorazepate, lorazepam, chlordiazepoxide, prazepam and diazepam.

Benzodiazepine users take doses in excess of those recommended for therapeutic purposes. Oral and intravenous doses of 100–150 mg of temazepam and diazepam are common. Some may take up to 50 tablets of temazepam (500–1,000 mg) for hedonistic effects. Benzodiazepines are widely available on the street and are relatively cheap. A major source is from a doctor's prescription pad. Some children obtain them from prescription bottles meant for their parents.

Effects

The most common reason given by multiple-drug abusers for taking benzodiazepines is that they enhance and often prolong the high obtained from other drugs, including heroin and other opioids, cocaine, and amphetamines.

Benzodiazepines can be used to alleviate withdrawal effects from other drugs. Users of stimulants, including cocaine, amphetamines, and Ecstasy, also take benzodiazepines as downers to help them overcome the effects of uppers and to combat hangover effects. In alcoholics, benzodiazepines are used partly to alleviate the anxiety associated with chronic alcohol use, but also because the mixture of alcohol and benzodiazepines produces a hedonistic effect. When taken alone in high doses, and particularly when injected, benzodiazepines can provide their own high. Although benzodiazepines in therapeutic doses seem to have little abuse potential compared with other drugs of abuse, their abuse liability may be greater at doses above the therapeutic range. Deaths following self-medication do occur, even when the drugs are taken alone, and a fatal outcome from overdose is more likely with flurazepam and temazepam than with other benzodiazepines. They can add to the respiratory depression caused by some other drugs. Their use increases the risk of traffic accidents resulting from relaxed or impaired judgment, especially when the user drives under the influence of higher doses. Mental disturbances caused by benzodiazepines include blackouts and memory loss, aggression, violence, and chaotic behavior associated with paranoia. Loss of judgment and amnesia may also be associated with high-risk sexual behavior, including casual sexual contacts and unprotected sexual activity—which appears to be a particularly strong characteristic of temazepam abusers. Cognitive impairment, including deficits in learning, memory, and sustained attention, has been proven in many long-term benzodiazepine users, even at therapeutic dose levels, and may persist after benzodiazepine withdrawal. Regular use of benzodiazepines, especially in high doses, can lead to physical dependence, evidenced by withdrawal symptoms on sudden cessation. The use of temazepam is associated with the practice of sharing injecting equipment, thus increasing the risk of HIV infection and hepatitis. Temazepam is extremely irritating and likely to cause tissue damage.

Symptoms of benzodiazepine withdrawal include depression, pins and needles, sensitivity stimulation from light and sound, sensitive eyes, and loss of memory.

Chapter Five

Drugs of Abuse, Part II

Inhalants

Common Terms for Inhalants: poppers, snappers, boppers, amys, bolt, pearls, rush, and whippets

What They Are
Unlike other drugs, inhalants can be found right in your own home. They can be in your household supplies in the kitchen, the garage, and even in your bedroom. If you think that your child or friend is using inhalants and you don't know what to do, contact your local physician, or call an ambulance in an emergency. If the child sniffs too much, they may go into a coma or even die. Some examples of inhalants are as follows:

+ **Gases:** butane, propane, aerosols, and other substances that can be used in household or commercial products, including ether, chloroform, halothane, and nitrous oxide found in medical anesthetic gases

+ **Nitrites:** amyl nitrate, butyl nitrite, and cyclohexyl nitrite are all volatile components that are found among organic nitrites. Amyl nitrate is used in diagnostic medical procedures.

+ **Aerosols:** spray paints, hair or deodorant sprays, fabric protector sprays, vegetable oil sprays, and computer protector sprays (compressed air).

+ **Volatile Solvents:** paint thinners or removers, degreasers, dry-cleaning fluids, gasoline, and glue are industrial or household solvents, along with correction fluids, felt-tip marker fluid, and electronic contact cleaners.

Effects
Inhalants can slow down the body's functions. A high concentration can lead to death due to the displacement of oxygen in the lungs. It's similar to the feeling you get when you're painting in a room without ventilation and become lightheaded. Chronic inhalant users can develop other problems such as "sudden sniffing death syndrome" (the heart overworks, beating quickly and

unevenly, which can lead to cardiac arrest), this occurs as a result of sniffing or snorting highly concentrated amounts of chemicals. This can happen if the user continues to sniff the chemical after he has already received a buzz. The syndrome is particularly common among users who inhale or sniff chemicals such as butane, propane, and other aerosol products.

Typical Symptoms:

> Slurred speech
> Drunk, dizzy, or dazed appearance
> Unusual breath odor
> Chemical smells on clothing
> Paint stains on body or face
> Runny nose
> Red eyes and/or change in pupil size
> Lack of coordination

(Note: Some of the above information was contributed in part by Astra Clarke of the Bahamas and the National Drug Intelligence Center: http://www.usdoj.gov/ ndic/pubs07/708/index.htm.)

Prescription Medications

Common Terms for Prescription Medications: ludes (methaqualone), hill-billy heroin (Oxycontin), Vitamin R (Ritalin), Sudafed® (Robo-tripping), and morphine (God's drug)

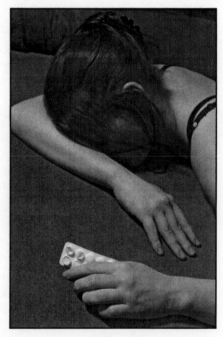

Source: www.dreamstime.com

What They Are
The ONDCP (Office of National Drug Control Policy) reports the most abused prescription medications are the following three classifications:

+ opioids, such as codeine, oxycodone, and morphine

+ central nervous system (CNS) depressants, such as barbiturates and benzodiazepines

+ stimulants, such as dextroamphetamine and methylphenidate

These medications have beneficial uses when obtained legally and used properly.

Effects
Prescription drug abuse affects many people throughout the world. Some trends of concern can be seen among older adults, adolescents, and women. In addition, health-care professionals may be at increased risk of prescription drug abuse because of ease of access, as well as their ability to self-prescribe drugs.

The misuse of prescription drugs is likely the most common form of drug abuse among the elderly. Elderly persons use prescription medications approximately three times as frequently as the general population, and they have been found to have the poorest rates of compliance with directions for taking a medication. In general, older people should be prescribed lower doses of medications, because the body's ability to metabolize many medications decreases with age. (http://www.drug-rehab.com/prescription-drugs.htm)

Several indicators suggest that prescription drug abuse is on the rise in the United States. According to the 2007 National Survey on Drug Use & Health, in 2007 an estimated 6.7 million Americans used prescription pain relievers nonmedically for the first time.

Many people become addicted to prescription meds. Often, a person has uncustomary pain (back pain, kidney pain, pain from an injury, surgery, migraines, arthritis, osteoporosis, etc.) and their physician prescribes a controlled medication like Oxycontin, Darvocet, or Talwin. The patient takes the medication, finds relief, and also is pleased with the sense of euphoria—the trouble-free high—and thus he continues to take the drug. He may ask the doctor to continue prescribing the drug even though he no longer has pain. Perhaps the patient fears stopping the drug will bring back the pain or that by not taking the drug he will lose that happy, peaceful feeling. Kids may become dependent on prescription medications because of an injury or other pain. If parents refuse to get a prescription filled for their child, because they suspect their son or daughter is becoming addicted, the child then may steal drugs from others or obtain them on the street. Some prescription meds, such as Oxycontin and hydrocodone, can be chemically altered (ground and snorted like heroin) to supply an immediate high, which makes them even more addicting.

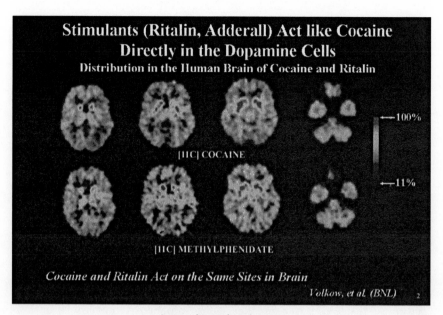

Source: http://drugabuse.gov

OTC (Over-the-Counter) Drugs

Common Terms for Over-the-Counter Drugs: generic aspirin, nurofen, orudis, enerjets, ACT-3, orange crush, red devils, Robo-dosing, dex, and skittles

What They Are
OTC drugs (over-the-counter medications) can be acquired without a doctor's prescription and can be purchased in pharmacies or local drug stores. Improper use of a combination of OTC drugs can be very harmful. The improper use of these drugs can also lead to addiction.

Misused OTC drugs include pain relievers, such as acetaminophen (e.g., Tylenol), ASA (e.g., Bayer or other aspirin products), nonsteroidal anti-inflammatory drugs (ibuprofen, such as Advil), cough and cold medications, antihistamines, antacids, and laxatives. These substances are generally purchased for medicinal purposes and often tend to be effective, but they may be later misused or overused.

Effects
Cold and cough medications may lead to symptoms of nervousness, stomach ache, heart palpitations, headache, and breathlessness. Antihistamine abuse may show up as dizziness, concentration problems, drowsiness, ringing in the ears, mild euphoria, and, possibly, nervousness and unusual excitement. Signs of abuse may also include confusion, muscle twitches, hallucinations, tremors, flushed or red face, irregular heartbeat, and faintness.

DXM is a cough-suppressing ingredient in several OTC cold and cough medications. Dextromethorphan (DMX), a semisynthetic narcotic, is found in cold medications with either "DM" or "Tuss" printed on the box. DXM acts centrally to elevate the threshold for coughing. At the doses recommended for treating coughs (1/6 to 1/3 oz of medication, which contains 15–30 mg dextromethorphan), the drug is safe and effective. At four or more ounces, dextromethorphan produces dissociative effects similar to those of PCP and Ketamine.

Something as mild as aspirin can be used for almost any type of pain, but many people may fail to realize that consuming more than the recommended amounts can lead to liver problems, internal bleeding, and, ultimately, death.

Antihistamines are used to prevent or lessen allergy reactions. They can also be found in OTC sleeping aids and Gravol (for motion sickness). Even at recommended doses, doctors and the drug manufacturers recommend that people do not operate heavy machinery or perform other skill-demanding acts. That is because these meds can cause dizziness, concentration problems, drowsiness, ringing in the ears, mild euphoria, and possibly nervousness and unusual excitement. These effects may be greater if higher doses are consumed. Signs of abuse may include confusion, muscle twitches, hallucinations, tremors, flushed or red face, irregular heartbeat, and faintness.

Laxatives are used to relieve constipation or aid in infrequent bowel movements. As with any drug, the major concern is developing an addiction. Laxatives should be used only when necessary.
(This information has been contributed in part by Astra Clarke of the Bahamas.)

Steroids

Common Terms for Steroids: juice, pumpers, roid rage, stackers, Georgia homeboy, Arnolds, gym candy, and weight trainer

What They Are

Steroids are related to the male sex hormone, testosterone, and affect muscle growth (anabolic effects) and the development of male sexual characteristics (androgenic effects). The formal definition is: Testosterone and its synthetic analogs are listed as controlled substances and include androstendols, androstendiones, their 19-nor versions, dehydroepiandrosterone, and designer anabolic steroids. They have been banned by major amateur and professional sports authorities. They are classified as Schedule III controlled substances in the United States.

Effects

Yellow tint to skin color, acne, gynecomastia (the development of enlarged mammary glands in boys or men), weight gain, accumulation of fluids, and psychological disorders, such as heightened aggressiveness, are all hallmarks of steroid usage. In females, a deeper voice, marked masculinity, hair on upper lips, and male-pattern hair growth occur. Use of steroids can cause liver dysfunction, cardiovascular disease, hypertension, and infertility. Steroids can be detected in urine, if the drug has been taken orally, for up to three weeks. If the drug is injected, it can be detected in the user's system from three months up to one year. The initial steroid effects are: noticeable muscle growth, improved physique and strength, and enhanced sex drive. Over time, however, chronic abuse compromises natural hormone production, and testosterone levels drop very low. Usage leads to many negative side effects, ranging from severe acne to permanent liver damage, cardiovascular disease, loss of fertility, injuries, mood swings, and psychological dependence. In women, they may cause irreversible masculinity.

The lack of steroid testing in schools leads many students to sincerely believe steroids, especially in the form of "nutritional supplements," are not drugs. The National Survey of Drug Use (http://www.monitoringthefuture.org) indicates that in 2008 the annual use of steroids for eighth, tenth, and twelfth graders was .9%, .9% and 1.5% respectively.

Our company can provide lab testing for detection of the following anabolic agents:

- Bolasterone metabolite

- Boldenone metabolite

- Clenbuterol

- Clostebol metabolite

- Danazol and/or metabolite

- DHCMT (Dehydrochloromethyltestosterone) metabolite

- Dihydrotestosterone

- Dromostanolone and/or metabolite

- Ethylestrenol/norethandrolone metabolite

- Fluoxymesterone metabolite

- Formebolone metabolite

- Furazabol metabolite

- Mesterolone and/or metabolite

- Methandienone (Dianabol, methandrostenolone) metabolite

- Methandriol and/or metabolite

- Methenolone and/or metabolite

- Methyl testosterone metabolite

- Mibolerone metabolite

- Nandrolone/norandrostendione/norandrostendiol metabolite

- Oxandrolone and/or metabolite

- Oxymesterone

- Oxymetholone metabolite

- Stanozolol metabolite

- Testosterone/androstendione/androstendiol/DHEA (T/E Ratio >6)

- Trenbolone metabolite

Masking Agents: probenecid, epitestosterone

U.S. Controlled Substances Act (CSA) of 1970

The CSA is part of a larger piece of legislation (the Comprehensive Drug Abuse Prevention and Control Act of 1970). It provides a legal basis to fight the ongoing war against drugs through closer monitoring and categorization. This allows the control of all classes of drugs, as determined by their addictive effect as well as their usefulness in medical situations.

The CSA categorized all drugs into one of five schedules. A substance's scheduling is based on three factors:

- its medicinal value

- its possible harmfulness to human health

- its potential for abuse or addiction

Schedule I drugs have a very high possibility for abuse. They are too dangerous to be used even under a doctor's care, and no medical reason exists for their use.

Schedule II drugs can cause severe psychological and/or physical dependence, have a high potential for abuse, and are permitted to be used medically.

Schedule III drugs can be used medically, can lead to mild psychological and/or physical dependence, and are less likely to be abused than drugs in either Schedule I or II.

Schedule IV drugs can be used medically, could lead to limited psychological and/or physical dependence, and have a low potential for abuse.

Schedule V drugs can be used medically, carry a low potential for abuse, and are less likely to cause psychological and/or physical dependence than drugs in Schedule I, II, III or IV.

Pseudoephedrine, found widely in antihistamine OTC medicines, was being used in the manufacture of methamphetamine. As a result of this legislation, Congress placed restrictions on the sale of any medicine containing pseudoephedrine. Succeeding bills were amended to the Patriot Act, with additional stricter rules and regulations, such as requiring a customer to sign a log book and show a valid photo ID, and limiting purchases of pseudoephedrine products to no more than three packages. Some pharmacies only sell it from behind the pharmacy counter.

Information is taken from the following Web sites:
http://www.deadiversion.usdoj.gov/schedules/alpha/alphabetical.htm (accessed September 4, 2005).
http://www.enotes.com/drugs-substances-resources/highlights-u-s-controlled-substances-act-csa

Club Drugs

(Note: Club drugs are mentioned throughout this book in various references. This section, however, focuses entirely on them.)

Common Terms for Club Drugs: Club drugs, or designer drugs, go by a variety of names. *Roofies*, for example, is a term often used for rohypnol; *Ecstasy* is used for MDMA, and so on.

What They Are

"Club drug" or "designer drug" are vague terms that refer to a wide variety of drugs. Uncertainties about the drug sources, pharmacological agents, chemicals used to manufacture them, and possible contaminants make it difficult to determine toxicity, consequences, and symptoms that might be expected in a particular community. The information in this alert will be useful, whatever the local situation.

Some club drugs include Ecstasy, GHB, Rohypnol, Ketamine, methamphetamine, and LSD. Most of these drugs are discussed throughout this book. Club drugs acquired their name because they are often used by young adults at dance parties called raves or trances, at dance clubs and bars. Research shows that club drug use can cause serious health problems and, in some cases, death. Used in combination with alcohol, these drugs are even more dangerous. No club drug is benign. Because some club drugs are colorless, tasteless, and odorless, they can be added unobtrusively to beverages by individuals who want to intoxicate or sedate others. In recent years, the use of club drugs has been increasingly used to commit sexual assaults.

Effects

Club or designer drug usage causes mental damage, increased heart rate, poor coordination, visual disturbances, and much more. Chronic abuse of MDMA appears to produce long-term damage to serotonin levels, resulting in a variety of behavioral, cognitive, and memory disturbances.

The most common club or designer drugs include:

1. Club Drug: METHYLENEDIOXYMETHAMPHETAMINE (MDMA)

(Refer to the charts in the back of the book for detailed information.)

Common Terms for MDMA: Ecstasy, XTC, X, Adam, clarity, and lover's speed

What It Is

MDMA is a neurotoxin (nerve toxin) that was developed and patented in the early 1900s as a chemical precursor in the synthesis of pharmaceuticals. Chemically, MDMA is similar to the stimulant amphetamine and the hallucinogen mescaline. MDMA can produce both stimulant and psychedelic effects.

Methylenedioxyamphetamine (MDA) and methylenedioxyethylamphetamine (MDEA) are drugs chemically similar to MDMA. MDMA (Ecstasy) is taken orally, usually in a tablet or a capsule. MDMA's effects last approximately three to six hours, though confusion, depression, sleep problems, anxiety, and paranoia have been reported to occur even weeks after the drug is taken.

Effects

Chronic use of MDMA has been found to produce long-lasting, sometimes permanent, damage to the released serotonin. It consequently causes memory impairment, as well as a significant increase in heart rate and blood pressure and a sense of alertness like that associated with amphetamine use. It can cause a marked increase in body temperature (malignant hyperthermia), leading to the muscle breakdown and kidney and cardiovascular system failure. MDMA use may also lead to heart attacks, strokes, and seizures in some users, and may also cause dehydration and hypertension. MDMA can be extremely dangerous in high doses.

2. Club Drug: GAMMA-HYDROXYBUTYRATE (GHB)

Common Terms for GHB: grievous bodily harm, G, liquid Ecstasy, and Georgia homeboy

What It Is

GHB can be produced in clear liquid, white powder, tablet, and capsule forms. It is often used in combination with alcohol, making it even more dangerous. GHB has been increasingly involved in poisonings, overdoses, date rapes, and fatalities. The drug is used predominantly by adolescents and young adults, often at nightclubs and raves. GHB is often manufactured in home labs, with recipes and ingredients found and purchased on the Internet. GHB is usually abused either for its intoxicating, sedative, and euphoric properties or for its growth hormone–releasing effects, which can build muscles.

Ingredients in GHB, gamma-butyrolactone (GBL) and 1,4-butanediol, can also be converted by the body into GHB. These ingredients are found in a number of dietary supplements available in health food stores to build muscles and enhance sexual performance. The U.S. Food and Drug Administration offers: "Nationwide, the government's Drug Abuse Warning Network has tracked an increase in GHB-related emergency room visits from 20 in 1992 to more than 750 in 1997. (See graph below.) But these statistics are the "tip of the iceberg," warns rave drug specialist and former narcotics detective Trinka Porrata, who adds, "Kids are dropping like flies."
(From: "The Death of the Party: All the Rave, GHB's Hazards Go Unheeded," by Tamar Nordenberg, U.S. Food and Drug Administration.)

GHB-Related Emergency Department Episodes (1992-1997)

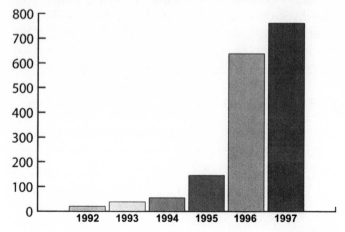

Females, especially, should be aware of this drug's possibilities because of its potentially lethal consequences (memory lapse, etc.) and its use in some molestation and rape cases. Because college campuses are seeing expanding widespread use, they are making a point of informing women about it. Make sure you share this warning with your daughters. People who use GHB or its precursor, GBL, to stun and anesthetize others for the purposes of molestation or rape face criminal charges of poisoning, with a maximum sentence of life in prison.

Effects

GHB's intoxicating effects begin ten to twenty minutes after they are taken. The effects can last up to four hours, depending on the dosage. At lower doses, GHB can relieve anxiety and produce relaxation. GHB is eliminated from the body relatively quickly, so it is sometimes difficult to detect in ERs and treatment facilities.

Overdose of GHB can occur quickly, and the signs are similar to those of other sedatives: drowsiness, nausea, vomiting, headache, loss of consciousness, loss of reflexes, impaired breathing, and, ultimately, death. GHB, a central nervous system depressant, can relax or sedate the body. At higher doses, it can slow breathing and heart rate to dangerous levels. At even higher doses, its sedative effects will result in coma or death. When slipped into a person's drink, GHB may cause a form of amnesia and stupor, which lowers defenses and inhibitions, putting the user at risk for rape. With high doses, the drug's sedative effects may result in sleep and eventual coma or death.

3. Club Drug: KETAMINE

Common Terms for Ketamine: Special K, K, Vitamin K, and cat valiums

What It Is

Ketamine is an injectable anesthetic that has been approved for both human and animal use in medical settings since 1970. About 90 percent of the legally sold today is intended for veterinary use (http://www.drugabuse.gov/ClubAlert/

ClubDrugAlert.html). It gained popularity with abusers in the 1980s, when people realized that large doses caused reactions similar to those associated with use of PCP, such as dreamlike states and hallucinations. Ketamine is produced in liquid form or as a white powder that can be snorted or smoked with marijuana or tobacco products. In some places, Ketamine is reportedly being injected intramuscularly.

Effects

At higher doses, Ketamine causes delirium, amnesia, impaired motor function, high blood pressure, depression, and potentially fatal respiratory problems. Low-dose effects from Ketamine are impaired attention, learning ability, and memory loss.

4. Club Drug: ROHYPNOL

Common Terms for Rohypnol: roofies, rophies, roche, and forget-me pill

What It Is

Rohypnol (flunitrazepam) belongs to the class of drugs known as benzodiazepines (others in the benzodiazepine category include Valium, Halcion, Xanax, and Versed). It is not approved for prescription use in the United States, although it is approved in Europe and is used in more than sixty countries as a treatment for insomnia, as a sedative, and as a pre-surgery anesthetic. Rohypnol is tasteless and odorless, and it dissolves easily in carbonated beverages. The sedative and toxic effects of Rohypnol are elevated if used with alcohol. Even without alcohol, a dose of Rohypnol as small as 1 mg can impair a victim for eight to twelve hours. Rohypnol is usually taken orally, although there are reports it can be ground up and snorted.

Effects

The drug can cause profound anterograde amnesia; individuals may not remember events they experienced while under the effects of the drug. This may be why one of the street names for Rohypnol is "the forget-me pill" and why it has been used in sexual assaults. Other adverse effects include decreased blood pressure, drowsiness, visual disturbances, dizziness, confusion, gastrointestinal disturbances, and urinary retention. The Community Epidemiology Work Group (CEWG) reports that Rohypnol use has been reported in Miami, Houston, and cities along the Texas-Mexico border.

5. Club Drug: METHAMPHETAMINE This topic is discussed in detail throughout the book. Refer to the various sections on meth as well as the charts.

Common Terms for Methamphetamine: speed, ice, chalk, meth, crystal, crank, fire, and glass

What It Is
Methamphetamine is a toxic, addictive stimulant that affects many areas of the central nervous system. The drug is often made in clandestine laboratories from relatively inexpensive OTC ingredients. It is being used by diverse groups, including young adults who attend raves, in many regions of the country.
(*Source: The National Institute on Drug Abuse [NIDA], http:// www.nida.nih.gov/DrugPages/methamphetamine.html]*

For more information on each type of club drug presented here, please check the Internet resources as well as other texts and aids.

Chapter Six

Adolescents, Drugs, and the Internet

Overview

Sadly, there is no shortage of reports about young people who have fallen victim to predators on the Internet or unthinkingly have met a stranger from cyberspace. Online predators can lure gullible and naive children to meet them with promises of everything from friendship and gifts to parties and drugs. While there are endless motivations, many predators are specifically interested in sexual exploitation of children and often introduce them to drugs. Another possibility is the introduction of a drugged or addicted child into the world of sex and slave trade. Child slave and/or sex rings are more common than you would think. Often missing children are caught up in this underground world, never to see their homes, parents, friends, or siblings again.

Source: www.thinkstock.com

Online predators are not the only danger associated with your children and the Internet. Kids may use their knowledge of the Internet not only to buy drugs, but also to connect with other drug users, play games forbidden by their parents, view pornographic material, and find ways to cheat drug tests. Many sites geared specifically toward helping users and addicts pass drug tests are available to anyone willing to look for them. Please check the following article regarding drugs and the Internet, concerning access and information to many illegal drugs via the Internet:

> http://www.drugstory.org/feature/drug_internet_QR.asp#ref#ref
> http://pediatrics.aappublications.org/cgi/content/full/109/6/e96

Often, Web-savvy young people develop their mentality about sexual activities through their contact with the Internet. Therefore, it is important that you closely monitor your children's computer habits—so you, and not the Web, are the primary influence in your children's development. The Internet can be extremely valuable for research, but its drawbacks are extensive, particularly when it comes to young people, who are easily influenced and very impressionable.

The Internet is the perfect vehicle for illegal drug sales. Major syndicates and other seedy elements can use cyberspace to peddle drugs and are often very successful at it until—or if—they are caught. Even then, it is a simple task to create another Web site under a different name. Marc Kaufman, in an article in the April 21, 2005 edition of the *Washington Post*, discussed the arrest of twenty people responsible for the online sale of millions of doses of illegal drugs (narcotics, steroids, and amphetamines). Over two hundred illegal drug Web sites were involved in the purchase of these drugs.

Youth and the Internet

The best way to ensure your children are safe, wherever they may be, is to be *involved* with every aspect of their lives. Today's world is an unsafe one, and to let your children wander through it unsupervised leaves them vulnerable. You, as a parent, are responsible for helping your children safely navigate not only the wonderful discoveries in life, but also the dangers.

Here is vital information from http://www.med.umich.edu/1libr/yourchild/internet.htm and the University of Michigan: "Internet Safety."

> Internet messages about alcohol and tobacco abound, and many are targeted to kids. Teach your children to be media literate, and keep tabs on the sites they visit. Talk with them about advertisers' messages on the Internet and learn if they agree or disagree with the message, and why they feel the way they do, and if their friends have commented on the ad or on the subject matter. This is important to understanding your child. (http://www.media-awareness.ca/english/parents/internet/kids_for_sale_parents/index.cfm).

> To protect your children on the Internet:

> 1. Share your e-mail account with your children rather than allowing them to have their own. An alternative is to create an account for your children, so you control the password. This way you can monitor your children's Internet communications.

> 2. Encourage your children to tell you if they run across suspicious contacts or unsettling, disturbing, or threatening Web sites.

> 3. Emphasize to your children that they must never go into any chat room without permission and must never agree to meet anyone in person whom they have contacted online.

4. Purchase parental monitoring software that lets you prohibit or allow access to certain sites. Talk with computer experts about how to go about this. Do some research, and learn which programs are the best and most suited to meet your needs.

5. Forbid your children to use the Internet at friends' homes, and make sure their parents know your rules regarding Internet use. If other children's parents don't monitor their Internet access, your children may have unrestricted access to material you prohibit.

6. Buy filtering software. This is similar to blocking software, but it restricts access to sites with certain key words in their domain names.

7. Procure tracking software to determine where your children are online. While not totally foolproof, many programs have very strong features to track, block, and filter potentially dangerous Web sites.

8. Look into purchasing special browsers that allow you to limit your children's access to sites. Outgoing filter programs can prevent personal information such as names, addresses, and phone numbers from being sent online.

9. Place your computer in a common area where you can monitor what your children are browsing. Do not allow children to have computers in their private areas.

10. Talk to your children about the types of sites you will allow them to explore and which ones are off-limits—and tell them why. Children receive directions more openly if you explain your reasons. Spend time online with your children showing them positive Web sites, especially educational ones. Show them how to bookmark good sites, so they can click on those right away instead of spending time searching for them and perhaps coming across risky sites.

Use these question to start a conversation with your children about the Internet:

- Why do you like to use the Internet?

- What do you find that's positive and negative in using it?

- If you could change anything about the Internet, what would it be and why?

- What are your ideas for making cyberspace safer?

- If you came across an unknown chat room, what would you do?

- Do you think it's safe to apply for a job online or to display your resumé?

- If not, what parts would you omit, and why?

- What do you think about "diary spots" and personal profiles, like Facebook?

- How would you protect yourself in these?

- What types of sites do your friends go to?

- What do you know about drugs and the Internet?

- What kind of games, music, programs, pictures, or any material would you or your friends download? Do you investigate them first?

11. Make sure your children use a screen name and not their real name on Web sites. Their password should only be shared with you. Also stress that they should never, ever give out any kind of personal information online. As their parent, it is your job to protect your children's identity and thereby their safety online.

12. Enforce consequences if your children go to prohibited Web sites.

13. Don't allow your children to access or use profile or so-cial networking sites. (such as MySpace, Flickr, Twitter, LinkedIn, and Facebook). These are public sites, and they can put children, in particular, at risk, because predators are known to search these sites looking for gullible children or teens to exploit. Additionally, your children could uninten-tionally reveal family confidential information or post embar-rassing information on you and your family.

14. Warn your children about **cyber-bullies** who boss chil-dren around and try to intimidate them online, sometimes convincing them to do things they don't want to do. Check out http://www.stopcyberbullying.org for help.

15. Explain to your children that sometimes adults market products toward children and thus victimize them, because children may not be able to discern a real opportunity from a scam. Tell them not to purchase anything online without permission.

16. Teach your children that they should not believe every-thing they see online. They should check sources and docu-mentation to ensure it is from credible sources. Not every-thing online is accurate, true, or real, even though it may be easily found, viewable, or audible. Teach them how to exercise good judgment and to use discernment. The Internet can be a valuable and useful learning tool, but it requires good judgment.

17. Sit down with your children and work out an Internet-usage contract that you both can live with and that each of you will willingly sign. This should be in the form of a pledge and should state that your children agree to practice safe Internet usage under your guidance and will be responsible while surfing. Refer to "Unity Oath."

18. Go online yourself, and play detective by assuming the role of a child or adolescent. Befriend kids to learn what makes kids trust strangers online. Don't be aggressive with your research, but perhaps form a group of parents who can

use this detective technique to help work with and guard one another's families online.

19. Talk to the parents of your children's friends to learn what their positions are on their child's Internet use and whether they monitor their children's access to it.

20. Communicate not only with your children about Internet usage and its role in drug and alcohol experimentation and addiction, but also with your significant other, who should be your equal in helping to protect your children.

To determine if your children are visiting sites you do not approve of, here are some signs:

A. **Secretiveness**: If your child says little about his experiences on the Internet, keeps to himself about what sites he's visited, and shares very little with you about online experiences, exercise concern, because this may mean your child is browsing places he shouldn't be. Make sure your child isn't trying to hide sites.

B. **Excessive Computer Time**: Are your children spending an excessive amount of time on the computer? Are they staying up late at night to play online computer games? Maybe they're getting on the computer after school under the pretext of doing homework, while they are really visiting sites you've restricted them from. Set limits for your children's computer time, and make sure you monitor them frequently to make sure they are sticking to your Internet rules.

C. **Morality Issues**: Are you seeing links to pornography or other sexually exploitive sites in your child's browsing history? Is there any place your child is visiting that is worrisome to you? Be on the lookout for links to Web sites of religions or cults that contradict the spiritual morality you've chosen to teach your child, links to cult-based video games, interactive games you've not approved of, and anything that doesn't bolster the morality and high self-esteem you desire for your child. While moral curiosity is normal in developing children and teens, make sure your child understands that you will help him find answers to his questions.

D. **Supplementary Materials:** If you see or find pornographic magazines or drug paraphernalia, it is highly possible that your kids' sudden interest is being supported or prompted by what they are doing. Keep your eyes open for changes in their interests or behavior that might have been initiated by online information.

E. **Reception:** Is your child receiving questionable materials in the mail, by fax, or hand-delivered? Is your child receiving strange phone calls, especially at odd hours of the day? Monitor your child's mail and your phone bills to see if there are names, addresses, or phone numbers you don't recognize.

F. **Behavioral Changes:** This is a critical sign. If your child begins to withdraw from the family, introverts and goes places without telling you, or if she goes places you've prohibited and then lies to you about it, be concerned. This could signal some serious personality shifts and may be a sign your child is involved in matters and activities you would not approve of. Uncharacteristic disrespect and lack of attention or focus are also symptomatic of both drug use and overactive Internet influence.

G. **Money:** Keep a constant monitor on your checkbook and credit cards, as well as any PayPal or other merchant commerce accounts. If you start to see money being paid out for something you didn't order, be on guard, as your child might be involved in buying and selling online, possibly using the money for drugs.

The Web site http://www.family.samhsa.gov/monitor/internet.aspx reports that 76 percent of six- to twelve-year-olds say their parents are either in the room or nearby all or most of the time they're online; 35 percent of teenagers report the same.

Understand how risky the Internet can be, for it is possible that there is a predator in every Web site link. Stress this danger to your children. There are many stories about bad things that have happened to good people, especially children, who didn't practice caution and safety in cyberspace.

Conversely, the Internet can be a highly valuable and beneficial tool if used properly and with precautionary discretion. Share this information with your children as well, and show them how to tell the difference between helpful Web sites and dangerous ones.

The Internet and Drugs

Cybercults wholeheartedly believe in and promote drug use and all that is associated with it, and they use the Internet as a magnet for kids.

Government statistics (http://www.family.samhsa.gov/monitor/internet.aspx) report that marijuana is one of the top-one-hundred words looked up on search engines. People who advocate marijuana use know that teens spend more time online than any other age group, so they target much of their advertising to them.

Dangerous and addictive controlled substances can be easily acquired over the Internet without prescription by individuals of any age.

Check out the Web site http://www.family.samhsa.gov/teach/highonline.aspx. This government-endorsed site has information on substance abuse and mental health. Such information includes "The Internet acts as a megastore where young people: [17]

- Can purchase almost anything, including prescription drugs, marijuana, cocaine, club drugs, alcohol, and cigarettes

- Find online directions to concoct drugs, such as methamphetamine

- Learn how to get high on household products (e.g., cough medicine, aerosol sprays)

Legislators and law enforcement agencies are finding new ways to address drugs in cyberspace. Parents and caring adults must be on the alert to ensure their children don't buy drugs online or obtain them from other kids who are buying them online. After all, even if your children don't have Web access, nearly 69 percent of kids ages ten to fourteen and 80 percent of kids ages fifteen to seventeen *do* have access—so know where your children might go to get online."

Consider this information regarding youth and the Internet.

What to Know
Here are several points you should know. Keep in tune with your children and their Internet use.

> **Teens Online:** Teens spend an average of 16.7 hours online per week. This is more than they spend watching TV. Internet drug sellers know and use this fact to market directly to kids.

> **Web Purchases:** With a credit card, teens can buy drugs online as easily as they can purchase a book or download music. Many Web sites sell prescription drugs, such as narcotic pain relievers, stimulants, and sedatives—without asking for a written prescription or the age of the purchaser—and mail in unmarked packages.

> **Safety Concerns:** Some prescription drugs sold on the Internet have harmful ingredients, are fake, are stronger or weaker than listed, or are manufactured without proper safety standards. This just compounds the danger.

What to Look For
The Internet is one of the few centers of teen culture that promotes cough medicine abuse. Several Web sites promote the abuse of cough medicines containing dextromethorphan (DXM), recommending how much to take to get high, suggesting other drugs to combine with DXM, explaining how to extract DXM from cough medicines, and even selling a powder form for snorting. Marijuana, as well as pipes, seeds, and other related items, also can be bought online.

Busted!
People who buy and sell illegal drugs online risk being scammed or busted in sting operations, even though dealers and buyers work hard to mask their identities.

The article "You've Got Drugs! Pushers on the Internet" appeared on About. com as a CASA (the national Center on Addiction and Substance Abuse) news release at Web site address:

http://www.casacolumbia.org/absolutenm/templates/PressReleases. aspx?articleid=356&zoneid=61. About.com's health, disease, and condition content is reviewed by Steven Gans, MD. (http://www.about.com/health/p4.htm).

In its piece titled "CASA White Paper Outlines Threat to Children," CASA stated the following:[18]

1. CASA considered the threat to children too immediate to wait until the full study was completed at the end of 2004. CASA and BDA (Beau Dietl & Associates) released this part of the report to alert parents, teachers, and others of the grave risk that Internet drug pushers present to American children.

2. During a one-week analysis, BDA identified 495 Web sites advertising controlled prescription drug sales: 338 portal sites that led to other sites for purchase of such drugs and 157 anchor sites that directly sold dangerous and addictive drugs.

3. Drugs available over the Internet included opioids and other pain-killers, such as Oxycontin, Percocet, Darvon, and Vicodin; stimulants, such as Dexedrine, Ritalin, and Adderall; and depressants, such as Valium and Xanax.

4. Only 6 percent of the Web sites selling drugs said they required a prescription to complete a sales transaction, and not a single site placed any restriction on the sale of these dangerous and addictive drugs to children.

Among the study's findings about the drug-selling Web sites are the following:

+ 49% offered an "online consultation"

+ 4% made no mention of a prescription

+ 4% requested a prescription be faxed

+ 2% requested a prescription be mailed

+ 47% of the selling Web sites said drugs would be shipped from outside the United States

+ 28% said the drugs would be shipped from the United States, and 25% gave no indication from where the drugs would be shipped.

+ 94% did not require any prescription (41% stated that no prescription was needed.)

"These Internet pharmaceutical predators pose a dangerous and immediate threat to our children," said Joseph A. Califano Jr., CASA's chairman and president and former US Secretary of Health, Education, and Welfare. "These drugs are as readily available to our children on the Internet as candy. Anyone, including children, can easily obtain addictive prescription drugs online without a prescription. All they need is a credit card, and if parents' credit card information is saved on a home PC, today's tech-savvy kids will know where to find it."

Beau Dietl, chairman of Beau Dietl & Associates, offers, "The wide availability of controlled prescription drugs on the Internet is an open floodgate of drugs of abuse and the tide is rising ever higher—and the ease of creating sites—[makes] it extremely difficult to regulate ..."[19]

The Web site http://alcoholism.about.com/cs/prescription/a/blcasa040226. htm offers a detailed article on how kids get drugs on the Internet. Other sources that will be of help to you include:

SAMHSA's *A Family Guide to Keeping Youth Mentally Healthy and Drug Free*. Know What Your Child Is Doing on the Internet, (http://www.family.samhsa.gov/monitor/ internet.aspx), referenced December 29, 2006.

SAMHSA's *National Clearinghouse for Alcohol and Drug Information, 2004*. Tips for Teens: The Truth about Marijuana, (http://ncadi.samhsa.gov/govpubs/phd641/), referenced December 29, 2006.

FBI.gov. A Parent's Guide to Internet Safety, (www.fbi.gov/ publications/pguide/pguidee.htm), referenced December 29, 2006.

Raves and the Internet

(Refer to club drugs elsewhere in this book)

The term "rave" gained popularity in the 1980s to refer to long dance parties, some of which last all night. These parties may occur at someone's house—particularly when parents aren't home—or in other spots, like warehouses and nightclubs. Loud music and dancing are not unusual pastimes for teens and rarely damaging to anyone—other than to a person's hearing. The danger in raves, however, is the drug subculture associated with the gatherings. The main goals of hard-core rave-goers are to get high and have fun, which sometimes includes drinking, drugs, and sex. The use of synthetic hallucinogens—some of which are so new they haven't yet acquired street names—is common at raves.

Dangerous synthetic substances used at raves are usually manufactured in small home-based labs, which are illegal. Their long-term health effects are unknown and unpredictable. The Web site http://www.usdoj.gov/ndic/pubs2/2161/index.htm#Prevalence,[20] the USDOJ says:

> Drug-related activity is widespread on the Internet, and even the novice user has easy access to all the information needed to produce, cultivate, purchase, sell, or use any illegal drug, even relatively obscure ones. Many of the users participating in these drug-related activities are adolescents and young adults. Individuals who use illegal drugs or are contemplating their use can readily access information about them on Internet sites, including explanations of drug terminology and methods of use. Many of these sites popularize and glamorize drug use, and others promote use and experimentation. Drug distributors and customers utilize Internet sites to post and discuss drug prices. They also use Internet bulletin boards and chat rooms to arrange the sale of drugs or chemicals, which are then shipped to the customer for an agreed price.
>
> Recipes and detailed instructions for producing illicit drugs also are easily obtainable on the Internet. Many sites offer

chemical formulas for drug production as well as easy-to-follow guidance about where and how to obtain the required chemicals and necessary equipment without arousing the suspicion of law enforcement. Much of the online information about drug production refers to marijuana, drug paraphernalia, or club drugs, which are all popular among young people.

Information on these common drugs (and others) is readily available online: marijuana and its paraphernalia, MDMA (Ecstasy), LSD, GHB, psilocybin mushrooms, and Ketamine.

It appears that some Chinese pharmaceutical companies are marketing to young people, even minors, in making drugs available on the Internet,[21] particularly those chemicals used at raves.

This website offers valuable information:
http://www.usdoj.gov/ndic/pubs2/2161/index.htm#Prevalence.%20%20the%20USDOJ

Raves

Throughout the 1990s, high energy, all-night dances known as raves, which feature hard-pounding techno music and flashing laser lights, increased in popularity among teens and young adults. Raves still occur in most metropolitan areas of the country. They can be either permanent dance clubs or temporary "weekend event" sites set up in abandoned warehouses, open fields, empty buildings, or civic centers. Club drugs—a group of synthetic drugs that includes MDMA (Ecstasy), GHB, LSD, Ketamine, and others—are often sold at raves and dance clubs. MDMA is one of the most popular club drugs. Rave managers often sell water, pacifiers, and glow sticks at rave parties in order to enhance the effects of MDMA or to offset the negative effects of the drug. Many raves are advertised on the Internet. Rave promoters often avoid using the term *rave* in their advertisements and may advertise these events as techno parties or music festivals in order to avoid detection.

Some have posted notices on the Internet which claim that the parties are Christian gatherings where drugs and alcohol will not be available, although subsequent law enforcement actions revealed that club drugs were being distributed and used by many attendees. Rave promoters usually do not reveal the exact location of the rave until the day of the event. Updated information regarding raves usually is disseminated through e-mail and prerecorded phone messages.

From:
http://www.usdoj.gov/ndic/pubs2/2161/index.htm#Prevalence,%20%20 the\%20USDOJ.
This site gives this precautionary message: "The Internet provides access to a vast amount of information about drug production, including processes, recipes, ingredients, and substitutes, and this information can be easily accessed by any individual with an Internet connection—the most inexperienced drug producer can easily obtain the instructions, chemicals, and equipment needed to synthesize many illegal drugs in a kitchen, bathroom, or basement laboratory. Misinformation is fairly common and can lead to serious injury, illness, or death."

Raves can prove very expensive for party-goers, as the chemicals used are sold per "hit"—per tablet or capsule or other form. MDMA, for example, can cost twenty-five dollars or more per capsule (at the printing of this book). This expense can lead teens who want to experiment with them to steal or sell stolen items to procure the money needed to use the drugs. Doing drugs at such parties presents a serious problem, as many young people decide to "just try" a drug so as not to be considered unpopular, as illustrated in this article: (http://www.cmaj.ca/cgi/reprint/162/13/1864-a.pdf) "Raves Worry Edmonton MDs, Police." Nouvelles et al analyses; 1864 JAMC, 27 JUIN 2000; 162 (13)

> Following a rave in March, several people had seizures and one became hypothermic ... The rave ideal is PLUR—peace, love, unity, and respect. Raves frequently use drugs, such as Ecstasy, to achieve the heightened sensitivity...idealistic ravers don't understand the increasing presence of drug dealers jockeying to control the flow of drugs at raves, and the growing potential for gang violence.

On the same Web site (http://www.cmaj.ca/cgi/reprint/162/13/1864-a.pdf) "Raving on the Internet." Nouvelles et al analyses; 1864 JAMC, 27 JUIN 2000; 162 (13) Greg Sullivan offers more information:

> The Internet's most predominant rave sites have grown out of the tight-knit communities within cities possessing a large

rave subculture. These sites, which provide an important voice for individual ravers, often include discussion groups, party reviews that allow members to decide which rave promoters to avoid, and a strong sense of community...The online rave community is well aware of the drug use that exists at raves.

Clearly, the Internet is treacherous for people who employ it to get drugs and drug equipment for themselves or to produce addictive substances for others. This, coupled with the promotion of ingesting perilous chemicals at raves, should concern every parent and spur them on to learning just exactly what their children are viewing and doing online. Some useful sites for getting a clearer picture of rave culture are:

http://www.techno.xvi.com

http://www.purerave.com

http://www.dancesafe.org

http://www.ravesafe.org.za/

http://www.cmaj.ca/cgi/reprint/162/13/1864.pdf

By their very nature, raves have become social gatherings that trigger parents' fear—and rightly so. Raves are certainly not the only social gatherings where drugs are present, but they have a long track record of being some of the most conducive to drugs and drug-related activities. Be certain you know where your children are and who they are with at all times, and periodically check in on them without warning.

Legal Challenges

Parents are faced with a multitude of concerns in protecting their children. They may question what is and isn't legally right and whether they can get into trouble for their discipline. We live in a highly litigious society today, where kids understand they have rights and frequently use those rights as a threat against loving parents who only want what is best for them.

What does the law have to say about all this? Parents have the absolute right to test their children for the presence of illegal drugs. In fact, the Supreme Court, on June 27, 2002, not only upheld but also broadened a previous 1995 ruling that schools may, under certain circumstances, test for the use of drugs. Some New Jersey schools should be commended for their actions in this regard. This is in recognition of the widespread nature of drug use among young people and the responsibility that parents and educators have to raise healthy drug-free kids. While it is important to respect your children's individuality, no claims of right to privacy can or should prevent you from taking rational steps to ensure your children's safety.

Other threats also exist on the Internet, such as the growing trend toward selling kids counterfeit drugs. Consider this information found at: http://medicine.plosjournals.org/perlserv/?request=get-document&doi=10.1371/journal.pmed.0020100&ct=1&SESSID=3db6e0881113d154dbb0d483bd95ed38:

> Parents have the legal right to test their children, especially if they are under the age of eighteen, in most states. Many school districts have taken it upon themselves to test their students in order to cut back on drugged and drunk kids in the classroom. If parents took a more active role in preventing drug and alcohol use and abuse, including testing their children, our country's drug/alcohol problem would be significantly more marginalized, and our kids would be healthier.

If you have concerns regarding the legality of drug testing your children, don't be afraid to contact an attorney or a legal aid society to obtain current information on the law and drug testing. Do whatever is necessary to protect your children. They're your responsibility. Responsibility for their upbringing and safety does not reside with schools or neighbors, or with your kids' friends. You must step up to the plate and take action to keep your children out of harm's way and to keep them away from the influences of all harmful chemical substances and illegal drugs.

The Scale of the Problem

It's been estimated that up to 15 percent of all drugs sold are fake; in parts of Africa and Asia, this figure may well exceed 50 percent (from "The Scale of the Problem," http://medicine.plosjournals.org/perlserv/?request=get-document&doi=10.1371/journal.pmed.0020100&ct=1&SESSID=3db6e08-81113d154dbb0d483bd95ed38#JOURNAL-PMED-0020100-G001#JOURNAL-PMED-0020100-G001)

Web site references can assist you in researching these statistics, including those listed below; also see the resources section in the appendix of this book.

R. Jones, FDA spokesperson, stated in an e-mail that the FDA estimates fake drugs comprise approximately 10 percent of the global medicine market (R. Jones, FDA spokesperson, e-mail statement, 18 November, 2004). This estimate suggests annual criminal sales in excess of thirty-five billion dollars in the United States alone.

The graph below represents the number of investigations of possible counterfeit drugs by the FDA, which has jumped from about five per year in the 1990s to more than twenty per year since 2002. Reproduced with permission from the Public Library of Science (PLoS), according to their terms of agreement. Chart and info taken from the following:

Figure: Margaret Shear, Public Library of Science

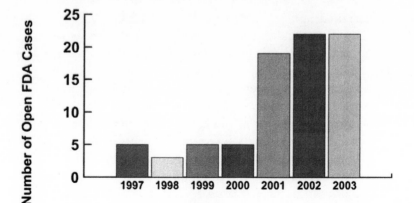

In addition to the headaches that agencies, counselors, and other drug-battling warriors face, parents confront a massive collection of other legal challenges. Consider these other questions:

1. **At what age can parents legally test their children?**
   The general consensus is that if the child is under age eighteen parents have a legal right to know what their children are doing and to test them for drugs and alcohol. Check with your state for more information about legal ages of consent.

2. **Can guardians test children living with them?**
   If they are deemed to hold legal responsibility for the children, then guardians should have the right to test them. It's wise to check your area's laws, as extenuating circumstances surrounding guardianship could come up in court at a later time.

3. **Can parents test children who are age eighteen and over if the children are still living in their house?**
   This is a tough question. Much of the answer rests with the arrangement the parents have made with their legal-aged children. If you've established the rule "You do as I say while you live under my roof" (and this can be proven through an agreement signed by both parties), then it is likely the parents have the right to enforce testing of a person over eighteen. However, it is wise to consult with an attorney on this matter.

4. **Can parents decide if they want their children on or off a certain drug?**
   Even if the child is under age eighteen, many parents face an uphill legal battle in deeming their child should be on a certain medication or, on the flip side, should be off a certain medication. Government has interceded in these situations time and time again, ruling that parents cannot withhold medications from their children or force them to take something that is not universally accepted as beneficial for them. Before you enter this court melee, learn the laws in the area where you live, and consult an attorney who can inform you of any precedents that may have already been set with regards to your situation. This issue may also involve religious beliefs.

5. **Can parents enforce their rules through physical discipline?**
We do not recommend physical discipline. It is better to try to talk your children, and if they are still defying you, then begin taking away privileges from them: no extracurricular events, no going out with friends, no talking on the phone, no TV, no computer time, no being allowed to use the car, and so on. Your goal should be to keep your kids safe while taking matters into your own hands to protect them and others. Berating your children, calling them names, or using other demeaning tactics are considered emotional abuse; stay away from this, as well. Just keep in mind that you must be consistent in punishment. Criticize the act, not the child.

6. **Can parents force their child who is on drugs to go to a treatment center?**
As long as the facility is accredited and highly rated, a parent should have the right to force their child to get help, but the child must be under eighteen. Again, check the laws in your state. If parents are sending their kids to treatment sites lacking good reputations, or if they're employing unusual techniques to fight drug abuse in their kids, they're likely not going to win court battles on this subject. It's best to work out a plan of intervention with a professional or a team of counselors first.

7. **If I know my children have drugs in the house, in their possession, or in the car, do I have to turn them in?**
By law in most states, parents don't have to turn in their kids, but if you find the paraphernalia or other telltale signs of drug use, you must hand it over to the police. Some states deem you can destroy it. Check your state's law.

8. **If my child is in possession of solvents, is that illegal?**
It's serious if your child shows signs of huffing or inhaling solvents, but, legally, possession of these items is not prohibited. Your job is to get help for your children before they risk severe lung and/or throat damage, or even death.

9. **How can my children be held accountable, or we, as the parents, be held responsible, if they have illegal drugs?**
You are legally accountable for your underage children and open for a criminal record, retribution, and jail time

should your children commit illegal acts. If your child is in possession of illegal drugs, alcohol, or prescription drugs not prescribed for them, the chances are extremely high that your child is aware of the rules about illicit drug possession or trafficking. They may know enough to try to adulterate any urine samples you may take to test for drugs. Kids involved in drugs are not naive. They generally know exactly what is lawful and what isn't. They start out innocent about which drugs cause the most damage and about which drugs are or are not controlled substances. If they've been around other kids who do drugs and alcohol, and they have done drugs themselves, it is very likely they understand what the law permits and what the law punishes. Many states now arrest parents of underage children who commit crimes.

10. **Do parents have legal rights over their children who are using the Internet?**

A superb summary is offered in the article, "Potential Legal Challenges to the Application of the Children's Internet Protection Act (CIPA) in Public Libraries: Strategies & Issues" (Paul T. Jaeger, Charles R. McClure; *First Monday*. Vol. 9, no. 2, February 2004). http://firstmonday.org/issues/issue9_2/jaeger/index.html:

When the United States Supreme Court upheld the constitutionality of the Children's Internet Protection Act (CIPA), the ruling was limited to issues of whether the statute, as written, was an unconstitutional limitation of freedom of speech. In holding that the wording of the law did not present an unconstitutional limitation on the exercise of free speech, the Supreme Court did not address the constitutionality of the application of the law.

Before taking any steps that may result in legal consequences, consider every step you think you should take, and double check your thoughts with an attorney or even a drug counselor.

We authors are not legal experts, so the advice in this book is offered from a perspective of drug testers.

The chart below, as included in the above article, illustrates these areas:

Table 2: Potential Challenges to the Application of CIPA in Public Libraries

Legal Challenge to CIPA	Legal Basis of Challenge	Approach to Challenge
CIPA creates more restrictions on free speech than are necessary	Least Restrictive Alternative	Research regarding what filters are actually blocking
The requirements of CIPA limit access to too much speech	Overbreadth	Research regarding what filters are actually blocking
The requirements of CIPA are too vague as a regulation of free speech	Vagueness	Research into how terms are generally being defined and applied
CIPA inappropriately infringes on political speech	Political Speech	Research about the types of information patrons are not reaching due to filters
CIPA forces adult patrons to request access to information that they would otherwise be able to receive unimpeded	Information Request Policies	Research that examines the process of requesting access to unfiltered Internet access
CIPA places inappropriate constraints on a public benefit – free Internet access in public libraries	Public Benefits	Research into the amount the Internet is used in public libraries and the reasons that it is used
CIPA prevents adult patrons from reaching information before the constitutionality of that information has been evaluated	Prior Restraints	Research about the decision-making process of librarians of whether to disable filters
The public library could be considered a public forum where information is intended to be freely available	Public Forum	Legal analysis of precedents regarding public forum
CIPA curtails the public's right to freely receive information	Right to Receive Information	Legal analysis of precedents regarding the right to receive information

What it comes down to, then, is whether parent's rights in caring for their children supersede the children's rights, as interpreted by the courts. Apparently, a minor, based on the summary above, can make sound, logical choices for himself and has the right to do so, even if the child is under age eighteen, supplants the parental decisions of the child. It is likely this very decision will be challenged again in the future. It is best to read Jaeger's and McClure's article in full to grasp a better understanding of the issue.

11. **Can parents do anything to stop pharmaceutical sales to kids?**

In the words of legal counsel Davis Wright Tremaine, LLP, in the article "Pharmacy and the Internet: The Challenge and Opportunity of eHealth" by Keith M. Korenchuk; (http://www.dwt.com/practc/hc_ecom/bulletins/03-00_Pharmacy.htm. March 2000, expired link) and (http://www.dwt.com), here is the answer:

> The challenges of the Internet, however, are significant when it comes to providing safe and reliable information to the public concerning health choices and information. Pharmaceuticals are at the center of the complex legal issues associated with the use of the Internet for health care. The use of online pharmacies to provide prescription drugs to patients raises both traditional and novel legal issues, as the role of traditional health-care regulation is challenged by the new medium that cuts across state lines, jurisdictional authority, and international boundaries.

In essence, parents could attempt to sue a pharmaceutical company or an entity that sold drugs to a minor only if they could prove damages. Even then, they might well have a hard time proving that the particular company sold a particular drug or drugs to an underaged child and caused the distinct damages incurred. In the end, it might mean a lot of time spent in courts and a lot of money gone out the window.

12. **Can parents demand that their children's doctors test them?**

In essence, no. You can certainly *urge* them to test your child, pleading your concerns and what you have observed, along with showing the physician your log of your child's behavior and activities, but you can't demand the doctor test your child for drugs and alcohol. Of course, if you have expressed your concerns sincerely to the doctor and—God forbid—something happens to your child, you may have some legal recourse, but the problem would be in proving you stressed this urgency to the doctor and then in showing that the medical professional was negligent in not heeding your concerns. It is best to prevent such issues by being proactive rather than reactive.

13. **What if we don't know our child is growing marijuana or manufacturing drugs in our home, or trafficking from it?**
No matter how you slice it, it is illegal to manufacture or promote illegal drugs, even in the privacy of your home. Legally, parents may find themselves paying fines or serving jail terms for their children's drug manufacture or use in the home. (There are a few states that condone marijuana for medical use, but strict adherence to a doctor's prescription is required. Check with your state and with your doctor for more information.)

14. **If my child gets mixed up with drugs—even if she isn't aware of the seriousness of it—will she have a criminal record, even if it's her first offense?**
If your child is caught with drugs at school or anywhere else, then, by law, your child can earn a recordable crime status for this. Keep in mind that there are ways your child's record can be cleaned up (varies by state and court).

15. **What if my child is underage and becomes involved with drugs/alcohol?**
Some states and countries regard children at age sixteen as adults; others mandate age seventeen or eighteen, though children committing serious crimes are now often prosecuted as adults. The Web site *SafeKids.com* (http://www.safekids.com/child-safety-on-the-information-highway/) offers that kids who do drugs and are caught may "face a criminal trial. Being found guilty could not only result in possible imprisonment, it means a criminal record for life. That will affect their job prospects, stop them visiting certain countries (such as the United States), and can affect their ability much later in life to obtain life insurance or a mortgage."

16. **If I don't know my child is involved in drugs, can the police still search my home?**
Absolutely! All they need is a search warrant.

The above sixteen questions discuss issues that face parents and kids. Drugs are dangerous, and everyone is affected by them. It's best to prevent your children from becoming involved with them; if they are caught, their bright future could collapse. Their schooling, sports, career, voting, jobs, reputation, and much more could be lost. If you don't stop them, you might not only be part of the problem—you might face legal woes and criminal charges as well.

Parents' Job

It is not easy being a parent today. You worry about your children when they're in school, when they're out with friends, when they're involved in some extra-curricular activity—and you worry about them when they're on the computer. Certainly, you can monitor what comes in the mail for your children. Many parents feel this is an invasion of privacy, but if your child is purchasing drugs or drug products or becoming involved with strangers in cyberspace, you're better off stopping it quickly rather than not knowing about it. Of course, that doesn't thwart your child from having his drugs or devices sent to a friend's home where the parents may not monitor their children.

The Kind of Friend You DON'T Need

Source: www.dreamstime.com

While the Internet offers a vast wealth of information, it also provides a lot of dangers, and drugs are one of those dangers. Children today are savvy and know how to find drugs online. Equally disturbing is how they know where to go to find products that will hide, change, or distort drug tests so that results return false negatives (show negative to drug use). It's wise not to inform your children ahead of time that you plan on testing them, as they could try to eliminate any substances from their systems more quickly or taint (adulterate) the sample so that accurate results can't be obtained. Unfortunately, there are Web sites that offer agents and chemicals that can help them with this, although testing technology generally keeps ahead of the game.

Monitoring what your children do on the Internet is difficult, and, yes, one more thing to worry about. But there are ways to prevent your children from visiting some sites in cyberspace. If you know the Web sites your children are using, you can lock them out by going to the Security tab in the Internet Properties window and listing those sites as Restricted. If you are not sure of the sites, you can go into your children's computer and check the Web sites they have visited. If you find any that are objectionable, you can set them as a restricted site in the Internet Properties window. The problem is discovering which sites your children can go to, to get drugs or to purchase products that will invalidate a drug-test sample (urine, hair). Programs can track where your children have been on the computer, but that doesn't stop them from going to someone else's home and clicking on those sites. Prevention is the key.

Many parents have tragic stories of having lost their children through death or via kidnapping by an online predator. Drugs are often part of the scenario. There are tons of parental control programs offered online to help you oversee what your child is doing, but the clearest and easiest solution is to talk to your child. Here are some suggestions:

1. **Do your research first.** Determine if your children are watching unhealthy television shows, playing violent or suggestive video games, or viewing computer sites you deem unfit. Monitor their travels, and look for uncharacteristic activities. Trust your instincts if you sense they're hanging around the wrong crowd. Go online after your child has been at the computer and find out where they've been surfing. Limit their computer time; some children today no longer get a full night's sleep because they are overstimulated.

2. **Talk to experts.** Talk with ministers, counselors, and computer gurus. Learn what you should be on the lookout for where your child's behavior and habits are concerned, and then learn how you can prevent or stop bad behavior and habits.

3. **Use the Internet to your advantage.** Search for parental control software to help you monitor and limit your child's activities on

the computer. The drawbacks here are that software is quickly outdated, kids know how to beat some of the programs, and they can go to a friend's house to access the online sites you're blocking.

4. **Pick a time to communicate.** Choose a time when you and your children are at ease to chat, not when there's a lot of homework to be done or when you and/or your significant other are in the midst of something else. Make the discussion informal and nonthreatening. Your goal is to stress to your children your concerns about the Internet and drugs, and let them know what your disciplinary plans are if they violate computer rules. Have a dialogue with your children about what they like to explore online and what the dangers are of giving out personal info and going to risky sites, such as interactive games and diary-style sites. Cite specific examples to back up your concerns. Children respond better when they are given documentation that supports a premise. If you can lay out specific examples or situations that have resulted from kids getting into trouble on the Internet, they will respond more positively. Teach your children that the Internet is unregulated and not all the information on it is accurate.

5. **Know exactly where your children are going.** Have your children communicate with you every time they leave the house or a friend's home to go elsewhere. Know everything about their friends and their friends' families and their locations. Check on where they say there're going and who they say they will be with.

6. **Have regular meetings.** Meet regularly with your children about their use of the Internet. Have them keep a log of what they're surfing and doing every fifteen minutes, and then discuss this log with them. If they've written down something they did on the Internet, you have a record of it, and you can always go back and track it to determine if your children are telling the truth. Tracking software helps you to achieve this. Don't be concerned about interfering with your kids' privacy; their safety comes first. Call a family meeting at least once a month, or more often if there are issues to settle and concerns to clear up. Just as it is a good idea to sit down at dinner with your children and have everyone take turns and tell about their day, you should have regular family

meetings where everyone gets to talk., Just remember that you, the parents, are in charge. And, just as it is a good idea to set a rule that no one leaves the dinner table without first being excused, and that no one begins eating until the rest of the family is at the table, you should also set the rule that no one leaves a family meeting unless a parent calls for an adjournment.

7. **Stress to your children that passwords are to be kept secret.** Make sure they understand that passwords are not to be shared with friends or others, and illustrate the results if someone uses their passwords. Tell them that it is not only their own information that becomes accessible to their friends and even strangers—everything the family has on the computer becomes jeopardized, along with your personal family records or financial recordkeeping. It is wiser to put important data on a removable thumb or flash drive that you can keep private.

8. **If you know your children's friends' parents, work with them.** Work with other parents to learn what your children do online when they're at each others' homes. If other parents aren't concerned about what children do on the Internet, then restrict your children from using the computer at their house or from going to that friend's home at all. Violations should result in your planned disciplinary actions. It is difficult to keep track of what your children are doing online when they're on someone else's computer. It falls to you to observe your children's behavior and check their belongings for any signs that your children are doing things without your permission.

Being the bad cop is always hard. The instant you challenge your children, they're going to fuss. Some will balk a tad, depending on how they were raised and how much you let them get away with when they were younger; others may act out and become melodramatic. No matter what your children's reactions to confrontation, you must hold firm, even if "Johnny's mother lets him surf the net anytime he wants!"

You may not be the popular parent or the popular household, but you will be confident you've done everything you can to keep your children safe. It is your job to do that. Kids truly want to believe, regardless of age, that they know everything—but they don't. You didn't know everything at their age, and even though they seem more advanced than you were when you were a kid, they are, quite simply, still children. They are *your* children and *your* responsibility. Take charge; take control. Don't back down if they fuss, fight, cry, scream, challenge you, sneak behind your back, or try to manipulate you in other ways. *You* are the parent, even if your child changed and you don't seem to know him, or particularly like him at that moment. Just remember though, to always love your child.

Maybe your charge of your children and the Internet will set a precedent for the more relaxed and less concerned parents you know. You might even want to give talks on it once you have a smooth-running plan in motion. Your most precious blessing is your children. Protect them.

Protecting Your Children

This section will look more closely at sites that offer valuable information for protecting your kids while they're on the Internet.

1. **The best way to protect your children is to be involved in their lives.** Pay attention to what they do, and keep the lines of communication open. Some of the protection products available are listed below. These products vary greatly in their sophistication. Some software vendors provide a subscription service with regular updates of blocked sites (usually for a fee). The best product will depend on your needs, your children's ages, and the computer and operating system they are using. Review parenting and computing magazines and *Consumer Reports* magazine or Web sites to compare the different packages available.

   * Search or browse for Internet safety products (http://kids. getnetwise.org/tools/) with this tool from Get Net Wise (http://www.getnetwise.org/).

   * Internet Content Rating Association (http://www.icra.org) is an international, independent organization that helps parents make informed decisions about electronic media through open and objective labeling of content.

2. **Monitor your children's computer time.** Many young people today will sacrifice sleep to be on the computer or to play video games on systems like Wii and PlayStation.

3. **Remind your children about cyberbullies.** These Internet bullies are no different than real-life bullies. They order people around, intimidate, and demand things such as money, loyalty, obedience, or almost anything. Also, discuss with your children the nature of ads they may come across while online, some of which are for mature audiences, others of which are vulgar, and still others of which may try to sell them drugs.

Internet reading suggestions (from http://www.med.umich.edu/1libr/yourchild/internet.htm; also read:

- "Teen Safety on the Information Superhighway" (http://www.safekids.com/child-safety-on-the-information-highway/), which is also available in a Spanish PDF version.

- http://www.missingkids.com/missingkids/servlet/PublicHomeServlet?PageType=ContentMain&LanguageCountry=es_US) Spanish

- You and your teenager can visit the SafeTeens site, (http://www.safeteens.com/) for lots more resources and information.

- Teens are getting lots of their health information from the Internet: (http://www.kff.org/entmedia/Press%20Release.pdf). This Web site is under maintenance at the printing of this book. Make sure your kids are getting facts, not fiction. Point them toward the KidsHealth.org Web site (http://www.kidshealth.org/index.html), which has a teen area (http://www.kidshealth.org/teen/) with reliable and interesting information on the kinds of things that teens want to know.

4. **Tell your children not to send photos of anyone out over the Internet (Facebook, social networks, etc.), not to purchase anything (especially with a credit card), and not to give out ANY personal information.** Additionally, you should remind them not to open e-mails from strangers. Share an e-mail address with your children, so you can keep tabs on what communications they are sending and receiving.

5. **Make using the computer a family adventure.** Remember what you do on the computer serves as a model for your children, so be sure to keep yourself safe online, and ensure you don't make the mistakes you're warning your children against.

6. **Keep in mind that you are a parent and not a pal.** Your job isn't to be liked by your kids or be popular with their friends. Your job is to protect your children; keep them safe; teach them; help

them to develop into productive and moral citizens, to be kind, compassionate, and thoughtful, and to have initiative; and—most of all—to love them. So there will be times you won't be popular or liked, but it is your responsibility to do what's best for your kids.

7. **Know the warning signs of drug/alcohol experimentation and use.** Reread this book, and highlight the places where signs and symptoms of drug use are given. Memorize these, and observe your children to see if they are exhibiting any of these signs. If you think they might be using drugs, then talk to your children and test them. We offer a variety of valuable and reliable instant tests that can be done in the home.

8. **Monitor everything your children do.** Watch everything your children do online, and use the other tips given in this book that fit your situation. Make sure you also monitor your children's other activities and behavior. This includes, but isn't limited to, the following:

   • Where they go and who they go with

   • What goes on, wherever they are, when they're away from home

   • Their friends' homes and parents

   • Nature of school activities and after-school activities

   • Their academic status and progress

   • The CDs they listen to and the DVDs they watch

   • How they dress

   • The possessions they acquire and how they acquire them

   • How they behave both in the home and outside the home

   • Their physical demeanor (eyes, for example)

- How they interrelate with others

- What they eat and how much

- The phone calls they make and receive

- How they drive and who they ride with

- Their personal hygiene

- Games (especially electronic) they play and with whom they play

9. **Talk to other parents and school officials.** Get feedback from the parents of your children's friends. This list also includes teachers and staff, who may have heard something you haven't. You don't want your children hanging around friends who aren't good for them, don't have a respectable reputation, or are into things you don't want your children doing. Talking to those parents might not yield the information you want, so it's best to talk to other parents who might know your children, especially the parents of kids who *used* to be your children's friends. They might be able to give you some added insight.

10. **Constantly review safety rules.** It never hurts to remind your children about the safety rules in your home, from not talking to strangers, to not walking alone, to exercising caution on the Internet, and so on. If you come across something in the newspaper or on the Internet that offers examples of good or bad safety habits, share it with your children. Even something as simple as how to put out a grease fire on the stove is valuable.

11. **Encourage your kids to tell you immediately if they find something on the Internet that makes them feel uncomfortable.** Discuss with them what's making them uncomfortable. Make sure they know not to return to that Web site. Use a software program to track and curtail Internet browsing, if necessary.

12. **Enforce the Internet rules you lay down for your kids.** Develop a list of rules you want your children to obey. Research the Internet for examples of good Internet rules and make sure you write them

out to suit your situation. Discuss them with your children, print them out, and post them on the computer monitor. These rules could consist of

- reminding your children not to give out their passwords to anyone;

- forbidding your children to download software or do anything with your computer that could cause malfunctions and result in crashes or other electronic problems;

- having your children show you the new things they've learned on the computer, as well as games they play or other things they do online;

- forbidding your children to give out personal information or purchase anything online; and

- limiting their computer time.

Knowing specific works to read, besides this book, to learn about drug and alcohol use is not nearly as important as it is to communicate with your kids at all times and to do as much research as possible. The more you know, the better armed you are as a caring, loving parent.

Internet Lingo

There is an entire language for use in e-mails, chatting, and text messaging. Some children use it when talking to one another. The Web site NetLingo (http://www.netlingo.com/index.cfm) has an incredibly extensive list of acronyms used on the Web. It can help you understand the language of online communication.

The majority of Internet crimes are sex related, and begin with communications between teenagers and older adults. Pedophiles stalk the Internet and online video games. It has been reported that 80 percent of offenders were quite explicit about their sexual intentions; 73 percent of cases include multiple sexual encounters; in 50 percent of the cases, victims are described as being in love with the offender or feeling close friendship; in 25 percent of the cases, victims had actually run away from home to be with the person they met online (from: "Sex Offender Stats," http://www.marshalsforkids.com/offender.cfm). Parents, if you don't know about the need to protect your kids online, read these statistics: http://www.netlingo.com/statistics.cfm

Educating yourself in the language used online can help you protect your children from online predators. Some of the terms, abbreviations, and codes used in online or text message communications are listed below. This list was put together by the authors of this book by culling numerous resources.

Language of the Internet

459, 143, ILU, ILY	I love you
8	Oral sex
WUF	Where Are You From?
WYRN	What's Your Real Name?
;)	Winking
SMEM	Send Me an E-Mail
KPC	Keeping Parents Clueless
WYCM	Will You Call Me?

ASL	Age/Sex/Location
Banana	Penis
CD9	Parents around (Code 9)
MorF	Male or Female
KFY	Kiss For You
MOOS	Member(s) Of the Opposite Sex
ADRA	Address
HAK	Hugs And Kisses
FB	F***ing Buddy
:-><	Puckered up to kiss
:/i	No smoking
P911	Parent Alert
PAW	Parents Are Watching
Kitty	Vagina
SMIM	Send Me an Instant Message
:*(	Crying
#-)	Wiped out, partied all night
%*}	Inebriated
1174	Nude club
DUM	Do you masturbate?
%\	Hangover
:-d~	Heavy smoker
POS	Parents over Shoulder
KOTL	Kiss On The Lips
8-#	Death
RUH	Are you horny?
J/O	Jerking off
GYPO	Get your pants off
RU/18	Are you 18?

TDTM	Talk dirty to me
420	"Let's get high." (marijuana)
Tweaking	High on amphetamines
CM	Call me
F***U, 4Q	F***ing you, F***
:(	Sad
(-:	Smiley from the southern hemisphere
=^*	Kisses
:.(	Crying
LOL	Laugh out loud
:|	Bored, sad
}:[	Angry, frustrated

Internet Resources

The information below is specific to the Internet. The resource offers other places to look for help. It is not a bibliography but a listing of additional sources to check out. The Web site http://www.med.umich.edu/1libr/yourchild/internet.htm, from the University of Michigan: "Internet Safety" offers the excellent resources and links below, as well as a host of other great info. Go to their site and learn:

Internet Safety

What do I need to know about the Internet and my child?
Use of and access to the Internet has exploded over the last ten years. The World Wide Web has enabled us to do things from the comfort of our homes like never before. The Internet can be a useful tool *and* lots of fun. When your child goes online, he can

- access educational resources, including encyclopedias, journals, and more;

- obtain up-to-the-minute information on current events;

- send mail instantly to people around the globe;

- learn about places around the world and be exposed to other cultures and other points of view;

- participate in real-time forums on topics of interest;

- get help with homework through all kinds of references and resources; and

- have fun playing games, sometimes with people thousands of miles away.

The Internet does carry some risks. It is largely unregulated, and not all the information on it is accurate. Advertisers market to children, just as they do in any media. Your children may have their privacy invaded by some Web sites or individuals they come across online. In addition, there are many sites that contain material inappropriate for children, including pornography, hate speech, and gambling. Finally, criminals can use the Internet with the intent of financially or sexually exploiting kids or harming them in other ways.[22]

The site offers tips on how to protect your child online, such as tracking them to maintain their safety, discussing the good and bad sites online, and using the Escape and Back buttons to get out of nasty sites. It advises to always keep passwords secret (do not give out your passwords that offer full access to all Web sites or hold your private financial and other family records). Give your children their own screen name, so that offenders can't track them to your home; there are stalkers online. Add to this security by stressing that they should never give personal info to anyone online or in person. People take such info and track kids to their homes and to parents' business places to get to your child at an appropriate time. Tell your kids to stay away from chat rooms, not to engage in social sites (Facebook, Twitter, etc.) or talk to "friends" they meet without telling you—and, certainly, to never meet anyone without your presence.

This book is filled with info on keeping your child safe on the computer. There are many different types of software available that give parents ways to block sites they don't want their children visiting. There is also a rating system for Internet content and products. The University of Michigan site (http://www.med.umich.edu/1libr/yourchild/internet.htm) suggests you browse for "Internet safety products with this tool from Get 'Net Wise." They also encourage parents to visit The Internet Content Rating Association for safety products. Keep on top of cyberlingo that kids use to fool their parents as to what they're saying. This book offers examples of that and sites you can visit to get more lingo translations.

Just keep in mind that you must be involved in every aspect of your children's lives. This encompasses protecting them from vulgarity, pedophilia, sexual perversion, online theft, stalking, pornography, and other unhealthy and immoral problems. The University of Michigan site informs parents that if they think their child has been cyber-abused, they should call the Cyber Tip Line, or call 1-800-843-5678. The University of Michigan is a valuable site for all parents. There is lots of good stuff there.

Having said all that, you should also know that the computer could be a useful tool for your child's fun and education. It's advisable, though, that you, the parent, spend time with her at the computer for educational reasons and for fun things to do on the computer. Some fun sites are listed in the following sections.

Fun Web Sites:

America's Story, from the Library of Congress (http://www.loc.gov) has truly fascinating stories to explore. This is a great family site.
     http://www.americaslibrary.gov/cgi-bin/page.cgi

Exploratorium: The Web site of the San Francisco museum of science, art, and human perception includes interactive activities and video segments.
     http://www.exploratorium.edu/

The National Gallery of Art kids' page has neat art-related activities for kids.
     http://www.nga.gov/kids/

Sesame Workshop: This was created by the Children's Television Workshop. This Web site has activities for kids, as well as useful parenting advice.
     http://www.sesameworkshop.org/home

At PBS Kids, children can play games based on popular PBS TV shows.
http://www.pbskids.org

Funbrain: This site contains educational online computer games for school-aged kids.
     http://www.funbrain.com/

KidsHealth is a site with health info geared toward kids, teens, and parents.
     http://www.kidshealth.org/index.html

Mr. Dowling's Electronic Passport is a cool social studies site by a Florida teacher.
     http://www.mrdowling.com/

The Yuckiest Site on the Internet: This site answers questions on a wide range of "yucky" topics, from worms to ear wax.
     http://yucky.discovery.com/noflash/index.html

Refdesk provides access to sources of current information, from news to weather to history.
     http://www.refdesk.com/

The Internet Public Library: Youth Division This is worth checking out.
http://scout.wisc.edu/Projects/PastProjects/NH/95-03/95-03-23/0000.html

Kid Pub shares more than forty thousand stories by kids.
http://www.kidpub.com/

The National Wildlife Federation kids' page is fun and informative.
http://www.nwf.org/kids/

Find more cool sites for kids at the Association for Library Service to Children (ALSC),
http://www.ala.org/gwstemplate.cfm?section=greatwebsites&template=/cfapps/gws/default.cfm

Teen Safety on the Information Superhighway is timely.
http://www.safeteens.com/safeteens.htm

Find cool games to share with your kids. They teach about online marketing, protecting online privacy, chat room pitfalls, and critical thinking about online content, alcohol advertising, and online hate speech. Each game has a recommended age group, from age eight to fourteen.
http://www.media-awareness.ca/english/games/index.cfm

Internet Safety Tips for Parents comes from the Kentwood (Michigan) Police Department.
http://www.ci.kentwood.mi.us/police/pdf/Internet%20Safety%20Tips%20for%20Parents.pdf

Safe and Smart: Research and Guidelines for Children's Use of the Internet Video and Computer Game Ratings: Entertainment Software Rating Board (ESRB) rates Web sites and online games for ensuring online privacy protection and for reviewing.
http://www.med.umich.edu/yourchild/topics/internet.htm

Video and Computer Game Ratings: Entertainment Software Rating Board provides services for rating Web sites and online games, for ensuring online privacy protection and for reviewing advertising created by the interactive entertainment industry.
http://www.esrb.org

If you think your child may be a victim of an online crime, or if you want to report suspicious online activity involving children, you can go to CyberTipline: http://www.missingkids.com/missingkids/servlet/PublicHomeServ let?LanguageCountry=en_US, or call 1-800-843-5678.

> Parents, if you don't know about the need to protect your kids online, read these statistics: http://www.netlingo. com/statistics.cfm

Drug Lingo

Sometimes abbreviations represent entire words or even entire sentences, such as BF for best friend. Similar to the online world, the drug world has a language all its own. Even knowing the lingo isn't foolproof, as users will change terms routinely or add and delete. Children who use drugs may find other ways to communicate when they realize their parents are catching on.

As new drugs and chemical are synthesized, the composition of drugs changes, along with their potency, cost, and street names. It is wise to keep apprised of new drugs, as well as the ingenious ways they can be distributed, as in candy (looks like Pop Rocks) and on postage stamps (LSD), as well as Four Loco and so-called "whipped cream.".

Drug lingo or slang is used on the Internet, in text messaging, as well as in conversations. Drug lingo is also included in the back of this book The authors researched many sites to offer examples of the drug lingo.

Take a look at this conversation, and see if you can figure out what really is being said:

> BOY: How about 420 tonight?
>
> GIRL: Got 007s and 3050s?
>
> BOY: Yep; 2-4-1.
>
> GIRL: I have 80s and 40s and 51s.
>
> BOY: You got an author for those?
>
> GIRL: Some. Others from my "friends."
>
> BOY: Great! AC/DC will be there, and Aunt Hazel, Aunt Nora, Angel, Bay T, and Beamers.
>
> GIRL: Okay, but I don't want to get amped out tonight.

Have you figured out the slang conversation above? Below is the translation:

> BOY: Wanna get high tonight? Especially got marijuana.
>
> GIRL: Got MDMA and marijuana and crack rolled in a joint?
>
> BOY: Yep; selling them on special as a two-for-one deal.
>
> GIRL: I have Oxycontin pills, and a combination of crack cocaine with marijuana or tobacco, and LSD.
>
> BOY: Did you get a doctor to write the prescription?
>
> GIRL: Some. Others are from dealers and traffickers.
>
> BOY: Great! Codeine cough syrup will be there, and heroin, cocaine, PCP and crack cocaine.
>
> GIRL: Okay, but I don't want to get wiped out on amphetamines tonight.

In the appendix, in the charts section, you will see some of the most common slang terms used by young people online, in text messaging, in snail mail, and in conversations dealing with drugs. Be familiar with slang, so if you hear your child speaking it to a friend or someone else, you'll be aware that your child may be trying to keep something from you. Combine your familiarity of drug lingo and Internet lingo, so you can more fully understand your child's communications.

Chapter Seven

Testing

Windows of Opportunity

There are two "windows of opportunity." The first is the time period parents have to find out if their child is using or considering using. Once your child starts using, the problem becomes *much* more serious. This window is open until the child starts to use. As discussed before, marijuana is indeed a gateway drug. If you used it in your earlier years, please know the strength of marijuana has increased dramatically, as have the poisonous (possibly deadly) effects of the materials used to cut it. You need to test your child before they use, and you need to educate them as to why you're concerned and why you're testing.

If you miss this opportunity, you have moved from a preventive situation to a recovery situation. Your problem in a recovery situation is exponentially worse. We plead with you to not let your child's complaints of "You're invading my privacy" and "You don't trust me" get in the way of your responsibilities as a parent. These are just typical arguments a child will use to get out of discussing drugs with you.

The second window of opportunity is a generalized measurement of how long a drug remains in the system. In reality, this is dependent upon a number of factors, such as:

- The amount of the drug used

- The drug's potency

- Whether the user has eaten or drunk anything before or after using the drug

- The user's physical health (size, metabolism, activity)

- The user's emotional health

- The location where drugs are being used

- The user's experience

- The user's drug tolerance level

- The drug's purity

There are many other factors involved, and they vary by individual.

The following chart gives a good sense of how long a substance may last in a person's system, and how effective testing will be based on that time period. The chart also offers information on the various specimens used to detect drug abuse.

Quick-Glance Chart

(Drug Detection Times)

Drug Name	Detection time for urine	Detection time for saliva	Detection time for hair
Alcohol	2 – 80 hours	up to 14 days	N/A
Amphetamines	1 – 3 days	1 – 1 ½ Days	Up to 90 days
Anabolic Steroids	Oral – up to 21 days injectiable – 90 days - 1 year	N/A	N/A
Barbiturates	1 – 21 days`	N/A	N/A
Benzodiazepines	1 – 14 days	N/A	N/A
Cocaine	1 –3 days	1 – 1 ½ Days	Up to 90 days
Ecstasy	2 – 4 days	1 – 1 ½ Days	Up to 90 days
GHB	Up to 72 hours	N/A	N/A
Ketamine	1 – 2 days	N/A	N/A
LSD	Up to 8 hours	N/A	N/A
Marijuana	1 – 30 days	Up to 24 hours	Up to 90 days
Methaqualone	1 – 7 days	N/A	N/A
Methadone	1 – 3 days	N/A	N/A
Methamphetamine	1 – 3 days	1 – 1 ½ Days	Up to 90 days
Opiates	1 – 3 days	1 – 1 ½ Days	Up to 90 days
Oxycodone	2 – 4 days	2 – 4 days	N/A
Phencyclidine (PCP)	1 – 30 days	1 – 1 ½ Days	Up to 90 days
Propoxyphene	1 – 3 days	N/A.	N/A
Rohypnol	1 – 3 days	N/A	N/A

What Are the Elements of a Drug-Testing Program in Schools?

Many workplaces have had drug-testing programs in place for years, and recently some school districts have implemented programs for testing their athletes. Successful programs typically share a number of common elements, beginning with a clear written policy. Parents and teachers sign a statement declaring that they understand the policy, which is typically announced at least ninety days before testing begins (this time period can vary drastically). An effective policy addresses questions such as the following:

- Which students, if not all, can be tested for drug use?

- What type of testing will be done?

- What is the process for selecting students for testing?

- Who will conduct the test?

- What are the consequences of a positive drug test?

- Are steps clearly articulated for helping students who test positive for drugs?

- Will a second confirming test be done for those testing positive initially?

- Who pays for the test?

- Will subsequent positive tests result in suspension or expulsion from extracurricular activities and/or school?

- Are test results cumulative throughout a student's tenure at the school, or is the slate wiped clean each year?

- What happens if a student refuses to take the test? Will refusal be construed as a drug-positive test? This is true in the world of corporate testing programs.

- Who will see the test results?

- How will confidentiality be maintained?

- How and when will parents be informed about positive test results?

- How does a student contest the results of a positive test result?

- What mechanism is in place to protect students whose prescription medication triggers a positive reading?

The Most Commonly Used Tests

Urine

Urine test results show the presence or absence of specific drugs or drug metabolites (drug residues) in the body some time after the effects of the drug have worn off. Positive urine tests don't always mean the subject used drugs at the time of the test. Rather, it detects use of a particular drug within the historical "look-back" time of each drug ingested. The historical time depends on the drug. Most drugs will show up in urine. Technology has invented what is commonly referred to as "instant tests," which are also often called integrated "urine cups." These cups incorporate detections for several different drugs into one test. Though many states permit such a device in workplaces, several others don't. They are invaluable for home use, and many schools and workplaces use them.

Hair

Analysis of hair provides a much longer detection window for the presence of specific drugs and drug metabolites, giving a drug-use history of approximately ninety days, depending upon individual hair growth. A hair test uses one and a half inches of hair length from the scalp. Hair follicle testing doesn't provide evidence of current impairment, only past use of a specific drug. It cannot be used to detect alcohol use. Hair testing can detect amphetamines, cocaine, methamphetamine, marijuana, opiates, and PCP.

Blood

Blood tests are basically used with law enforcement. Blood testing shows current impairment. Sending your child to a lab for such a test is always a possibility. Testing the blood for drugs is also more invasive than saliva, urine, or hair testing.

Sweat

This test utilizes a skin patch that measures drugs and drug metabolites in perspiration. The patch, which looks like a large adhesive bandage, is applied to the skin and worn for a length of time. A gas-permeable membrane on the patch protects the tested area from dirt and other contaminants. The sweat patch is sometimes used in the criminal justice system to monitor drug use by parolees and probationers, but so far it has not been widely used in workplaces or schools. It will show use of amphetamines, methamphetamine, marijuana, cocaine, PCP, and opiates. The drawbacks to this type of test are its varying degrees of accuracy and the fact that the user could remove the patch and then attempt to place it back on before the test is done.

Sprays and Wipes
There are sprays and wipe devices that detect drugs by evaluating perspiration left on hard surfaces touched by the user. The user's perspiration leaves remnants of the drug(s) on any hard surface they touch. This works fine as long as the area being tested isn't accessed by other people who could have contaminated the surface areas.

Breath
Breath analyses (i.e., breathalyzers) are valid testing devices, for they detect and measure current alcohol levels. In this test, the subject blows into the breath-alcohol test device, and the results are given as a number known as the blood alcohol concentration (BAC), which shows the level of alcohol in the blood at the time the test was taken. To maintain accuracy, these machines are calibrated on a regular basis. These tests measure the amount of substance in the body based on how much of it is expelled by the lungs. Alcohol is commonly tested for in this manner, and police officers frequently use it on the road to determine if a driver is DUI (Driving Under the Influence) or DWI (Driving While Impaired). Breathalyzers come in portable and nonportable configurations and provide printed documentation of results.

Oral Fluids (Saliva)
Traces of drugs, drug metabolites, and alcohol can be detected in oral fluids, the generic term for saliva and other material collected from the mouth. Oral fluids are easy to collect; a swab of the inner cheek or the collection of saliva are the most common methods used to obtain a sample. They are difficult to adulterate or substitute, and collection is less invasive than with urine or hair testing. Because drugs and drug metabolites do not remain in oral fluids as long as they do in urine, this method is used for determining current/recent use and impairment. It will show amphetamines, methamphetamine, marijuana, cocaine, PCP, and opiates. Swab tests are also available for alcohol and DNA testing.

What Do Drug Tests *Not* Measure?
No standard test (that we are aware of) can detect inhalant abuse, a problem that can have serious, even fatal consequences. Inhalant abuse refers to the deliberate inhalation or sniffing of common household products—gasoline, correction fluid, felt-tip markers, spray paint, air freshener, and cooking spray, to name a few—for the purpose of getting high. The same problem exists regarding "magic mushrooms" (psilocybin).

Commonly Used Devices in Home and Workplace

What Do Drug Detection Devices Test?
Test devices work in two categories: property and people. Sprays and wipes are predominantly used to detect drugs on surfaces or properties, while oral (saliva), urine, blood, hair, and breath tests work to detect drug consumption in a person.

What Kinds of Tests Are Available?
Urinalysis, the most common drug-testing method, has been studied exhaustively and used extensively, has undergone rigorous challenge in the courts, and has proved to be accurate and reliable. Some employers use hair, sweat, and oral fluids. Each of these tests has benefits as well as drawbacks. The chart in the appendix outlines some of the pros and cons.

What Does Each Test Measure?
Drug tests are used to determine whether a person has used alcohol, illegal drugs, and/or prescription drugs. Some tests show recent use only, while others indicate use over a longer period. Each type of test has different applications and is used to detect a specific drug or group of drugs. The Federal Drug-Free Workplace Program relies on urine tests designed to detect the use of marijuana, opiates, cocaine, amphetamines/methamphetamine, and phencyclidine (PCP). Urine tests can also be used to detect a large number of other drugs, as well as alcohol and steroids. Cotinine, the major metabolite of nicotine, can also be detected through urine.

Drug Testing in Schools

Drug Testing: An Overview
When you consider the amount of time your children spend away from home and at school, your focus should be on ways to protect your children when they are out of your immediate supervision. Get together with other parents, and urge your school system to test students (within your state and local laws) as well as offer valuable information on drugs and testing to parents and the community. Many school districts are beginning to test their students. Some are also equipping parents with our SafeBox for their homes. If you are interested in bringing a drug/alcohol testing program to your school, please contact us at info@omnidrugscreening.com.

Some schools are relying on experts to spray or wipe down lockers, computers, and other surfaces. This type of testing program is used to determine what drugs exist in the school, and this can be determined without testing even one student. These tests will also show if there is a drug problem and which grades are doing which drugs. We can provide this service if you have an interest or feel there is a need.

What Should You Do *Before* You Begin Testing?
The decision of whether to implement a drug-testing program should not be left to one individual or even to one school board. It should involve the entire community. In fact, by making the effort to include everyone, a school can greatly increase its chances of adopting a successful testing program.

It is not enough to have a general sense that student drug testing sounds like a good idea. A need for testing can be determined from student drug use surveys; reports by teachers and other school staff about student drug use; reports about drug use from parents and others in the community; discoveries of drug paraphernalia or drug residue at school; and from prescreening school equipment via sprays or wipes (This is a noninvasive method of determining drug usage.)

> *Schools considering testing will want plenty of public input, bringing together anyone who has an interest in reducing student drug use.*

Before implementing a drug-testing program, the school should consult early in their deliberations with an attorney familiar with laws regarding student drug use and testing. They should seek the advice of drug prevention and treatment professionals and should also contact officials at schools that already have drug-testing programs in order to learn what works and what doesn't.

Schools considering testing will want plenty of public input. They should bring together members of the local board of education, school administrators and staff, parents, community leaders, local health-care agencies, local businesses, students, and anyone else who has an interest in reducing student drug use—as well as those who are against the idea. Listening to opponents and including their views can strengthen the testing program and improve its chances of success.

Pros and Cons of Various Drug-Testing Methods

Many factors determine the best test to use. Consider these factors:

- Many states have implemented strict laws about who can be tested in the workplace and in schools, as well as when they can be tested. Check your state regulations before you engage in any kind of testing, because it's typically a requirement that you have a drug and alcohol policy in place.

- Improper procedure in performing a drug test is always problematic. This can yield false negatives or false positives—invalid results. People who administer tests—such as hair, urine, saliva, spraying, blood, wiping, and breath analysis—are trained and/or certified. Drug cutoff levels have been established to eliminate false results. This means that specific drug/drug metabolite levels need to be reached before a result is considered positive.

- An expired instant test device can yield improper results; it is always important to check expiration dates prior to using.

- Spray-and-wipe tests are dependent on the residue in sweat, which allows for drug detection on hard surfaces touched by an abuser. A drawback is the possibility of surface contact with the skin of a person other than the suspected user.

- Urine tests are commonly accepted specimens for drug testing. It is possible they could be adulterated, though most instant devices are sophisticated enough today to make this possibility small. Be aware, though, that users are always working to find new ways to fool tests, and these are shared, mainly through the Internet.

- Breath test machines are not as widely available as urine tests, and they are expensive, but the results are extremely accurate and widely accepted.

- Reading test results properly is important in order to make sound judgments about what the test is revealing.

- Inattention to temperature control can invalidate a testing device that requires the device to be stored within a certain temperature range (usually 2–30 degrees Centigrade or 36–86 degrees Fahrenheit).

- Adulteration substances and devices are available online for those who want to try to alter or falsify test results. Most of these adulteration attempts are useless.

- Blood tests are invasive and have a short look-back period, but they do show current use.

- Oral tests are dependent upon acquiring a sufficient amount of saliva for the test to be valid.

- Hair follicle testing is extremely reliable, but it's more expensive than urine or saliva testing.

- Testing property rather than people spares legal headaches, in some cases, but doesn't pinpoint a guilty party, unless a person's personal area is swiped or sprayed separately.

- Each test used is selected specifically depending on what you want to test for and whom you are testing, as well as over what period of time.

- Every drug you are attempting to detect has its own window of opportunity. Each drug has a historical look-back period and is in the system for a specific period of time. In order to detect that drug, you must test within that period of time. Hair follicle testing is one of the few methods that can detect drug use approximately ninety days (dependent on speed of hair growth) prior to the test date. Each one and a half inch of hair growth gives approximately ninety days of drug-use history.

- There can be legitimate reasons for positive results (legal prescription medications); therefore, one should not immediately assume the person being tested is an abuser.

Each test has its own advantages and disadvantages. Investigate the best ones for your situation, or, if you like, we can suggest the proper test for your needs. When testing a loved one, especially your child, it is best to start with in-home testing devices, such as integrated test cups, alcohol swabs, or other types of test kits. You don't need to go through special training or certification to administer these tests. Read and follow the directions. This book serves as a major asset here.

Workplace Testing

For testing in the workplace, you must know the laws of your state regarding employee and employer rights. You should call upon a professional tester and/or a TPA (Third Party Administrator) who knows how to implement a drug-free workplace program, as well as how to perform the tests and do general and specific assessments. If you are interested in determining whether you have a workplace drug problem without testing individuals, please contact us to arrange a spray or wipe. If evidence of drugs should turn up, you can then determine what further steps you want to take. This generally involves the process of developing and implementing a drug-free program that includes testing, though this is entirely up to the parties involved.

Types of Drug Tests

	Pros	Cons	Remarks
Urine	☐ Reliable results ☐ Least expensive ☐ Most flexibility in testing for drugs, alcohol and nicotine ☐ Most widely used of all drug-testing methods	☐ Specimen may be diluted, adulterated, or substituted ☐ Limited window of detection ☐ Test sometimes viewed as invasive or embarrassing ☐ Biological hazard for specimen handling and shipping to lab only if urine contains blood	☐ Typically 1 to 14 days and up to 45 days for chronic marijuana use
Hair	☐ Longer window of detection ☐ Greater stability (does not deteriorate) ☐ Can measure chronic drug use ☐ Convenient shipping and storage (no need to refrigerate) ☐ Collection procedure not considered invasive/embarrassing ☐ Cannot be adulterated by shampoo, dye or bleaching	☐ More expensive. ☐ Test detects basic 5-drug panel (amphetamines, methamphetamines, PCP, opiates, and Marijuana) ☐ Cannot detect alcohol use ☐ Will not detect very recent drug use (1 to 7 days prior to test)	☐ Depends on the length of hair in the sample. Hair grows about a half-inch per month, so a 1½-inch sample would show a 3-month history. Body hair can also be used and will yield a much longer window of detection
Oral Fluids	☐ Sample obtained using direct observation ☐ Minimal risk of tampering ☐ Non-invasive ☐ Samples can be collected easily in virtually any location ☐ Can detect alcohol use ☐ Reflects recent drug use	☐ Drugs/drug metabolites do not remain as they do in urine ☐ Less efficient than other testing methods in detecting marijuana use	☐ Approximately 1 ½ to 3 days
Sweat Patch	☐ Non-invasive ☐ Variable removal date (generally 1 to 7 days) ☐ Quick application and removal ☐ Longer window of detection than urine ☐ No sample substitution possible	☐ Small number of labs able to process results ☐ People with skin eruptions, excessive hair, or cuts and abrasions cannot wear the patch ☐ Passive exposure to drugs may contaminate patch and affects results	☐ Patch retains evidence of drug use for at least 7 days, and can detect even low levels of drugs 2 to 5 hours after last use

Hair Testing

Hair testing is a good way to determine if drugs had been used over the past three months. Employers often use this in preemployment testing because of its accuracy. Hair testing analysis for drugs has held up in the courts for the following categories:

- Parole

- Employment

- Divorce

- Child custody

- Criminal cases

- Military cases

These Web sites provide backup information regarding the legal acceptability and court decision of hair testing for drugs:

- http://www.ncjrs.gov/txtfiles/hair.txt

- http://www.phila.gov/personnel/laborrel/FOPaward2000.pdf

- http://www.criminology.fsu.edu/journal/mcbay2.html

- http://civilservice.sheerinlaw.com/2008/10/articles/employ-ment-law-2/decision-to-allow-nypd-drug-screening-by-hair-analysis-instead-of-urinalysis-reversed/

- http://dsp-psd.tpsgc.gc.ca/Collection-R/LoPBdP/CIR/901-e.htm

- http://www.omegalabs.net/media/documents/pdf/Cases-7-03-net.pdf

- http://www.armfor.uscourts.gov/opinions/1996Term/96-1239app.htm

Hair testing serves as a vital instrument for detecting drugs. It can be used to determine drug usage in individuals, or incorporated into a drug-free workplace. Equally important is its use in legal cases.

How to Test for Drugs and Alcohol

Many kids think there's nothing wrong with smoking pot; they fail to realize it is a gateway drug and at least five to twenty times more potent than marijuana sold in the 1960s. Kids need to hear from you how wrong it is to try drugs. There are no inappropriate times to talk to your children about illegal drugs. Just talk whenever you can without preaching.

Kids do listen to what their parents say. They watch what we do and learn from that. When you make the decision to test for drugs and/or alcohol, we urge you do it when your child is not on legally prescribed medication such as cough medicine with codeine, or a pain reliever (Vicodin, Percocet, Percodan). This medication will show up as a synthetic opiate.

In-home instant testing is easy. The integrated test kit is a simple two-step process. The same-sex parent accompanies the child to the bathroom. Allow your child some dignity while he or she urinates into the cup, but make sure you are aware enough so you don't allow him or her the opportunity to adulterate (pollute) the urine sample by adding water, bleach, or an online adulterant.

Because a child may try to change the test results if he or she thinks it will be positive, it is important to check the temperature strip on the cup to make sure it is within the proper range of 90–100 degrees Fahrenheit. If the child is attempting to adulterate a specimen by adding water, the temperature strip will indicate a problem. We can also provide test kits with adulteration checks built in.

If the results indicate there are indeed drugs in the child's system, try to remain calm. Have a discussion with your child, something along the lines of: "This test shows you're positive for marijuana (cannabis/THC). Have you been smoking grass?" Your child will likely deny any drug use, but persist with him in a diplomatic and gentle, but stern, manner. If the child still says no, test him again with another of our integrated cups, or have a specimen submitted to a lab in order to obtain defensible results. If your child refuses to be tested, you probably already have a problem. If there is no guilt, there is no reason for your child to resist testing.

If the test is positive, you and every member in your family have a problem, as drug use and/or trafficking affects *everyone*—not just the user. You will need to take steps to help your child right away. Every community has local agencies that will help you, and you can go to http://dasis3.samhsa.gov/ and locate reputable rehab centers in your area. If the problem seems serious and urgent, your doctor might have other ideas for getting your child the right care. You can also contact us at info@omnidrugscreening.com and we will refer you to an appropriate lab for retesting and/or a rehab facility in your area. There have been situations in which the parents think their child is using marijuana and, after testing, find out that the child has been using heroin—so be prepared for anything. If your kids complain about your infringing on their privacy, tell them you're concerned about them growing up in a safe environment, and you don't want them participating in anything that could hurt them. Also pointedly tell them that their bedroom is part of the home *you* provide, and thus you have every right to make sure your house isn't being used as a place to use drugs. Additionally, let them know you don't like to go through their property or their bedroom, but it is your duty as a parent to watch over them and keep them healthy and safe. Stress that drug use will hurt them and everyone around them for the rest of their lives.

Specific Testing Directions
for Urine Test Kit

We offer numerous drug-test kits. The most comprehensive package, called SafeBox, includes three important components: an alcohol-swab oral test, a ten-panel drug-test cup, and our book on kids and drugs. If you want printed material on more specific subjects, then we strongly advise you to visit the Web sites listed in the appendix and throughout the book. You can request any print materials they may offer, as well as nonprint materials (videos, audio tapes, etc.). Most are free; some require payment for the products. Government agencies do periodically run out of literature, and some place limitations on the amount of materials you can request, so understand you may have to wait for reprints or substitute the items with other brochures (many of which the government now offers online in PDF format).

Ten-Panel US FDA 510(k) Cleared-Urine Drug Test

 Temperature Strip on back

Read Results

Image Courtesy of: Express Diagnostics International, Inc

The test cup shown above will detect cocaine, amphetamines, methamphetamine, marijuana, opiates, phencyclidine, barbiturates, benzodiazepines, methadone, and synthetic opiates (Percodan, Percocet, and Vicodin). The temperature-integrated drug-test kit is a rapid, one-step screening test for the simultaneous, qualitative detection of multiple drug metabolites at specific cutoff levels in human urine. This is a bit technical, but it serves as a description of how the detection method works. We hope your children will agree to voluntary testing. If not, we offer parents a way to test their children without their knowledge (see below).

For confirmation of a disputed positive test, the donor can be retested and the specimen submitted to a qualified laboratory at an extra cost. Contact our home office for the nearest qualified collection facility. False positives can occur if a person tested is taking other medications, so we recommend to all parents who get positive results that they take the child to an approved collection facility to conduct a confirmation test. We can provide this service.

The directions for testing are below, but you should always read the directions accompanying the drug-test cup. Some other urine cups may be used as well. They essentially all work the same way, but read the directions.

Step-by-Step Instructions
1. Remove cap (unscrew)
2. Donor provides specimen and screws cap on tight.
3. Check cap for tight seal.
4. Check the temperature strip to make sure it is within the range shown.
5. Set the cup on a flat surface.
6. After five minutes, peel the label to view the results.
7. Do not attempt to interpret results after ten minutes.

All of our drug-test kits

- are US FDA (Food and Drug Administration) 510(k) approved;

- adhere to SAMHSA (Substance Abuse and Mental Health Services Administration) cutoff levels (same as DOT— Department of Transportation—levels);

- are 99% accurate;

- include an integrated temperature strip to insure proper donor sample;

- have control markers for test validity;

- show results in five minutes (most results can be photocopied);

- offer a 12–18 month shelf life;

- have a new leakproof top for confirmation lab testing, if required; and

- allow you to keep control of the results and timing.

This book not only provides advice on dealing with drugs and your children, but it also offers vital information on testing your children. We work with various manufacturers to provide you with the most reliable, accurate, and easy-to-use test kits, which will detect up to fifteen different drugs. Our oral alcohol swabs are excellent in detecting alcohol usage.

Voluntary Testing

Voluntary collection and testing is the preferred method. If your child refuses to be tested, you may need to resort to involuntary testing. In voluntary testing, your child urinates directly into a cup, securely replaces the cap, and gives the container to the parent right away. The child must not attempt to adulterate (deliberately mess up) a drug test. It is advisable for a parent of the same sex as the child being tested to remain with the child in the bathroom while she/he is taking and completing the test.

How to Read the Test

(Below are simplified directions for interpreting test results.) The lines referred to below will be shown on each test cup and easily identified.

Negative

Two lines will appear if the test is negative. One red line should be in the control region (C), and another apparent red or pink line should be in the test region for each specific drug. This negative result shows that the drug is not in your child's system. The shade of red in the test may vary, but even a faint pink line indicates a negative result.

Positive

If there is no red or pink line—even a faint one—the result is positive. Each drug has a specific, standard cutoff level that must be exceeded before the specimen is considered to show positive for drug use. This level is established to eliminate false positive results.

Involuntary Collection

In the case of a child who refuses to cooperate, parents can collect a specimen from the toilet directly. This is easy to do and will avoid any confrontation. First, turn off the water to the toilet bowl at the valve behind the bottom of the water tank. Then flush. No water will be able to flow into the reservoir tank, but water will still show in the bowl. Next, when your child goes to the bathroom, flushes, and no water flows into the bowl, you'll probably hear, "Hey, the toilet doesn't work." This is your opportunity to get a urine sample from the toilet bowl by scooping liquid from the toilet into the cup. After you have collected your sample, open the water control knob and flush. You now have a urine sample to test.

Surprising your kids with a random test periodically allows you to perform a test before they've had the opportunity to adulterate or corrupt a specimen. Some of these adulteration methods include drinking a massive amount of water to attempt to dilute or corrupt the sample, using cleansing solutions, substituting another's urine, and applying masking agents. You can read more about methods for test adulteration by typing some of the following phrases into an Internet search engine, like Google: (1) drug-testing adulterants, (2) drug-test cleansers, (3) drug-test detoxification, or any phrases similar to these. Check your child's possessions as well to see if they are carrying or stashing any known adulterant agents.

Just as reading and understanding the test results for the urine cups are easy, so is interpreting the results of the alcohol swab test.

The Alcohol Swab Test Kit

The alcohol swab provided in the SafeBox package is a unique and beneficial test. There is no urinating in a cup, no wait period to send a sample off to a lab, no breathing into a machine or any other mechanical means, and no invasive blood draws or other test formats. Instead, all that has to be done is the following:

+ Check the expiration date on the container to make sure the test kit is still viable.

+ Keep the container. You will need this to compare the swab color with the color shade chart on the back of the package. This will show the alcohol level.

+ Have your child sit for fifteen minutes without any drink or food.

+ Pull the swab (a stick with a cotton-like flat ball on the tip) out of the container (small bag), being careful not to touch the test ball.

+ Either hand it to your child to place inside her cheek or have your child open her mouth and let you scrape the inside of her gums and mouth with the swab until the swab is saturated.

+ Let the swab lie flat on a hard, clean surface for two minutes.

+ After two minutes, match the color of the tip of the swab to the color shades on the back of the package. This will give you the level of alcohol (if any) in her system.

If your child tests positive, it is important to implement consequences as well as to give serious thought to getting your child help, especially if she admits to using alcohol and particularly if your child is underage. Don't take a positive test lightly. Alcohol is an addictive drug, even though it is legal (with age restrictions), and its use is widely accepted in today's world.

This sample illustration shows how color indicates the blood-alcohol level in the alcohol test swab:

Alcohol level chart

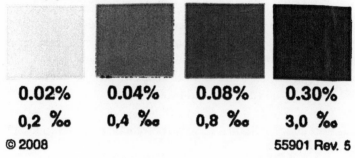

Image courtesy of Chematics, Incorporated; N. Webster, IN

Typical Alcohol Swab Test Kit

Image courtesy of Chematics, Incorporated; N. Webster, IN

Alcohol Test

The oral swab is an excellent, noninvasive way to find out if your child has been drinking. We can also provide other more sophisticated alcohol tests that have a greater time coverage (window of opportunity), such as the eighty-hour EtG alcohol urine lab test.

Additional Testing Information

Each cup provided in our test kits comes with directions specific for that brand of test. Some require you to push a key into a hole in the cup; others have you tilt the cup upside down; still others may have you do nothing but put the lid on the test cup and wait to read it within a proper time frame. Just check the accompanying directions. Nearly all the cups we provide in the SafeBox correlate to the comments and cautions listed below:

Although the integrated cup test is 99.0 percent accurate, it is not 100 percent foolproof.

+ Some kids will attempt to adulterate (contaminate) the specimen.

+ The test may not be correct if it's used past the expiration date, if the kit is stored at too high a temperature, or if it's not properly administered.

+ The test may not have been read within the proper time period (Read after five minutes but not after ten minutes.)

+ The test may read invalid if the urine was insufficient in amount.

+ Your child may attempt to dilute (adulterate) it with water from the toilet or sink. This is why we encourage a parent or guardian of the same sex as the child to be with him in the bathroom when she/he is giving the sample.

+ Positive results do not always equate to drug use. If your child has been ill recently and been given legal prescription medications, he might test positive for drug use. For example, if your child has taken certain cough medications with codeine, pain medications containing Percodan, Percocet, Vicodin, or attention deficit disorder medications (Adderall), he could test positive for opiates or benzodiazepines.

- Positive results do not mean your child is an addict or even a drug user; it just means he tested positive for a certain category of drugs. When given a prescription for your child, always ask the doctor if it could show up in or affect the results of home drug tests. Discuss testing-cutoff levels with the physician.

The competed test should be placed on a level surface and allowed to sit for five minutes before you read it.

Your child should be with you while you are waiting for the five minutes to pass. This gives the child time to consider the ramifications of testing. The child will likely be a bit nervous if he has been doing drugs, so he might decide to confess to drug use before the test results are evident. While waiting, remind your child that the test is 99 percent accurate and that if he has anything to tell you, he should do it at this point. It is better to hear from your child personally rather than learning of drug use from the label on a test cup. Emphasize that lying to you is as bad as being on drugs or alcohol. You might want to talk to your child about drugs, although sitting with him in silence is often an effective way to get him to begin speaking to you about his actions.

Consider this hypothetical conversation:

YOU: Bobby, what results do *you* think I will see?

BOBBY (SHRUGGING): I don't know.

YOU: Do you think I'll be surprised, upset, happy?

BOBBY (NERVOUSLY): I don't know.

YOU: Is there anything you want to tell me before we look at the results?

This could yield a confession or a protest. You should discuss the consequences of a positive test prior to testing. The next section details how we suggest you react to test results.

YOU: If the results are positive, we will discuss your use in detail and what we plan to do to help you get clean. If the tests are negative, then we will know that you listened to what we taught you and are doing what you should be doing—staying away from drugs. We will be very proud of you if we see a negative result.

Even if your child confesses that he has been doing marijuana or some other drug, you must still read the test results to determine if there are other drugs in his system. Many times the drug kids confess to might not actually be the drug they are using, or there may be another drug they're using and not admitting.

If the test results come out invalid, you will need to retest your child with a new test cup that is sealed and not past the expiration date.

If your child opposes taking the test, the likely reasons are either that he is very principled in terms of trust or that he is doing drugs. Constantly remind yourself that your child will get over the feeling that you don't trust him, but he *won't* get over addiction.

So how should you react to the results you witness after your child takes the test?

Negative results.
Give praise, and let your child know he will be tested from time to time on a random basis. Also explain that this random testing is a great excuse for him not to take drugs if they are offered. All he has to say is, "I can't. I get tested at home, and I never know when." This allows him to not take drugs and doesn't put him in a position to be ridiculed by his peers for saying no.

Positive results
Be sure you conducted the test properly. If the results indicate signs of drug use, you can retest your child to be sure. Certain factors, such as your child taking prescription cough medicine with codeine, medication for ADD, etc., may affect the results. Also, if he tested positive, consider having confirmation test done. We work with a variety of approved labs and would be able to supply you with proper lab forms for your area.

Invalid results
If the C line (the control line) doesn't appear, the test is invalid. This could be to the result of a number of reasons (see previous sections), such as improper technique, adulteration of the urine by your child, a temperature that is too high or too low, a dysfunctional test cup (past expiration date), a faulty cup (though unlikely), or other causes. You should retest immediately with a new cup if you get invalid results. Keep in mind that if the control line is absent on the drug cup, the test is invalid. Do not use the kit past the expiration date.

Getting help

If the test is positive and the control line is valid, chances are your child has one (or more) drugs in his system (remember that a positive can result if your child is taking a prescription medication). Don't neglect this critical indicator; don't be an enabler to your child or make excuses. If he tests positive, something is going on. Remember that even illicit use of prescription drugs can make a child an addict (and they are becoming more popular all the time). Regardless of which chemical your child is being tested for, positive results mean usage, and you have to take action. We urge you not to treat marijuana as a minor drug. There is no such thing as a minor drug. Marijuana is a gateway drug and can (and usually does) lead to the harder drugs of abuse. Don't make excuses or try to justify your child's use. Marijuana addiction is serious.

DNA Testing

Unfortunately, sometimes drug and alcohol abuse may lead to unwanted pregnancies. In the case of multiple recent partners, it is extremely important that the mother, child (children), and potential father(s) find out who the biological father really is. DNA testing can provide two types of results: informational and legal (court admissible). There are several good DNA labs, but exemplary is GTL (Genetic Testing Laboratories), which is AABB and ISO 17025 accredited (DNA testing industry standards and requirements). GTL's phone number is: 575-646-3465.

Overview of DNA testing

DNA test samples can be collected from family members by simply swabbing the inside of their cheeks with a special collector that looks like a large cotton swab. This is quick and painless. Home DNA testing kits are available for both informational and legal verification. Saliva is the typically utilized, but DNA can also be obtained from many different types of body specimens.

Here Is What to Look For

Having to find a treatment center for your loved one who is addicted is always difficult, especially in an emergency situation. When possible, research all the treatment centers near you and, if need be, go beyond your own perimeter, even into another state. But before you make any decision as to where to place your child, consider these criteria:

Accuracy

When seeking a reputable lab, always look for the highest-quality paternity tests in the industry, preferably those using sixteen genetic markers, backed by an accuracy guarantee.

Affordability

While DNA testing technology for human identity is a powerful tool, there is no need to overpay for the service. Shop for labs with experience, sophisticated and quality equipment, proper accreditation, offer certification, and reasonable price.

Convenience

When looking for a DNA lab, consider convenience. The easier the lab makes it for you to send them the test and for the lab to return your results, the better off you are. Included shipping and FedEx "overnighters" are a major help, too, along with a quick turnaround in getting you the results.

Easy Directions

You'll want to locate a lab that provides easy-to-follow directions for implementing their tests. In most cases, DNA testing is a simple procedure, but you'll want to make sure you understand all aspects, especially when performing the test for legal causes, as when you are attempting to prove paternity and for court-admissible evidence. Legal DNA testing requires third-party involvement. Therefore, good directions with supporting images are vital. You also want to be able to do the test quickly and accurately. The kit should also allow you to test additional people, even though you should expect to pay an additional fee per extra person in most cases.

Frequently Asked Questions about DNA Testing

Below are questions fielded by GTL, a respected genetics lab.

How is a DNA test performed?
A stick with a swab at the end of it is swiped in the inner cheek (buccal) area, placed in an envelope, and secured with a tamper-proof tape. The sample(s) is then sent to a lab for genetic analysis.

What is a buccal swab, and is it as accurate as blood testing?
A buccal swab is soft and resembles a large cotton swab. It is used to collect a sample of cheek saliva by simply rubbing the inside of the cheeks. It is as accurate as blood testing, as the DNA is similar. A person should, however, abstain from drinking coffee for a few hours before taking a sample, and smokers should rinse and brush their cheeks with a toothbrush before swabbing.

How does the DNA or Paternity Home Test Kit work?
The GTL Home Test Kit contains illustrated instructions and a consent form to be filled out with information about each person providing a sample. A photograph, proof of identity, and sometimes even a fingerprint may be required. Except for infants and very young children, each person collects his or her own samples; the collection process is simple. Buccal sampling takes about forty-five minutes for three people, with an additional fifteen minutes needed for the swabs to dry completely. The samples are then returned to labeled tubes and containers. The samples, plus the paper forms, are placed in the included prepaid mailing envelope and sent by mail back to the laboratory. Home Test Kits for DNA cannot be used as court evidence. Third-party collection is required for results to be used in court.

Where are DNA tests performed and what are their restrictions ?
You can order home DNA or paternity test kits over the Internet, or you may call to make an appointment for us to take samples in your area. By definition, home (or self-collected) paternity tests are not accredited (legal for use in court) unless they meet specific requirements. Many families opt for a home DNA/paternity test kit because it is more affordable and because they wish

to be discreet. If any laboratory advertises an "accredited home test" without meeting these requirements, they are being deceitful and violating AABB standards. Home tests do not require proof of identity or the assistance of a disinterested third party and are therefore not an AABB accredited test. The Legally binding Home Paternity Test, however, is an accredited DNA test. It comes with full instructions on the duties of the witness, informs you what qualifies as proof of identity, and will hold up as court evidence (Third-party collection is required in this case.)

Are results from the Home DNA or Paternity Test Kit admissible in court?
The basic Home DNA or Paternity Test Kit is intended as a discreet and private way whereby families can resolve questions without involving outside parties. It is *not* legally binding. We do offer, however, a GTL Legally binding Home Test Kit for an additional charge.

Do I need a court or doctor's order for a paternity test?
No, you do not need such an order to perform a parentage test.

How old does a child need to be to undergo a DNA paternity test?
A newborn infant can be tested. Taking a sample with a buccal swab is painless and is not traumatic for the child. Blood is an alternative method for a newborn baby.

How does a DNA parentage test work?
A DNA parentage test works by identifying the specific DNA sequences in the mother, child and father. If the mother and father are the parents of the child, the DNA in the child's chromosomes must have been inherited from both parents. Determining paternity and maternity is possible from these DNA sequences. In almost all paternity cases, if the alleged father is the biological father, all fifteen genetic markers will match those of the child (the sixteenth genetic marker is used to confirm the sex of the person). It is possible for the tested father to be the biological father and still have one or even two exclusions (mismatched genetic markers) because of mutations in the father's DNA. If a paternity test includes only one parent and the child, labs cannot guarantee a minimal probability of parenthood. In most cases, these probabilities are greater than 99.99 percent. Labs that are AABB accredited for DNA testing can perform all DNA tests, both court admissible and informational, using the most stringent control protocols in the industry. This provides clients with the security that they are receiving the most accurate DNA test results available.

Can a paternity test be performed without the mother?
Yes, although results will not be as conclusive.

Why is it better to include DNA from the mother when performing a paternity test?
In a matter as important as paternity, especially in legal cases, it is never good to leave room for doubt. Ideally, the mother, child, and potential father(s) should all be tested. Children receive half of their DNA from their mother and the other half from their father. Because the DNA half the child receives from the mother will match the mother's DNA exactly, the remaining unmatched DNA will match that of the biological father. Without the ability to remove the mother's DNA from the equation, the possibility increases greatly that results will not be conclusive. This may require testing of additional genetic markers, thus extending the time and cost needed to achieve conclusive results. In general, if the mother is available for testing, she should be included.

What if I want to test more than one child or alleged parent?
Additional potential fathers can be included in the tests.

What happens to the samples after the test?
Most labs retain the samples for six months, in case additional testing approved by the customer is necessary, and then they destroy the samples. If you wish, however, you may request that all samples containing the tested person's DNA be destroyed immediately upon completion of the test.

Chapter Eight

Home Base

Safety Starts in Your Home

Parents, you play the most important part in the decisions your children will make with respect to drugs and alcohol. Government statistics show that children whose parents talk to them about drug/alcohol abuse are five times less likely to use. If you don't discuss drugs and alcohol with your children, they'll get their knowledge from their friends and off the street. We find it remarkable that many parents don't understand that they are the primary and preferred source of information for their children. Many parents consider these conversations to be taboo. They are either embarrassed or afraid to have these discussions. Whether you like it or not, you are responsible for your children, and you need to have these conversations. Don't be afraid of your children—talk to them.

It is also important to discuss your past experience with drugs and alcohol. Some parents believe that if they discuss this, their children will think less of them, or they'll think, "If my parents did that, then I should be able to do it, too." This is a possibility, so, ultimately, you have to decide what's best to tell your children based on knowing your children. You can use your own experiences to talk about how drugs and/or alcohol harmed you or affected your life, along with how much more dangerous drugs and alcohol are now than when you were a teenager. Just be sure your children are at the right age to understand and differentiate your activities in your childhood from the risky activities of today's children.

Children know you aren't perfect as parents and you weren't angels when growing up, so sharing some of your experiences may help your children face some of the same or similar situations confronting them today. On the other hand, they could try to use your experiences as "ammunition" against you. The decision is yours. Parents should not think that, because they used drugs when they were younger, their children could use and still turn out as successful adults. This is not true for a variety of reasons, though your children may try to manipulate your past use to justify their current use.

We urge you to tell your children that marijuana is five to twenty times stronger now than when you were a teenager. Let them know that some marijuana is being cut with heroin or cocaine in order to get kids addicted to heavier drugs.

Stress to them that illegal drugs are often made under clandestine and unsanitary conditions; with illegal drugs, there is no such thing as "portion control," and there is no governing body to administer and control dosage amounts. They should also be aware that dealers sometimes cut their drugs (prior to sale) with various poisonous substances. They also cut them with nonpoisonous substances, but they really don't care which they use. If it is available, they will use it. They do this to make their supply stretch, and they have absolutely no regard for the harm this will do to the users. Also discuss the unsafe places drugs are sold and the dangerous people selling them.

An extremely crucial area you need to be involved with is helping your children choose the right kinds of friends. Know the friends and know their parents. This is your first line of defense in the battle to keep your children drug-free. Childhood marks the beginning of peer pressure, something every child has to deal with. Your children's friends are the most important risk factor for drug use.

As parents, you can take your children to many places to see the effects of drug and alcohol use/abuse. Visit rehab facilities, methadone clinics, and known open-air drug selling locations. Walk along the front of a meth clinic, and you may be approached by someone (typically a user) asking if you have a "jug" to sell. *Jug* is a term given to a take-home dose of methadone. They sell for about $150 (at the time of printing) on the street. Some users want to sell them and aren't taking the methadone they are supposed to be taking. They do this because they are in the methadone program but not taking it seriously. They are not ready to stop. Some buyers want to use the dose to get high or set up their own quick detox dosage.

Arrange with your community police to take your children, and perhaps other children, on tours to the police station and lock-up where other kids are being held for illicit drugs and drinking. This will give them the opportunity to see the dark side of drug use, see what people going into a methadone clinic look like, or how meth users have completely destroyed their appearance. Your children need to see what happens to users, how they look, how they live, and how they eventually end up. We encourage you to impress upon your children that those users who don't stop using generally end up dead or in prison.

Some children think drug usage is glamorous. This notion can come from TV, movies, and/or their friends, so you, as their parents, have the unfortunate chore of showing them the sinister side. Let them watch reruns of Dr. Drew Pinsky's *Celebrity Detox*, which will show them that using drugs and/or alcohol is not as glamorous as they may think. They will see celebrities going through the horrors of trying to detox. It is not a pretty picture, and it could be the visual your children need to help them understand how ugly drug use can be. Drugs and alcohol can ruin anyone's life—rich or poor, celebrity or not.

Faces of Meth™ is a project of the Multnomah County Sheriff's Office, and it shows before-and-after pictures of crystal meth addicts. These will definitely make an impression on your children (and you). Look at their Web site along with your children (these before-and-after pictures are scary): http://www. oregonlive.com/news/oregonian/photos/gallery.ssf?cgi-bin/view_gallery.cgi/ olive/view_gallery.ata?g_id=2927

Realize that your children learn by mimicking; they will do the things they *see* you do before what you *tell* them to do. You know the old saying: "Practice what you preach." Actions do speak louder than words. Children despise hypocrisy and are quick to see it, though they may not be able to verbalize it as such. They need and want your guidance and structure, but, most importantly, they want a good example to follow.

Don't be misguided into thinking schools will be teaching your children about drugs and alcohol use and abuse. Schools are established to teach the three Rs. They do much more than this, but the bottom line is that schools are not equipped to teach about drug and alcohol abuse; schools are not set up to be remote parents. In some areas of the country, schools are not allowed to even *approach* the subject of drugs and alcohol, so it ultimately falls to you to teach your children about the hazards of use and addiction.

Parents' Responsibilities

As a parent, your job goes beyond just testing your children for drug and alcohol use. In fact, if you follow the guidelines below, you may be able to nip the problem before it has a chance to blossom.

We brought our children into this world, and we bear the responsibility for their upbringing. It is important that we take our jobs seriously. Every parent faces similar experiences. There is the uncertainty about what to do in specific situations, exhaustion from needing two incomes to make ends meet, inconsistency in discipline, need for patience, single parenting—and the list goes on. You're not alone. Most moms and dads parent by gut feelings—not by following a training manual, special classes, or some magic formula. So, a lot of our actions and reactions toward our children are spontaneous, instinctual, compulsive, intuitive, and impulsive. But there are steps we can take to become better role models for our children, to discipline them in a proper way, and to prevent drug addiction from taking over their lives.

Below are some tips for heading off drug addiction in your children:

Prevent.
Prevention allows you to win the battle before the war is even declared. If you can head off drug and alcohol abuse, then you will not have to get dragged through the misery of addiction. Addicts can irreversibly alter family dynamics. They create dysfunction. They destroy loved ones, not purposely, but simply through the process of their addictions. Parents have gone absolutely bankrupt trying to save their child from drugs and alcohol. It is shocking, but important to remember: statistics say that usually by the time parents realize their child has a substance problem, the child or adolescent has been on drugs/alcohol for approximately two years. If your child does become a user, don't entirely blame yourself. Even the best kids—from the best homes, from religious families, from middle-class, loving parents—can become addicts. We want to help you head off the problem before it becomes extremely difficult to manage by offering you drug and alcohol test kits and drug and alcohol abuse education. Get a drug-test kit, let your children see it, and remind them that you could choose to test them at any time.

Deter.
The presence of the kit in your home serves as a preventive measure and deters your children from thinking they can get away with trying drugs. Equally important is that it offers an excuse for kids to shrug off peer pressure. They can say to their friends, "I can't try that! My parents test me!" Let them be right; do random tests on your children just to let them know you're on top of things, and you're watching them. Though they might not realize or admit it, most kids want their parents to present them with guidelines and rules and to enforce them.

Therein lies part of the secret to success in raising children. No matter how tired you are, no matter how many times you've said the same thing over and over, you *must be consistent* in disciplining. Even if it means you are pulled away from whatever important thing you are doing, you must still consistently and persistently discipline your children. They need to understand that if they do something wrong they'll be appropriately punished every single time. It is harder on you as the parent to discipline than it is on the children to receive discipline, but nowhere is it written that parenting is or should be a cinch. An important aspect of being a parent is quite simply that YOU are in charge, not your children. Don't let your children intimidate you, but don't jump to conclusions, either. You have the upper hand, because you are the parent. The law recognizes that you are in control of your home and its minors (your children), so you are the one who should make decisions. Parenting is the toughest, and yet most important, job you'll ever have. Just remember to temper your discipline with love and encouragement.

Know Your Children.
If you spend time with your children, you will pick up on their nuances and will be able to detect when something's amiss. This means interacting with your children, spending time with them, and being with each child independent of the others. If you have several children, you'll need to work out a time schedule where you're giving each child individualized attention. Mothers, especially, who regularly spend time with their children are able to develop a sense of what their children are thinking and can anticipate their actions many times. At the dinner table, let each person discuss his or her day. Show interest in each, and ask questions.

Working parents have it especially hard, because they have limited time to spend with their children, and the younger their children are, the more likely it is that nonparents play a large role in raising the children (nursery schools, day care, after-school programs, neighbors, grandparents, relatives, and so on).

Some parents don't have the opportunity to arrange work schedules to be home with their children all the time. Raising children is a serious job. If financially possible, don't let other people do it for you. The younger the children, the more impressionable they are, and their parents are their primary role models. If your children are under the care of others while you work, make sure they share your values and morals. Talk with your children. If kids are on drugs, they'll tend to pull back from their family, so having any dialogue with them could be trying—but you need to establish good communication with your children before they start using.

During puberty and the teen years, most children become somewhat introspective and sometimes introverted, making communication very difficult. This is a hard time for parents, and sometimes we can't see how to reopen the lines of trust and communication with our children. Often, we can seem smothering to children who are testing their independence. We might attempt to smooth things over for our children, or make quick judgments, or offer advice that our children internalize as criticism. When children feel they are under the microscope and everything they do will be judged unfairly, they end up retreating from contact with us. Parents often don't mean to yell when they discipline, or lose their tempers with their kids, or give advice that seems derogatory, but we sometimes do. We generally mean well, but many times we make the wrong choices about what to say or do. Sometimes it just comes down to swallowing our pride and saying we're sorry when we're wrong. This teaches our children to do the same. Respect goes both ways.

We parents walk a very thin line between doing right by our children, helping them to avoid the mistakes we made, and giving them the right advice while realizing they might take what we say as criticism or what we do as being unfair to them. Embarrassing them alienates them from us even more. It is difficult doing what we think we should do for our children while trying to retain our children's dignity when we have to discipline them. Sometimes tough love is the only real answer, but always, *always* let your children know you love them, no matter what they do, and you are there for them. You must, however, stand your ground and implement discipline and authority when your child breaks the house rules or the law. Like the old saying goes, "Criticize the act, not the child." One important factor is to always follow through on your threats. If you tell your children they will lose a privilege if found to be using, make sure you take away that privilege. If you don't follow through on your threats, they will know it, and you will lose your leverage, respect, and power to change their behavior.

Model Your Role.
This is where that saying "Actions speak louder than words" comes into play. The classic story of baby ducks learning to walk and quack rings true, because ducks imprint (that is, they copy the mother duck's actions). This is a prime example of role modeling.

Because young children lack a huge knowledge base of vocabulary and word nuances, they learn more from how we act than what we say. This is why inconsistency terribly confuses them and sends them conflicting messages. If you teach your children something, practice it yourself. If you say you're going to do something (or that you're not going to do it), follow through with what you've said. Children learn self-responsibility and accountability from their parents. If you're not modeling it, they're not going to learn it or exercise it. You, as parents, must be good role models at all times. If you don't do what you tell your children to do, they will think you are acting unfairly to them and won't believe your own advice.

Just as you discipline negative behavior, you should reward good behavior. If children do chores in a timely and proper manner, reward them in some way. Even something as minor as a compliment is a reward to a child. Negotiating with your children need not be a negative thing. If your child wants to stay up an hour or two beyond bedtime for an important event, then you might yield a little by meeting her halfway, and letting her stay up forty-five minutes later than usual. Other times you should not negotiate on anything; your word should be law. The important thing is that you weigh each issue in regard to each child and make good decisions based on the child's personality, maturity, degree of responsibility and trust, and what the issue really entails. Children need to learn what is negotiable and what is not negotiable.

Expand your children's responsibilities and allowances as they grow, and continue to prove that you are the boss in all of this—not your children. Play that role with seriousness but with an abundance of love. Your trust is to be earned by your children.

Be Aware.
Observe your children, their moods and attitudes, their grades, and, especially, their friends. Take note of any changes in their appearance and hygiene. Investigate their friends and their friends' families. Keep tabs on your children's academics and after-school activities. Talk to their teachers and classmates. Require your children to bring home test results and other school

papers. Learn the nature of homework, review it with them, and make sure they are doing it.

Know what's going on in the drug scene. Ignoring the problem and thinking your children won't get into trouble is denial, plain and simple. Any child can get into trouble, no matter what the quality of his home life, income stratum, religion, or school. You must be on guard as to what is going on, not only in the world regarding drugs and alcohol, but also particularly in your community, and especially in your own backyard. Learn about all the different types of drugs, both prescription and illicit (including designer or club drugs). This book offers all that.

Keep abreast of what new things kids and dealers are coming up with. Inhalants are an easily available source of danger. Kids' sniffing and huffing can be extremely hazardous. Constantly keep in mind that longer-standing drugs, like marijuana and heroin, are many times more potent than they were in the 1960s and 1970s. Sometimes the only difference between the city and the suburbs is the cost of the drugs. Part of being aware is understanding how the drug scene has changed—worsened—since you were a child.

Educate.
Learn all you can about drug abuse and alcohol intoxication. Go online (government agencies offer a wealth of information; see the resources throughout this book). Visit libraries, read relevant books, talk to therapists and counselors, visit schoolteachers and administrators, talk to other parents, and, if possible, confer with former addicts. They can teach you a lot of the tricks of the trade. Watch documentaries on the drug/alcohol problem, attend sessions offered in your community on drug use, and get involved with organizations and agencies that are trying to fight the problem. The more knowledge you possess, the better you are prepared to discuss drug and alcohol abuse with your children.

Besides educating yourself, teach your children and other family members the information you've learned. Have family discussions on the topic, and take the time to listen to what your kids have to say. If your children's school is not implementing a drug-free program, offering test kits, or performing random testing or wiping down of school property, make a point of getting your community involved in making these things happen. Knowledge is power!

Test.
Our SafeBox has everything you need to test your children for drugs and alcohol, even if you're not suspicious they may be using. Randomly testing them

will keep them on their toes. Tell them that at any time you can exercise your authority to perform instant testing to determine if your children are involved with drugs or alcohol. If they are not guilty, they shouldn't refuse to be tested. Your keeping the kit visible in the house reminds your children that they can be tested, while also providing an "out" for them against peers who pressure them to try drugs.

Follow the test directions properly, as explained in this book, and read the test instructions that accompany each test kit. Not doing so could result in an invalid test, though there may be other causes for invalid results as well. Whatever the results may be, you need to have a serious conversation with your children. If they test negative, you should praise them and figure out a reward system, but you should also reinforce the dangers of experimenting with drugs and alcohol.

The law on testing is fairly uniform nationally. It allows parents to test their children under the age of eighteen. Those over eighteen cannot be forced into testing, because they are considered to be adults. However, many parents give their children aged eighteen or over and residing at home the ultimatum of either being tested or moving out. Privileges can also be taken away from your children should they refuse testing. As the parent, you must be in control. You are the authority. You are the decision maker. Your child is dependent upon you, and thus the responsibility resides with you to keep him safe from harm. Our experience has shown that a large number of drug/alcohol abusers over eighteen are still living at home. In that case, they are still your responsibility.

Confirm.
If your child tests positive for any of the drugs shown on the test kit (the number of drugs tested for varies by cup selection), you'll need to bury the heart-sinking feeling that your child is an addict. Instead, focus your thoughts on how to save your child. Confirmation can be done by a lab test, which is available through the authors of this book, through your family physician (in some cases), or other resources. Just be sure that the follow-up confirmation test is reliable, sensitive, and gives results within a reasonable period of time.

Seek Help.
A confirmed positive test requires immediate help for your child. Learn about the treatment resources in your area and talk with each. Costs, insurance coverage, methods of treatment, time required, type of individual or group therapies, and other factors will enter your decision-making process. the longer you wait to get help for your child, the worse the problem will become.

Monitor.

Once you've managed to get your child off drugs and alcohol, your job isn't done. It is just beginning, as you will need to implement a regular monitoring program to ascertain that your child doesn't return to his old habits. Monitoring means not only observing your child's behavior, physical coordination, and academic progress, but also maintaining an ongoing dialogue with him about drugs and alcohol. This includes periodically testing your child. The goal is to keep your child clean. You should monitor your child even if he hasn't indicated irregular behavior or tested positive for drugs. This should be an act that you perform randomly. Testing is just something you need to do.

Intervene.

If your monitoring indicates your child is using or has returned to using drugs, then you must confront him and tell him he needs to get help now. If your child refuses (users deny), you should plan an intervention through a professional therapist. The abuser's loved ones confront him in an honest and straightforward, but loving and supportive, framework. The loved ones tell the abuser how he is damaging his life and that his usage must stop. An intervention requires the user/abuser to go for help at the time of the intervention—not the next day, or the next week, or a few months later. Interventions are painful for everyone involved, but they are a crucial tool in helping save the user, the user's family, and everyone else involved with the addict. There needs to be a serious penalty if he doesn't accept help.

Use the Unity Oath.

You and your family should sit down and discuss the Unity Oath offered in this book. As a signed oath, it promises that each and every person will not do drugs or alcohol. Should one of you be caught doing so, then that person must agree to get the necessary help, parent and child alike. Please feel free to modify the Unity Oath to your family's needs.

Enforce Consequences.

As hard as it may be, you have to be firm with your children who have gone astray or who are likely to. The earlier you start indoctrinating your kids on the dangers of drugs and alcohol, as well as doing your job of monitoring and protecting them, the better the odds your children won't do drugs. Lay out rules for zero tolerance on drugs and alcohol, and then enforce those rules.

Parents' Drug Check List

With gratitude to Charter Fairmount

All parents today need to be aware that a serious drug and alcohol problem exists among teenagers (and some younger than teens), and their own child may be involved. Most young people today experiment with drugs; some develop harmful dependencies. Listed below are some common problem areas, which you may have begun to notice in your child. If your child's behavior matches any of the warning signals listed below, drug or alcohol abuse may be the problem.

Personality:
- Are you observing noticeable mood swings?

- Does your child seem very giddy/very depressed?

- Is your child very irritable or hostile without reason?

- Does he/she have an extremely negative or apathetic attitude?

- Does he/she appear to have no motivation to do things?

- Does your child spend a lot more time alone, in his/her room?

Appearance:
- Have you observed a change in your child's appearance?

- Have you noticed red eyes or dilated pupils?

- Does your child seem unusually hyperactive? Sluggish?

- Has his/her look become sloppy?

- Does he/she look unusually pale; are there dark circles around his/her eyes?

- Have you noticed the smell of alcohol or marijuana?

Family Relationships:

+ Is your child refusing to participate in normal family activities?

+ Has your child stopped talking to you about his/her feelings and activities?

+ Is your child fighting more with other family members?

+ Is your child refusing to do his/her share of chores?

+ Is your child defensive or evasive when you try talking about drugs or alcohol?

Friends:

+ Has your child stopped spending time with old friends?

+ Is he/she hanging out with kids you don't know?

+ Is your child reluctant to introduce you to his/her friends?

+ Do your child's friends immediately go to your kid's room, avoiding everyone?

+ Does your child receive many short phone calls?

+ Have you checked on your kids and found they're not where they should be?

School:

+ Is your child having more problems than usual at school?

+ Are grades dropping?

+ Is your child avoiding extracurricular activities, such as sports, clubs, etc?

+ Is your kid skipping school, sleeping in class, arguing with teachers, or being tardy?

+ Have you caught your child forging notes to his/her teacher?

+ Are you having problems getting your child to go to school or do homework?

Legal:

+ Has your child begun to experience legal problems?

+ Has he/she been caught breaking into neighbors' homes?

+ Have you begun to miss money from your purse/wallet?

+ Are you missing items from the house that could be sold or traded for drugs?

+ Has your child been caught with drugs or drug paraphernalia?

The above list is offered on behalf of the generosity of Charter Fairmount Institute. If you have answered yes to several of the above, you need to seek help from a professional. Charter Fairmount provides a free, confidential interview assessment. If you have any questions, or would like more information, call us. We can help.

Maryville, Inc.
Charter Fairmount Institute
561 Fairthorne Avenue
(800) 235-0200
(215) 487-4100

A member of the Charter Medical Corporation
Family of Quality Health Care Facilities
Philadelphia, PA 19128
For local information, call (856) 935-9305.

FAQs

1. **How can I tell if my child is using drugs?**

   By using our easy testing devices, you can tell within five minutes whether your child is doing drugs. This book, along with the testing devices, will help you interpret the results and inform you on how to recognize drug usage and effects.

2. **If the results come back positive, what should I do?**

   First, have a discussion with your child to find out how long she has been using. Based on the answer, tell her the side effects of using that substance. If she claims she was just experimenting, you need to stress the seriousness of that and how it can lead to addiction. If your child has been exposed to the harmful substance on several occasions, you should seek professional help. Don't always believe what your child says. Users lie. Confirm all answers. If you find your child is lying to you, make sure she understands she has to earn your trust back. This book offers insight on treatment. Even if your child swears, gets on her knees, pleads with you, and promises to never do drugs or alcohol again, you must still be strong and get your child into a treatment process.

3. **How can I prevent my child from using drugs?**

   You cannot prevent your child from using, based on the simple fact that you are not with her twenty-four hours a day. But once you have warned her several times about the effects of drugs, you can hope she heeds your advice when approached by peers or dealers. If she is using, you MUST act and get help for her. You can, however, help deter her from using by having our SafeBox visible in your home. Try to be a role model.

4. **I know my child would not use drugs, so should I still get the kit?**

   It is impossible to know that your child has not used drugs, or that she never will. Once again, you cannot be with your child all day, every day, so the safest thing to do is to get the kit and test. If you have the feeling she has been using any illegal substances, you'll know within five minutes whether or not your suspicions are correct. If the results are negative, good!

You will then know your child is listening, and she, in turn, will know you care enough about her well-being to test.

5. **Does it really help to talk to my children about drugs?**
Children can learn about drugs from their parents, or they can learn about them from users and dealers in the streets. If you talk to your children about drugs, they are five times less likely to use. They need to learn correct information from their parents.

6. **I don't know anything about drugs. What should I tell my kids?**
This book contains a wealth of information. If you are afraid of misinforming your children, contact a professional who has experience with children and substance abuse. There are many resources on drug and alcohol abuse on the Internet. This book offers many examples, detailed explanations, and various suggestions for initiating the discussion. Always feel free to call on the services of a professional counselor.

7. **Aren't schools supposed to tell my children the dangers of drugs?**
This depends on where you are located. Some schools are *supposed* to tell your children about the hazardous effects of drugs, but there is no law dictating this. Many school administration departments are extremely liberal and believe they should not have any control over drug issues. Some even believe that marijuana should be legal. That is so wrong. Many school systems won't get involved, and they expect you, the parent, to initiate the conversation on drugs and alcohol when your children are still young.

8. **How do I get my child's school to test for drugs?**
As a parent, you can do two things to encourage schools to take on drug prevention programs. One is to press for a formal program in the school, and the other is to ask them to consider testing students, or at least school property, to determine the degree and type of drug use going on in the school or on its premises. However, the ultimate burden rests with you, so you need to test your child randomly on an ongoing basis, as well as consistently educate them and warn them about drug and alcohol use.

9. **How do I find the right treatment center?**
This book has the answers on how to find the best center, how to relate to your child's counselor, what questions to ask the rehab center, and what your role will be. Take this step seriously, because you're going to be investing money to cure your child. Understandably, you'll be distraught and worried once you discover your child is doing drugs, but you must get

beyond that and focus on healing your child. Start by checking with your insurance carrier on their drug- and alcohol-treatment policies. This online source is excellent: http://dasis3.samhsa.gov/

10. **Is alcohol considered a drug and why?**

Yes! Alcohol is the most commonly used and widely abused psychoactive drug in the United States. It reduces reaction time, slows thought processes, and lowers inhibitions. Underage use of alcohol is extremely dangerous.

11. **At what age should I begin drug testing my children?**

Every family situation is different. Some children experiment with drugs as young as eight and nine years old. We suggest implementing a program of random drug testing of youth before they are twelve years old. Unfortunately, the transition from grade school to middle school is a time when most children start using drugs. They are vulnerable and want to fit in with their peers, so testing during this transition period is important.

12. **My child isn't willing to give a urine sample. How do I obtain one?**

A involuntary specimen can be collected directly from the toilet. First, turn off the water to the toilet bowl. A knob is usually located between the tank and the wall. Then flush. No water can flow into the reservoir tank, but the bowl remains full. Next, when your child goes to the bathroom, flushes, and no water flows into the bowl, you will probably hear, "Hey, the toilet doesn't work." This is your opportunity to go and get a urine sample from the toilet bowl. After you have collected your sample, open the water control knob and flush. You now have your sample to test.

13. **If I get the kit, won't my children think I do not trust them?**

Trust has nothing to do with it. You are still a parent (or guardian) who need to look out for you children's welfare. You are responsible for their health and safety, period. Children do not possess the maturity to know how to make the right decision when confronted with offers to use drugs. The issue here is more safety than trust. How would you feel if your children overdosed on an illegal drug? Wouldn't you think they had betrayed your trust? Don't wait for something bad to happen—act now!

14. **How soon should I be talking with my children about drugs?**

It's never too early to share how you feel about drugs and what your expectations are in terms of zero tolerance of drug use by your children. A study showed that 74 percent of fourth graders wished their parents would speak with them about drugs.

15. **How big is the drug problem?**

    The scope of the problem is staggering. Have a look at some of the numbers:

    - Eighth graders' 30-day use (at least one use in the last 30 days) of an illegal drug was 7.6% in 2008.

    - Twelfth graders' 30-day use of an illegal drug was 21.3% in 2008.

    - The average age kids begin experimenting with illegal substances is 13.

16. **Would my child lie to me about using drugs?**

    Absolutely! If your child is using, he/she might lie about anything. Kids typically use drugs approximately two years before their parents are aware of their using. The only way to be certain of your child's drug-use status is to test him/her randomly and often.

17. **Are inhalants dangerous and why?**

    Lifetime use of inhalants showed a slight increase among eighth graders, from 15.6 percent in 2007 to 15.7 percent in 2008. But even a single session of inhalant abuse can disrupt heart rhythms and cause death from cardiac arrest or lower oxygen levels enough to cause suffocation. Regular abuse of inhalants can cause serious damage to the brain, heart, kidneys, and liver, and even one use can result in death.

18. **Is marijuana dangerous?**

    Today's marijuana is at least five to twenty times stronger than it was in the 1960s. It *is* a gateway drug. Statistics show most hard-drug users started with marijuana. Constant use of marijuana permanently destroys brain cells (as does any voluntary use of an illegal drug).

19. **Do drug users return to their old habits?**

    Drug users will almost always return to their habits at some point. It may not be right away, but, at some point, even those who swear off drugs and alcohol will relapse. Relapses are always a distinct possibility and happen more often than not. Treatment can help reduce the incidence of relapse and can help provide a support system for recovering addicts that allows them to enter recovery with more confidence and with an increased possibility of success. It is usually necessary for them to move away from their friends who are using. It is crucial you determine good and bad friends.

20. How do I tell if a child is on a controlled substance?

Here are some things to look for if you think a child is using drugs or alcohol (see elsewhere in this book for more information):

+ Discipline problems

+ Personality changes; unusual outbursts or displays of temper; unexplained changes in overall attitude, including depression; withdrawal or apathy; acting up and acting out in classes, when out with family, or at home; lying, meanness, lethargy, and apathy

+ Shirking of responsibilities

+ Deterioration or sudden change of physical appearance or grooming habits

+ Sudden secretiveness or inappropriate concerns for privacy; poorly concealed attempts to avoid attention and suspicion, such as frequent trips to the restroom or basement, which may be an attempt to conceal drug use

+ Wearing sunglasses or frequently using eye drops to clear the appearance of the eyes; the sclera and pupils often can give clues to substance use

+ Association with known drug users or "problem" students

+ Unusual borrowing of money from friends, siblings, or parents

+ Stealing, either at home or through shoplifting

+ Possessing unexplained valuables

+ Increased absences from school or work

+ Drop in academic grades or achievement levels

On Discovering Your Child's Use

It's painfully true that parents sometimes are unaware of the things that go on in their homes. Generally, kids who use drugs or alcohol have been using for at least two years before parents realize what is happening. By the time you put all the pieces together, analyze the changes in your child's behavior and appearance, take note of how your child is negatively reacting to you, discover that grades are slipping or that friends are questionable, your child may already be mired in drug use. Discovering use early in the game allows for a quicker, steadier, and more stable recovery for your child. Here are some pointers to help guide you through the recovery process:

Pretreatment

1. Talk to your child, and listen for reasons why they became involved in substance abuse. You may have to read between the lines, as your child may not even know the real reason they turned to drugs. Drug use is an addiction. You will want to find out what caused them to turn to drugs. If you don't fight the cause, you can't properly fight the addiction.

2. Check with your insurance company to find out what they'll cover regarding treatment and medications, as well as in-patient and out-patient care.

3. Research area rehab and detox centers. The appendix offers information on where to start.

4. Work with your spouse or significant other (if you have one) to help your child. Make sure any heated discussions and fighting between the two of you regarding your child's situation are done in private, as this can put additional pressure on your child. The child will also try to pit one parent against the other as a diversion.

5. Visit rehab centers. Take questions with you (shown as item number ten in the following section, "Dos and Don'ts in Your Role as a Parent of a Child in Treatment") to the treatment center to ask counselors and therapists.

6. Practice tough love with your child. Your heart may be breaking, but you must be firm and strong, but loving, to get everyone through this tough time. You'll have to tighten your rules and enforce each and every one of them, without exception. Again, make sure you are an exemplary role model for your child. Do not make idle threats.

7. Talk to school officials to determine how your child can stay current in academics while undergoing treatment. If there is no way for your child to keep up with schoolwork while undergoing treatment, make sure school officials are aware of what's going on, and work out a plan for your child to catch up with academics at a later time. They won't realize how important it is to their future that they finish school. Tell them.

8. Attend twelve-step programs or other self-help groups. There are many organized local support groups for the parents/guardians/friends of addicts. Check the phone book.

9. You might talk to the parents of your child's friends to see if they are aware of your child's drug/alcohol problem, or if they are experiencing the same with their own child. Chances are they've never considered the fact that their own child might be doing drugs, so sharing information with them and asking them questions could be beneficial to their family, as well. Ultimately, though, you are on a fact-finding mission. The last thing you want is for your child to return, after treatment, to people and conditions that encouraged his substance abuse in the first place. You need to make sure your child changes people, places, and things from negative influences to positive ones.

10. Encourage your child to constantly work on staying in recovery. Recovery is a lifelong process. Support him, and be loving, but firm, in what you have to do.

11. Work on correcting the things that got your child into this position to begin with. If his grades have dropped, you'll want to work with the school faculty. If there is tension between you and your spouse or significant other, you'll both need to work to improve your relationship for the benefit of your child. Learn what the contributing factors are, and repair them. Drug use is usually a reaction to a situation. Addiction is often a symptom of more extensive issues.

12. Don't ignore your other children while focusing on the addicted child. Siblings are also affected, and you don't want them to turn to drugs and alcohol, as well. Addiction is a problem that affects the dynamics of the whole family.

13. Lock up alcohol, drugs, or inhalants that could be accessible by your children, including prescription drugs.

14. Test your child.

15. Talk to respected local agencies and rehab/treatment centers. Normally, they have an interview and admissions procedure (intake assessment), whereby you can discuss treatment as well as insurance and payment information. They may offer local assistance if you don't have insurance or to complement insurance. Work closely with them. Some centers offer help and/or meetings for both the user and his loved ones. These meetings may even be a requirement for visitation.

Be sure the treatment center you choose fits your budget, that it medicates and practices the type of therapy according to what is most beneficial for your child, that it has ongoing out-patient programs, and that it keeps you and your other children involved and always in the loop.

Monitor your child's therapy. Make sure your son or daughter isn't forced to undergo a treatment that might injure or humiliate him or her. If something doesn't look or feel right to you, talk to the responsible party. If you're still unhappy, move your child to another facility.

Posttreatment
Posttreatment is not a one-time event. It's ongoing for the life of addicts and their loved ones. Once he has been addicted, you'll work to keep your child in recovery. There is no permanent healing.

1. You will always need to monitor your child for future signs of drug use or abuse.

2. Always keep your medicines, alcohol, inhalants and other potentially harmful substances locked up.

3. Keep in constant touch with your child's therapist.

4. Keep track of your child's school and after-school activities and associates.

5. Watch for transference of addiction. If your child was using drugs or alcohol, and you've managed to see them him treatment to recovery, you'll want to make sure he hasn't traded that addiction for another substance, such as prescription medications or other illicit and/or dangerous substances. All addicts have a drug of choice, but they don't mind substituting, if they can't obtain the substance they want.

6. Keep your child close to you. It is better to let your child invite friends (those that are not bad influences) to your home rather than allowing them to venture out unsupervised, especially right after treatment. If the friends are at your home, you will have more control over what your child and their friends are doing. In any case, always keep your child and their friends in sight. Don't let your child have closed-door meetings with his friends.

7. Talk to your child's friends; get to know them. Investigate them and their families.

8. Keep an ongoing dialogue with your child, not only about drugs, but also about life in general: happiness and mood levels, interests, goals, and so on. Just remember to not constantly lecture. Let your child speak, and really listen to what he has to say.

9. Monitor computer usage, text messaging, cell-phone usage and land-line calls, snail mail—any other communications that might tempt him back into using.

10. Check your child's room and possessions periodically to make sure nothing is present that would lead you to believe he is using again.

11. Test your child.

Dos and Don'ts for Parents
of a Child in Treatment

As the loving guardian of your children you want to do everything humanly possible to help them beat their addiction. There are a lot of things you can do right in this pursuit but, as with almost everything, there is the chance things can go wrong. Below are suggestions (some of this information is provided by a section of the Bright Futures Web site titled Tools for Professionals):

1. **Serve as a good role model for your children**. Develop a rescue plan with your child or adolescent. A rescue plan should specify that the child or adolescent can call you for a ride home if they find themselves in an unsafe situation, including being intoxicated or high or riding with someone who is. Agree that you will not question or punish your child at that moment, but will delay discussion until the following day. Then, discuss their behavior with him or her, and at that time, if necessary, take disciplinary action.

2. **Above all, do not enable the user!** If the child or adolescent refuses to stop using, you will need to get them into treatment. In most states, if they are under the age of eighteen, you can put them into a treatment facility.

3. **Do everything you can to help your child in treatment. More detail follows in the section "Basis for Effective Treatment."**

   - *Outpatient treatment* includes community and school resources, twelve-step groups, peer-support clusters, and individual counseling. These may be used for children and adolescents who are motivated to change behaviors and are not physiologically addicted to substances. They may also be used as a transition from more intensive treatment settings. After discharge from inpatient or residential substance abuse-treatment programs, 60 percent of teens who attended weekly community support groups remained drug-free for the first year.

- *Partial or day hospitals* may be considered for children and adolescents who need more intensive structure and support in order to break the cycle of substance use, if they are motivated for treatment and are not physiologically dependent. This may also be used as a transition from more intensive treatments.

- *Residential treatment* should be considered for youth who are unable to stop using drugs or alcohol if they remain in their home environment, including those who may be at risk for withdrawal or those with a history of treatment failures in less restrictive settings.

- *Inpatient Treatment* is for children or adolescents who are at significant risk for withdrawal symptoms, who have serious psychiatric disorders or symptoms (suicidal, homicidal, psychotic, or acutely dangerous behaviors), or who have failed in other treatment settings.

4. **If your child continues to show signs of relapse.** Immediately get help for her again. Contact a formal treatment program (residential or outpatient). It is difficult to admit treatment may be failing, but it does happen more often than not. You have to be aware of your child's progress in recovery at all times. It is easy for her to slip back into drug use, especially once she's out of a treatment center. It can take several treatment attempts to maintain an ongoing recovery.

5. **Continue to follow your child closely.** Even with professional help, you cannot step out of the picture. This is a hands-on process for parents.

6. **Monitor your child's treatment plan.** Make sure that you support and encourage your child and that you're monitoring her treatment program with the counselor. You, as the parent, along with other family members—even grandparents and aunts and uncles—are key elements in helping your child recover. Even if your relationship with your child is rocky, you are still the dominant factor in her life. She depends on you for structure, support, boundary-setting, financial shoring up, forgiveness, and love. She needs you to help her make the transition from a drugged life to a

clean, moral one. Parental involvement is crucial during recovery, especially because most children live at home with their parents. Parents should be unwavering points of support, there to encourage their children to learn to live without drugs and alcohol. This is not to say that parents should enable their children. Support and enabling are not the same things. Parents should make sure the child doesn't return to old friends who were drug users. They should participate in counseling, educational sessions, meetings, and caregiving. Children have a much higher probability of success in beating the vicious cycle of drug abuse when their parents care enough to stay involved. As they say in treatment, "The user has to change people, places, and things," meaning that the user has to give up the people they did drugs with, stay away from the places where drugs were available, and forego anything and anyone that was associated with drug use. This is extremely crucial to the success of treatment and recovery, and parents can help their child through the process. Once someone is addicted, recovery is a lifetime process.

7. **Keep in mind that relapses are part of the recovery process.** Don't give up on your child as a lost cause if she relapses. Instead, help your child get back on the right road, and this, again, means professional help. However, do not coddle or baby your child if she relapses. You need to make her understand that though you support her recovery process and know relapses occur, you do expect her to get back on track immediately. Don't make excuses for relapses, but accept them as part of the recovery process, and move forward.

8. **Be realistic about treatment.** There is no overnight cure. Your child may reach a point where he has to be hospitalized in order to move forward in his treatment.

9. **Never give up hope for your child.** Your children are a very real part of you. If you give up on them—if you quit, if you let them fall between the cracks—you have taken away the one connection they need to be able to rely on unconditionally: the bond between a parent and a child.

10. **Ask questions.** Here are some questions to ask when you are working with treatment centers, counselors, or other involved

professionals. You need to have detailed conversation with these professionals.

- What types of therapy methods do you employ? Are they conventional or radical in nature?

- What can we, as parents, do to enhance your work with our child?

- What is your educational background, and what are your credentials? Are you a certified drug/alcohol addiction counselor?

- How much experience do you have with youth and addiction?

- Can you give us a list of references to contact?

- What sort of success rate do you have?

- How soon will we start noticing signs of recovery in our child?

- Will our child's privacy be respected? Who will have access to her records, and why?

- Will we receive regular reports from you?

- Should we also expect to undergo counseling while you're treating our child?

- Will you be prescribing any medication for our child, and how will that affect her addiction problem? (You should always insist on consultation for any medications being prescribed or eliminated by the treatment program or professional.)

- Will my child be hospitalized? If so, will she be placed on a regular floor or in a mental-health section?

- How much will treatment cost, and what types of insurance or payments do you accept?

- How should we relate to or talk to our child while she is undergoing treatment? Will she act differently toward us for forcing her to get help?

- What will happen if you cannot help our child? What is next?

- What is the relapse rate, and what do we do if our child does go back to using drugs and alcohol after we believe she has controlled the problem?

- Should we test our child for drugs and alcohol randomly at home?

- Is it possible our child might attempt suicide while undergoing treatment? How common are severe depression and suicide among treatment patients? What are the warning signs of severe depression, and how can we help our child avoid it during this difficult time?

- Once our child begins recovery, what are the early signs of restarting use?

- Is treatment generally a one-time thing or an ongoing lifetime recovery process? (This is asking for the counselor's viewpoint.)

As hopeless and disheartening as addiction may seem, it is still treatable. Recovery rates vary greatly, depending on the personality of the user and the drug or drugs the user is addicted to. The key is to intercede immediately and get help for the user. The longer you wait, the harder it gets, and the more desperate and lost the addict becomes.

Unfortunately, recovery virtually always requires money, and a lot of it. Before taking money out of your pocket to finance a drug battle, check with your insurance company to find out if your child is covered for the services of a rehabilitation facility. Some communities may offer low-debt care facilities through special state or grant funding. Check out all the resources in the area where you live, starting at the local level and moving up to the state level, if need be. Sometimes private organizations offer funding for treatment or provide treatment through some type of community center (clinic, hospital, foundation, etc.). There are many facilities that will perform a free assessment to help you in determining your next step. They may also be able to help with funding sources.

The good news is that the external and internal struggles of addiction can be eased and, in some cases, halted through treatment programs and twelve-step groups. Treatment takes many forms, so be sure to check out the nature of the facility you're considering sending your child to. Learn about the types of therapies used and what types of methodologies the therapists employ to help the user reach a successful and sustainable recovery point. To learn more about the processes of addiction and recovery, have a look at http://www.drugfree. org/Intervention/WhereStart/Understanding_Addiction/

Do some research into treatment centers and their techniques, and do background checks on the physicians, nurses, and counselors working at the centers before you commit to one. This is important! Do not delay treating your child any longer than you must. The key is to get him help as soon as possible. Ask people who have known friends, children, spouses, or other loved ones in treatment (or who have been in treatment before themselves) what they approved of and what they disliked about the treatment centers they used. We don't recommend trying experimental facilities or programs that use unusual treatments, because their techniques might not have been tested and proven and could very well be dangerous. This doesn't eliminate new treatment options as possibilities, but please make sure those available to you have been tested and approved by respected medical authorities.

For those who wish to include religion and personal faith in treating their child, there are psychiatrists and therapists of virtually every faith who use religious grounding as a basis for their treatment offerings. Check with local houses of worship for more information on these options. Research everything you can on treatment, starting with the Internet (make sure the sources are trustworthy and reliable). The process of treatment and recovery works best when the addict truly wants it to work, *and* you are there for him with unconditional love and support.

Typical Questions Therapists May Ask Parents

Every therapist has individualized methods for assessing potential clients. Some may use interviews, others may rely on written forms, and still others will use both. Questions asked may differ from therapist to therapist, but here are some basic questions you're likely to be asked:

- Is your child on any medications?

- Have you seen any change in his personality and appearance and, if so, over what period? What has changed and to what degree?

- How many siblings are there? What are their ages, and how do they interact? Have you seen any radical changes in the way they relate/argue/play?

- How does your child do in school?

- What do you know about your child's friends?

- What is your relationship with your child's friends and their parents?

- Do you inspect your child's room and possessions on a regular basis?

- Do you always know where your child is when he is out of the house?

- Have you noticed your child with any extra money?

- Does your child have expensive items that you did not buy for him or don't remember him receiving as gifts from trusted sources?

- Have your child's grades in school been getting worse?

- How truthful do you think your child is with you?

- Do you have any evidence of drug use?

- Have you seen drug paraphernalia associated with your child?

- Does your child have any type of behavioral problems that have already been diagnosed (ADD, clinical depression, etc.)?

- Do you feel your child has an undiagnosed behavior problem? Why?

Below are some tips offered in their article, "Info Facts: Treatment Approaches for Drug Addiction." Refer to Web site address at end of this section. (Source: http://www.drugabuse.gov/infofacts/treatmeth.html.)

Effective Treatment Approaches

Treatment generally focuses on various therapeutic processes that aim to assist in detoxification and ease withdrawal symptoms while also helping to prevent relapse. Therapy can focus on all aspects of the user's life: psychological, physiological, family dynamics, job/career, community, and even religious relationships. Medications can be a key component in treatment. They are used to suppress withdrawal symptoms and assist the brain in reestablishing normal receptor functions. The brain is the first organ to react when its receptors are denied their chemical fix. Methadone, Subutex, and Suboxone are frequently used medications for treating opiate addiction (see the section in this book on Suboxone for more information).

Behavioral treatments operate in conjunction with medications to help the addict. These may include in-patient treatment, during which the addict undergoes a strict and structured program for anywhere from four weeks to a year. These are costly, and most insurance companies will only pay for a portion of them, so check your policy. A major point of behavioral treatment is the re-socialization of the addict that he no longer needs chemicals to get him through the day. The in-patient or residential program also focuses on the patient's physical and mental health. When a person is discharged from a residential program, he can (usually) be placed into an out-patient program (OP) or intensive outpatient program (IOP). Less severe cases often go straight into an out-patient program rather than an intensive residential one. Psychological counseling is the chief module in this form of therapy, though out-patient programs can/may offer medications as well.

You should be careful to look into every aspect of treatment, and reread the section on this topic as well. Newer treatment approaches may also include the criminal justice system, which assists users in understanding the criminality of their actions, how those actions can often lead to jail sentences, and how a user's criminal actions affect those victimized by his crimes.

Basis for Effective Treatment

Scientific research since the mid-1970s shows that treatment can help many people change destructive behaviors, avoid relapse, and successfully remove themselves from a life of substance abuse and addiction. Recovery from drug addiction is a long-term process and frequently requires multiple episodes of treatment. Based on this research, key principles have been identified that should form the basis of any effective treatment program:

- No single treatment is appropriate for all individuals.

- Treatment needs to be readily available.

- Effective treatment attends to multiple needs of the individual, not just his or her drug addiction.

- An individual's treatment and services plan must be assessed often and modified to meet the person's changing needs.

- A person's remaining in treatment for an adequate period of time is critical for treatment effectiveness.

- Counseling and other behavioral therapies are critical components of virtually all effective treatments for addiction.

- For certain types of disorders, medications are an important element of treatment, especially when combined with counseling and other behavioral therapies.

- Addicted or drug-abusing individuals with coexisting mental disorders should have both disorders treated in an integrated way.

- Medical management of withdrawal syndrome is only the first stage of addiction treatment and, by itself, does little to change long-term drug use.

- Treatment does not need to be voluntary to be effective.

- Possible drug use during treatment must be monitored continuously.

- Treatment programs should provide assessment for HIV/AIDS, hepatitis B and C, tuberculosis, and other infectious diseases. They should also provide counseling to help patients modify or change behaviors that place them or others at risk of infection.

As is the case with other chronic, relapsing diseases, recovery from drug addiction can be a long-term process and typically requires multiple episodes of treatment, including "booster" sessions and other forms of continuing care.

From: NIDA (http://www.nida.nih.gov/Infofacts/TreatMeth.html)

Gangs and Drugs

This section provides tips for keeping your children away from gangs.

Some of the most notorious and dangerous criminals in the United States are part of a gang called Mara Salvatrucha, commonly known as MS-13. They are mostly Salvadoran nationals or first-generation Salvadoran-Americans, but the gang also includes Hondurans, Guatemalans, Mexicans, and other Central and South American immigrants.

Rita Cosby, host of *Live and Direct* on MSNBC, says, "This gang has committed one of the [most] horrific crime scenes ever witnessed by law enforcement—young men, women, and children brutally murdered with machetes. These innocent victims were slaughtered and dismembered for no reason, at the hand of MS-13."

MS-13 is considered by the FBI to be the most lethal gang, leaving their mark from El Salvador, to Honduras, to Guatemala, to New Mexico. In the last decade, the United States has experienced a dramatic increase in the number of chapters and total size of this transnational street gang, which has quickly become a nationwide problem.

The majority of MS-13 members are foreign born and frequently involved in human and drug smuggling and immigration violations. Like most street gangs, MS-13 members also have committed crimes of robbery, extortion, rape, and murder. As well, they run a well-financed prostitution ring. They're known for their violent methods, are found in thirty-three states, and have an estimated ten thousand members and more than forty thousand in Central America. The FBI says MS-13 is the fastest growing and most violent of the nation's street gangs—even other gangs fear them.

You may be stunned to hear that this ruthless gang—many of whom will kill just for the sake of killing—has made its way to cities and suburbs across the country, even settling into small communities and boldly announcing its presence with violence. Northern Virginia is reported to have the strongest presence of MS-13 members in a single city. Many of our cities are infected by MS-13.

Tom Pickard, former assistant director of the FBI, offers, "These people are actually dividing up parts of the country to suit their drug network. What makes MS-13 so deadly is their skill with the machete—and most have had extensive military training in El Salvador, making them a double threat. The machete, typically used for cutting crops in El Salvador, is now the weapon of choice for this fearless gang. The MS-13 members are identified by the numerous tattoos on their bodies and faces. They wear blue and white, colors taken from the El Salvadoran flag. Children start joining the MS-13 at age twelve. It is imperative to get children on the right path early."

Death is frequently the only means of leaving the gang and escaping its clutches. One of the reasons for MS-13's success is its members' flexibility. When they enter a new area where they are not known, they will wear their colors in a flashy display in order to promote intimidation. Once the authorities catch wind of their presence, they may change their colors, carry their bandanas in their pockets, and change their markings to say 76 or 67 (individual numbers that, when added, total up to 13). Reports show that, as is typical of gangs, MS-13 members try to hide their existence from the authorities. They are powerful because of their numbers. Like any gang, when members are alone, they lack the nerve to go against authority. They use mob power, and they have to be stopped before they gain momentum due to the size of their group. If we remove their ability to smuggle and sell drugs, we can eliminate much of their effectiveness.

Federal law enforcement agents say the gang is adopting tactics used by major Mexican and Colombian drug-trafficking groups, and it has become a gun-for-hire entity for many major Central and South American drug-trafficking cartels.

"These gang members are some of the most brutal people we have ever encountered," said a DEA (Drug Enforcement Administration) intelligence officer on the condition of anonymity. "Whether they are unifying, well, that's more difficult to tell. In some cases, yes, and in other cases, no. But a unified criminal enterprise between all groups—it could happen. We'll have to wait and see. What we know is that they're getting stronger."

According to the DEA, the gangs' major sources of income are narcotics and arms trafficking. Human trafficking and extortion also are becoming lucrative enterprises for them, the DEA agent said. There are an estimated six to ten thousand members associated with 125 cliques in the United States alone. As of 2008, DEA and FBI officials have located groups in over forty-two states plus the District of Columbia.

Street gangs, Outlaw Motorcycle Gangs (OMGs), and prison gangs are primary distributors of illegal drugs on our streets. Gangs also smuggle drugs into America, and their activity is concentrated in major urban areas, though gangs also are proliferating in rural and suburban areas of the country. This is the result of gang members fleeing increased law enforcement pressure in urban areas or seeking more lucrative drug markets. This proliferation in nonurban areas is accompanied by violence and is threatening society in general.

According to a 2008 Department of Justice survey, an estimated 788,000 gang members and 27,000 gangs were active in the United States in 2007. In rural counties, the number of jurisdictions with gang problems increased by nearly one-quarter, and the overall number of gangs and gang members increased by 64 and 36 percent respectively between 2002 and 2007. Larger cities and suburban counties remain the primary location of gangs and gang members. They account for more than 60 percent of gangs and 80 percent of gang members.

(The following excerpted information is from the National Drug Intelligence Center http://www.usdoj.gov/ndic/pubs11/13157/):

What is the relationship between drugs and gangs?
Street-gang members convert powdered cocaine into crack cocaine and produce most of the PCP available in the United States. Gangs, primarily OMGs, also produce marijuana and methamphetamine. In addition, gangs increasingly are involved in smuggling large quantities of cocaine and marijuana and lesser quantities of heroin, methamphetamine, and MDMA (also known as Ecstasy) into the United States from foreign sources of supply.

Located throughout the country, street gangs vary in size, composition, and structure. Large, nationally affiliated street gangs pose the greatest threat, because they smuggle, produce, transport, and distribute large quantities of illicit drugs throughout the country and are extremely violent. Local street gangs in rural, suburban, and urban areas pose a low, but growing, threat; they transport and distribute drugs within very specific areas. These gangs often imitate the larger, more powerful national gangs in order to gain respect from rivals.

Some gangs collect millions of dollars per month selling illegal drugs, trafficking weapons, operating prostitution rings, and selling stolen property. Gangs launder proceeds by investing in real estate, recording studios, motorcycle shops, and construction companies. They also operate various cash-based businesses, such as barbershops, music stores, restaurants, catering services, tattoo parlors, strip clubs, and other businesses in order to comingle (launder) drug proceeds with funds generated through legitimate commerce.

What are the dangers associated with gang activity?

Large street gangs readily employ violence to control and expand drug distribution activities, targeting rival gangs and dealers who neglect or refuse to pay extortion fees. Members also use violence to ensure all members adhere to the gang's code of conduct or to prevent a member from leaving. In November 2004 a nineteen-year-old gang member in Fort Worth, Texas, was sentenced to thirty years in prison for fatally shooting a childhood friend who wanted to leave their local street gang.

Authorities throughout the country report that gangs are responsible for most of the serious violent crime in the major cities of the United States. Gangs engage in an array of criminal activities, including assault, burglary, drive-by shootings, extortion, homicide, identification fraud, money laundering, prostitution operations, robbery, sale of stolen property, and weapons trafficking.

What are some signs that young people may be involved in gang activity?

Some signs are changes in behavior, such as skipping school; hanging out with different friends; or, in certain places, spray-painting graffiti; and using hand signals with friends, though 2008 studies show that they are now adapting mainstream affectations so as not to be caught. In addition, individuals who belong to gangs often dress alike by wearing bandanas and clothing of the same color, or even rolling up their pant legs in a certain way. Some wear certain designer labels to show their gang affiliation. Gang members often have tattoos. Also, because gang violence frequently is glorified in rap music, young people involved in gangs often try to imitate the dress and actions of rap artists. Finally, because substance abuse is often a characteristic of gang members, young people involved in gang activity may exhibit signs of drug or alcohol use.

It's wise to investigate any changes in your community (vandalism, violence, graffiti, etc.). Gangs such as the Bloods, the Crips, OMGs, ABMs, Hells Angels, Pagans, Latin Kings, and MS-13 are rapidly expanding into small cities, towns, and suburbs.

Terror Links

Law enforcers around the world have long recognized the close connection between illegal drugs and terrorism, but a changing world and recent events have made this link more relevant in our daily lives. The bottom line is simple: terror and drug groups rely on a mutually beneficial relationship (money, tactics, geography, and politics).

Americans need to understand that our individual choices about illicit drug use have the power to support or undermine our nation's war on drugs. This is a war for survival of our way of life. Past President George W. Bush said, "It's so important for Americans to know that the traffic in drugs finances the work of terror, sustaining terrorists [and] that terrorists use drug profits to fund their cells to commit acts of murder. If you quit drugs, you join the fight against terror."

The annual terrorism report released on April 30, 2008, lists forty-two organizations designated as Foreign Terrorist Organizations. More have developed since then. Most of these groups have been identified as having links with drug trafficking:

- Abu Nidal Organization (ANO)
- Abu Sayyaf Group
- Al-Aqsa Martyrs Brigade
- Al-Jihad
- Al-Qa'ida
- Al-Qa'ida in Iraq
- Al-Qa'ida in the Islamic Maghreb (AQIM: formerly Salafist Group for Call and Combat [GSPC])
- Ansar al-Sunnah
- Armed Islamic Group (GIA)
- Asbat al-Ansar
- Aum Shinrikyo
- Basque Fatherland and Liberty (ETA)

- Communist Party of Philippines/New People's Army (CPP/NPA)
- Continuity Irish Republican Army (CIRA)
- Gama'a al-Islamiyya (IG)
- HAMAS
- Harakat ul-Mujahadin (HUM)
- Hizballah
- Islamic Jihad Group (IJG)
- Islamic Movement of Uzbekistan (IMU)
- Jaish-e-Mohammed (JEM)
- Jemaah Islamiya Organization (JI)
- Kahane Chai (Kach)
- Kongra-Gel (formerly Kurdistan Worker's Party [PKK])
- Lashkar e-Tayyiba
- Lashkar i Jhangvi (LJ)
- Liberation Tigers of Tamil Eelam (LTTE)
- Libyan Islamic Fighting Group (LIFG)
- Moroccan Islamic Combatant Group (GICM)
- Mujahadin-e Khalq Organization (MEK)
- National Liberation Army (ELN)
- Palestine Liberation Front (PLF)
- Palestinian Islamic Jihad (PIJ)
- Popular Front for the Liberation of Palestine (PFLP)
- Popular Front for the Liberation of Palestine-General Command (PFLP-GC)
- Real IRA (RIRA)
- Revolutionary Armed Forces of Colombia (FARC)
- Revolutionary Nuclei (RN)
- Revolutionary Organization 17 November (17N)
- Revolutionary People's Liberation Party/Front (DHKP/C)
- Shining Path (SL)
- United Self-Defense Forces of Colombia (AUC)

It may seem farfetched to you that your child could have the remotest links to terrorism, but remember—sometimes our children get involved in things in an innocent way and yet end up facing major criminal charges. For example, without realizing it, they may be delivering smuggled drugs into the country or across state lines or borders for a friend who, in turn, is involved in selling drugs. Just know how serious this can become. Keep your eyes on your child's every movement. You may also want to research the money sent to certain terrorist's groups by the U.S.—money that could be used to take care of our children.

Chapter Nine

Resources and Workplace Testing

A Word on Workplace Testing

Children who use drugs and alcohol, if they survive, grow up to be adults who still do drugs and drink. This poses a problem in the workplace. Preventing drug use and trafficking on the job is as important as preventing it during a person's younger years.

We could not close this book without briefly discussing workplace testing, which is vital in keeping safety and productivity at their highest points.

How much thought have you given to the company you hired to do remodeling in your home? How might you feel if the employer were to unwittingly send a worker to do the job who drinks every day? Under the influence, he fails to secure the load-bearing wall he's working on, which unexpectedly comes crashing down on you, or a family member, or a visitor.

How about a stoned lab tech giving false statements to your doctor saying that you have an incurable disease? Or the reverse, when a drugged tech entirely misses a treatable disease, which instead turns fatal because his error deprives you of life-saving treatment?

And how many times have you heard about a worker who was driving a company vehicle drunk and killed an innocent pedestrian or someone in another vehicle? There are instances of drunk drivers plowing through toll booths and killing the attendants.

Just as scary are pilots who get away with transporting planeloads of people while being alcohol or drug impaired. Maybe one has had insufferable back pain for days and took too much prescribed pain medication and then piloted a plane. After all, abusing prescription medication is becoming as big a problem as using illicit drugs.

Have you ever thought about the number of people we trust on a daily basis to do steadfast, commendable, careful jobs—who may drink or do drugs during their work to feel good, erase pain, or just maintain a "normal" feeling?

We worry about our kids doing drugs/alcohol, yet we often give little thought to what's going on where we or others work. Drug usage is high in the workforce, and it's dangerous, because employees could have jobs that affect not only other workers, but also the general public who rely on them for sound, safe, quality service or products. An employer's business can quickly fail if an employee has an accident while driving under the influence, or if a worker on drugs harms himself or others while on the job. The unknowing public needs to trust in employees, and if workers fail to perform to standards because they are drunk or high, then innocent patrons could get hurt or die.

More employers are coming to understand that they *must* implement a drug/alcohol testing policy to protect themselves, their companies, their employees, and their patrons, as well as the general public. Nearly all states permit workforce testing.

Every employee has the right to a drug-free workplace. Alcohol and other drug abuse certainly endangers the abusing employee, but it also imperils every other employee. In a nationwide survey performed for the Institute for a Drug-Free Workplace, the Gallup Organization reported that 28 percent of the full-time employees surveyed identified illicit drug abuse as the greatest threat facing America today. Consider these figures from SafeWork:

- Absenteeism is two to three times higher for drug and alcohol users than for other employees.

- Employees with chemical dependence problems may claim three times as many sickness benefits and file five times as many Workers' Compensation claims.

- On-the-job alcohol and drug use account for 15%–30% of all accidents at work.

An alcohol consumption study (Model and Mounts, "The Problem of Alcohol Use by Pilots," in *New England Journal of Medicine*, 1990) shows that "when airline pilots had to perform routine tasks in a simulator under three alcohol-test conditions, it was found that:

- After reaching a blood alcohol concentration of 0.10/100 ml, 89% could not perform all the operations correctly.

- Fourteen hours later, after all the alcohol had left their systems, 68% could not perform all the operations correctly."

Every day in small and large corporations around the world, the problems caused by substance abuse disrupt the workplace. There is a false perception that our nation's drug problem is youth-orientated. However, over two-thirds of drug abusers are employed. If you are in business you need to be aware of these facts gathered from government agencies, national surveys, newspapers, and various agencies (numbers as of the printing of this book):

- 41% of the workers surveyed stated that the drug abuse of fellow employees seriously affected their own job productivity.

- America accounts for approximately 6% of the world's population, yet it consumes approximately 67% of the world's illicit drugs.

- Over 35 million Americans are addicted to prescription and nonprescription medication.

- 18 million Americans are alcoholics; nearly 20 million use hashish or marijuana regularly.

- Over 5 million Americans use cocaine or crack *regularly.*

- Every day 5,000 people use cocaine or crack for the *first time.*

- In 2005, 74.8% of all illegal drug and alcohol users age 18 and over were employed either full or part time.

- 10% of all employees abuse drugs or alcohol on the job.

- 53% of employees state that drug use and drug dealing are major contributors to workplace violence.

- 44% of users support their habits by stealing from or selling drugs to fellow employees.

- About 10% of all full-time employees abuse drugs or alcohol on the job.

- In 2003, the U.S. Department of Labor estimated each impaired worker cost his or her employer $11,000 per year; this number is higher now.

- A user is 5 times more likely to file a worker's compensation claim and 16 times more likely to use sick leave than a nonuser.

- Abusers are 4 times more likely to injure themselves or another in a workplace accident and 5 times more likely to be involved in an accident off the job, affecting attendance, job performance, and innocent people.

- Drug and alcohol abusers are 35% less productive than unimpaired workers.

- A 2005 research study indicated that between 10 and 20 percent of the nation's workers who die on the job test positive for alcohol or other drugs.

The high risk of liability is a growing concern to businesses, especially in our litigious society. More importantly, abusers can harm or inadvertently kill co-workers and patrons. It only takes one mistake by an employee under drugs or alcohol to wipe out an entire company that an entrepreneur has worked hard to build and maintain a good reputation for. When a company goes under, this also causes all the non-drug users to lose their jobs. It hurts everyone.

Drug testing is the answer.
Employers need to have a drug policy in place that covers all aspects of testing: pre-employment, random, reasonable suspicion, post-accident, return to work, and follow-up. All tests must follow state regulations; otherwise, the employer risks a lawsuit. Careful consideration must be given to the type of testing, how it is done, the reasons for testing, and how results are reported. A drug and alcohol policy should be customized for each company and each separate state. Educational orientation and supervisor sessions should be provided, as well as the actual testing and discussion of the test results.

Additionally, hair testing (where permitted by the state in which the business operates) should be used for pre-employment, as hair testing gives a record (history) of any substance indulgence during the past three months. All employers should do pre-employment testing to avoid hiring someone who is already a user. Instant test kits, where allowed in your state, yield drug results in five minutes. Instant tests are extremely valuable, not only for employers but also for schools, parents, camps, sports organizations, and churches. When you consider the statistics given in this section on drug and alcohol use in the workplace, you can see how vitally important it is to set up a state-compliant, drug/alcohol testing program in your workplace.

Don't take the chance of having a co-worker harmed, or losing your business, or facing exorbitant lawsuits because of substance abusers in your company.

Department of Transportation (DOT) Drug Testing

The United States Department of Transportation (DOT), under the Office of the Secretary of Transportation, has established drug-testing rules for specific employees in the following groups of industries:

+ Aviation

+ Pipeline

+ Public Transportation

+ Railroad

+ Ships/Vessels

+ Trucking/School Bus/Tour Bus

Various occupations in the above industry groups are covered under specific rules and regulations of the DOT (including various sub-groupings). The definition DOT applies is employees who come into contact with the public, who have safety-sensitive positions, or who can cause harm to others in the course of doing their jobs. This is a general description, and the subgroups vary by industry. The DOT is very strict about testing and makes no exceptions in their rules regarding how subjects can be tested and through what methods.

All DOT drug testing consists of urine specimens collected by trained and certified collection stations/organizations or onsite collectors following strict guidelines. The urine specimen is tested for five groups of drugs: marijuana, opiates, cocaine, PCP, and amphetamines. Then the sample is submitted to a lab certified by HHS/SAMHSA (Department of Health and Human Services/ Substance Abuse and Mental Health Services Administration). Each sample is accompanied by a Custody and Control Form. This is a specific DOT form that follows the sample from the collection stage through the MRO (Medical Review Officer) stage. At the writing of this book, hair testing is not an approved method of DOT drug testing, but it can be used for pre-employment testing in most states. DOT employees can also be included in a non-DOT group, as long as they are tested under DOT rules first.

A different method of testing is required for detection of alcohol. DOT-approved instant saliva swab testing can be used for initial testing. Confirmation testing (if required) must be done using an approved BAT (Breath Alcohol Testing/Breathalyzer) machine. If the initial alcohol swab test shows negative results, the test is complete, and the employee is considered not to be under the influence of alcohol. If subsequent confirmation testing is required, an initial BAT test is performed. If this test comes up negative, the test is complete. If the initial BAT test comes up positive/non-negative, a second test is completed within approximately fifteen minutes of the first test. The employee can be sent to a collection center for BAT without first being tested by an instant alcohol swab test. Strict training, as well as rules and regulations, are in place for both collectors and MROs (Medical Review Officers).

Changes Coming to DOT Programs

As of May 15, 2009, the U. S. Court of Appeals upheld the District of Columbia Circuit decision regarding direct observation of drug testing for the following:

> Those who failed or refused to take a prior test
> Return to work and follow-up testing for those who failed a
> prior test
> (Note: observer must be of same sex as donor)

As of May 2, 2010, the following cutoff level changes for cocaine, amphetamines, and methamphetamine have been made (where *ng* means nanogram, or one billionth of a gram):

Cocaine:	Initial test cutoff level has been lowered from 300 ng/ml to 150 ng/ml. Confirmatory cutoff level has been lowered from 150 ng/ml to 100 ng/ml
Amphetamines:	Initial test cutoff level has been lowered from 1000 ng/ml to 500 ng/ml Confirmatory cutoff level has been lowered from 500 ng/ml to 250 ng/ml

Methamphetamines: Initial test cutoff level has been lowered from 1000 ng/ml to 500 ng/ml
Confirmatory cutoff level has been lowered from 500 ng/ml to 250 ng/ml

MDMA The new changes also allow checking for MDMA (Ecstasy), with the following cutoff levels:: Initial test cutoff level will be 500 ng/ml
Confirmatory cutoff level will be 250 ng/ml

Another recent change has been the addition of adulteration (tampering) checks. The lab will measure the specific gravity, pH, and creatinine levels to determine valid and reliable positive and negative results, as well as deviations in collected specimens.

Please refer to the following link for full information on DOT drug and alcohol testing:
http://www.dot.gov/ost/dapc/NEW_DOCS/part40.html.

Chapter Ten

Prevention and Summary

Steps to Safety

You've now read this book and have a much clearer understanding of what's involved with drugs and alcohol and your children. The rest is up to you. Your children are the most precious people in your life, and they should be protected at all cost.

It is true that no matter how much we try to keep our children safe, other factors can get in the way. We may suddenly find that they are still at risk—even with all our years of hard work in raising and shielding them from harm.

Much of the effectiveness of our nurturing depends on our children following our rules. Sometimes life isn't fair, and, yes, everyone has their own troubles. But drug and alcohol abuse is not a natural turn in life, and it can be avoided.

We come to accept and react based on how we are conditioned and how long we are exposed to that conditioning. Human behavior shows that even good people will do the wrong things if they've been conditioned long enough to do so. For example, if children are raised in a household where parents and siblings constantly criticize, berate, and chastise them, they may become conditioned to believe they are of little value, and they may act and react according to that belief.

Through the same methodology, if you condition your children to believe that drug use is bad, they will come to accept that and live their lives accordingly. But conditioning doesn't happen overnight; it has to start when the child is young and continue throughout his or her life. Here are some tips to help you instill healthy behavior in your child:

- Start talking about drugs and alcohol when your child is capable of understanding. Initially, your discussions don't have to be complicated; talk to your child with language appropriate to his or her age level.

- Teach by example. Most kids learn best through visuals, so if you have access to visual proof of the harm drugs and alcohol can do to people and property, share those. Again, make sure the material you share is age-appropriate for your children.

- Make reference to radio and television shows, DVDs, newspapers, and magazines—anything that will help reinforce your position on drug and alcohol use.

- Serve as a role model. Practice what you teach. The worst thing you can do is advise your children one way and then do the opposite. Children keep mental track of contradiction and dishonesty.

- Talk about drugs and alcohol on a regular basis.

- As your children mature, raise the level of your message. The older they become, the more capable they should be of understanding advanced ideologies and concepts regarding drug and alcohol misuse.

- Keep track of your children's activities. Even if they get upset because they think you're intruding, do it anyway.

- Make your children accountable for their actions. Once they know your rules and they break them, you must hold them accountable and discipline accordingly. Likewise, when they've done right, you should praise and reward them.

- Be consistent in what you teach and how you react to your children's violations. No matter how tired you are, you must consistently punish or reward, depending on the individual situation and the child.

- Not liking what your child does is not the same thing as not liking your child. Be sure to stress this to your child. Remember the old saying: "You may hate the sin but love the sinner."

- Make sure your children talk with you. When you discuss drugs and alcohol with your children, prompt them for feedback. Engage your children in exchanging thoughts and ideas.

- Check out your children's friends and their parents. If you have to ask other parents or school officials about them, do so.

- Respect your children's privacy, but monitor them all the same. No parent wants to admit to looking through a kid's backpack to see if there are signs of drugs, but sometimes you have to. It is better to begrudge them a little privacy, if it will keep them safe, than to leave them vulnerable to drugs and alcohol. Likewise, check their computer and Internet usage, phone calls, and text messages. Check your car or your teen's car for any signs of drug use or paraphernalia. Children have no privacy when they live in the parents' home.

+ Maintain and enforce a curfew.

+ Randomly test your child for drugs and alcohol.

+ Keep abreast of information about new drugs and various methods that kids are using to get high, especially inhalants and prescription medications.

+ Keep track of your money. Missing cash could signal that your child is taking your money to support a habit or to help someone who is an addict. Also keep track of your jewelry and other valuables.

+ Closely observe any changes in your child's behavior. This is a key point in protecting him or her.

+ Monitor your child's physical appearance, as well. A change in dress style could signify a problem. Physical appearance is an indicator of physical and mental health. Check your children over periodically to make sure there are no suspicious marks on their arms: bruising, needle marks, or any other signs that might cause you to worry.

Needle Marks

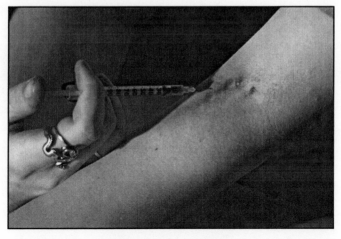

Source: www.dreamstime.com

- Discuss sex with them. Young people may end up at parties where friends are engaging in sex or other harmful behavior. They need to understand sex and the consequences, as well as your rules regarding sexual activity. Though the subject may be uncomfortable for you, it is important to make your rules regarding sex clear, as well as to teach your children the facts about unsafe sex and how to say NO!

- Emphasize that they should never leave their drinks unattended. Let them know that if they have stepped away from their drinks even for a second, they should *not* drink them. It is very easy to slip drugs into liquids, a situation that could result in inadvertent drug use. This is a common route to date rape.

- Clearly communicate your rules of zero tolerance for drugs and alcohol. Stand firm. This is important.

- Inform your children that drugs lead to crime and that substance use and crime lead to gangs. Stress the danger of gangs and how they can ruin their lives.

- Let them know you will not allow impertinent behavior or disrespect. You need to make your children understand that you are the parent, and they must obey you. Of course, you must also be reasonable with them. If they begin behaving rudely, wildly, or erratically, and this is out of character for them, let them know you won't hesitate to do whatever is necessary to correct their behavior. Let them know you will get the police or juvenile authorities involved in any serious drug and/or alcohol problem they might exhibit.

- Stress to your children that they must never, ever drive under the influence of harmful substances or get in a vehicle with anyone who is—including people who have smoked marijuana, taken other drugs, or even used inhalants. Let them know that if they are ever in that state of mind, they can call you, and you will pick them up with no questions asked until the next day.

- Check your household chemicals to make sure that solvents and inhalants aren't being used by your children. Better yet, lock them up, so your children do not have access to them. One use of an inhalant can cause death.

- If you discover—either by testing him or catching him in the act—that your child is trying or is addicted to drugs, call your doctor or a treatment center, and get help immediately. Check your insurance policy to see if drug and alcohol treatment is covered. Know the signs and symptoms of drug use. Most of all, know your child.

- Tell your children that you love them unconditionally, and you are there to help them. Don't hesitate to say the words "I love you," even as they get older.

- Monitor your children's co-curricular, extracurricular, and after-school activities. Keep on top of your kids regarding their homework, too.

- Keep track of your kids' online activities; limit their computer usage.

- Know and understand your children well. If you aren't communicating with your children, you won't know they're in trouble until it is too late.

- Keep your prescription medications locked up, even if you think your child would never take any of your medication. Your children's friends could take your medications if they are not put away.

- Do what you can to limit stress on your children by keeping arguments and adult discussions out of your children's sight and hearing. Remember, you're the adult and the one who should be in control. Build up your children's confidence by allowing them to see you as a confident, loving, and mature authority figure.

- If you find drug paraphernalia (needles, crack pipe, drug residue, etc), don't believe it when they say they're holding it for a friend. That does not happen.

While there are other ways to try to protect your children, the points here serve as a starting point. This is by no means an all-inclusive list. Your job as a parent is a serious one, perhaps the most serious and important endeavor you will ever undertake. Just remember, you made the decision to bring your children into this world, and you are responsible for them. It is important to be proactive in your children's lives. Often, we don't think about prevention until it is too late, and then we may become reactive and defeatist. Attend presentations on drug and alcohol abuse. Learn all you can. Keep current.

Summing it Up

Drug dealers come in all sizes and shapes: as individuals or big drug cartels, as strangers or as the child next door. When your child is confronted by a drug dealer who is a classmate, a friend, or an acquaintance, he may trust that person, because the dealer doesn't look like the stereotypical shady, disgusting drug dealer.

You, the parent, could be unwittingly acting as a drug dealer (rather harsh, but we're trying to make a point here) by having prescription and OTC medications easily accessible to your children. If you are taking prescription medications, lock them up; the same goes for OTC drugs and alcohol. Don't abuse your own medications, as this presents a bad example for your children. Keep in mind that illicit drugs are illegal for everyone, not just children.

Nearly every child, at some point, is offered drugs. The United States has the highest substance-abuse rate of all industrialized nations. One out of every two kids has tried drugs. Two out of every ten kids use illegal drugs and regularly abuse prescriptions drugs or alcohol.

Designer or club drugs are a serious concern for parents. These are synthetic/man-made illegal drugs that are produced in underground labs and sold on the street. They are particularly noteworthy, because they are generally introduced into social situations in which peer pressure to try them could be intense. The user has no idea of what the drug was cut with or if the manufacturing process (such as it is) was clean or sanitary.

Anyone can be fooled by drugs and by drug users, so you must be proactive in making sure your children remain free of drugs and alcohol. Home testing is a valuable tool in helping you achieve this goal. If your community doesn't have a drug-awareness program, you can initiate one. You can call a meeting of neighboring families around you and have a police officer talk about ways to prevent drug abuse in your neighborhood. Many neighborhoods and schools have employees whose sole job is to operate a drug-prevention program. These employees would be invaluable at this kind of meeting. Try to clean up your neighborhood if drugs are readily available. Get involved in your parent-teacher organizations/associations. Make sure everyone is informed on the damage drugs and alcohol abuse can do and what can be done to prevent it in our children.

Teach and reinforce the value of education. If your children are raised with a healthy respect for learning, and if you stress that you expect them to take school seriously and do something productive with their lives, they will aim for that goal. You need to start conditioning them to healthy behaviors and attitudes when they're young.

The family element plays a big role in whether or not a child resorts to substance abuse. Children may turn to drugs and alcohol to escape problems, such as a death in the family, divorce, illness, moving (relocation), physical and verbal abuse, or tension between parents. As they mature, it is crucial that you make their lives as free from unnecessary stress as possible and that you keep communication lines open with your children, so they can talk with you about anything that upsets them.

A key reason our society has a drug problem is that many parents don't want to take responsibility for teaching their children or for disciplining them. These parents often don't make time for their children. More kids are on drugs because of a lack of parental involvement than any other reason. Children whose parents talk to them about drug use and check on their activities and friends are five times less likely to use or even experiment with alcohol or drugs.

Prevention starts at home, and testing your children regularly and randomly helps ward off the issue. It is not easy approaching your children about difficult issues such as alcohol, drugs, and sex. Talking to your children about these subjects, however, is crucial in their development into informed, productive, and healthy young adults. Before you discuss drugs and alcohol, know what you're talking about. Read the appropriate sections in this book. Try maintaining an ongoing dialogue with them about drugs and alcohol. Be affectionate with them.

Drug and/or alcohol use can result in dreadful and appalling abuse, both to others and the abusers themselves. There are various types of abuse, such as physical, psychological, mental, and emotional abuse. Abusers and their families also often suffer financial abuse, sexual abuse, and much more. Drug and alcohol addiction opens the door for all types of abuse.

Kids who are on drugs or alcohol often get involved, either innocently or intentionally, with gangs and crime.

There are various stages of drug use. The longer the person indulges in drugs and alcohol, the deeper he or she will fall toward addiction. There is no cure for addiction, only the possibility for recovery, which is a lifelong process.

Addiction doesn't happen overnight. Typically, the user tries the drug, likes its effect, moves into social use (doing drugs and alcohol at parties) and then on to regular use—which turns into risky behavior. If you find your child has been doing drugs or alcohol, you need to intervene immediately and get professional help for your child.

Drugs are classified into groups, and each group has its own subdivisions. Specific types of drugs are discussed in detail throughout the book. Some groups of drugs give users a rush and a feeling of euphoria. Other groups may create depression. Still others may result in hallucinations. Controlled substances are heavily regulated by the United States to limit the opportunity for abuse. They are registered under the Substances Act of 1970.

Over-the-counter medications, or OTC drugs, can be acquired without a doctor's prescription and purchased in pharmacies or local drug stores. They may then be manipulated or mutilated (crushed, cut with other substances, combined, heated, altered, adulterated, etc.) to make them more potent. The United States Food and Drug Administration offers: "Nationwide, the government's Drug Abuse Warning Network has tracked an increase in GHB-related emergency room visits from 20 in 1992 to more than 1343 in 1998." As a result, the U.S. government put restrictions on Sudafed® (which contains pseudoephedrine). The U. S. government passed Section 1001 of Title 19 of the Patriot Act, requiring that any medicine with pseudoephedrine or ephedrine as an ingredient must be moved behind the pharmacy counter. To purchase the product, a customer must show a driver's license and sign a log book. This has made the raw ingredients more difficult to obtain and has led to a decrease in the number of meth labs in existence.

Methylenedioxyamphetamine (MDA) and methylenedioxyethylamphetamine (MDEA) are drugs chemically similar to MDMA. MDMA can be extremely dangerous in high doses. The drug is used predominantly by adolescents and young adults, often when they attend nightclubs and raves. This is also a prime setting for GHB and Rohypnol; both are date-rape drugs.

The number-one way to ensure your children are safe, whether on the Internet, on the street, at school, or at a friend's home, is to be involved with every aspect of their lives. That doesn't mean to be breathing down their necks on every little thing they do, but it does mean keeping track of where they go, who their friends are, how their grades are, and what they do on the Internet—among many other aspects. Internet communications about drugs, alcohol, and tobacco abound, and many are targeted to kids. Teach your children to be media literate, and keep tabs on the sites they visit. Here is some information regarding children and the purchase of drugs from the Internet:

> Legislators and law enforcement are finding new ways to address drugs in cyberspace. But parents and caring adults must be on the alert to ensure that their kids don't buy drugs online or obtain them from other kids who are buying them online. After all, even if your child doesn't have Web access, nearly 69% of kids ages 10 to 14 and 80% of kids ages fifteen to 17 do have access.[23]
>
> 47% of drug-selling Web sites said drugs would be shipped from outside the United States; 28% said the drugs would be shipped from the United States; and 25% gave no indication where the drugs would be shipped from.[24]
>
> Anyone, including children, can easily obtain addictive prescription drugs online without a prescription. "The wide availability of controlled prescription drugs on the Internet is an open floodgate of drugs of abuse, and the tide is rising ever higher," said Beau Dietl, chairman of Beau Dietl & Associates.[25] "Our research demonstrates that parents who are actively engaged in their children's lives, including monitoring Internet activities, have children far less likely to smoke, drink, and use drugs."[26]

Legal issues are always a concern when it comes to parents testing their kids for drugs and alcohol. Kids are savvy today and know how to find drugs online as well as on the street. Equally bad, they know where to go to find products that can hide, change, or distort drug tests to invalidate them. There is an old saying that goes, "When I was sixteen, I thought my parents were stupid. When I turned twenty-one, I was surprised how much they had learned in five years."

There are many parental-control computer programs offered to help you oversee what your children are doing, but it is most important that you constantly communicate with them.

Set rules you want your children to obey. Discuss the rules with your children. Remind them not to give out their passwords to anyone. Forbid them from giving out personal information or purchasing anything online or through their cell phones (downloading pictures, ringtones, etc.), and limit their computer time for games and entertainment. Younger children need strong guidance and rules. Older children need to know you're serious about enforcing those rules.

Young children don't possess the maturity to determine between good and bad Internet content. Other children frequently know the difference but will visit unhealthy sites because their friends are doing it, or they're involved with unhealthy activities. Some may play video games online that contain sex, violence, or simulated drug use.

As parent, you must monitor your children's habits and protect them from negativity. Research everything you can about drugs and the Internet. Realize that there are online sites that sell drugs to kids with no questions asked. This is one of the most serious threats to our children's mental, emotional, and physical well-being.

Keep in mind the power of spirituality in your children's development, and make it a point to educate them in your personal spiritual choices.

Parents have a window of opportunity to find out whether their child is using or considering using.

The decision of whether to implement a drug-testing program in schools or in the workplace should not be left to one individual or organization.

Drug tests are used to determine whether a person has used alcohol, illegal drugs, or specific prescription drugs. Each type of test has different applications and is used to detect a specific drug or group of drugs.

Results of a urine test show the presence or absence of specific drugs or metabolites in the urine. A positive urine test doesn't necessarily mean the subject is under the influence of drugs at the time of the test. Rather, it detects and measures use of a particular drug within the previous few days, depending on the drug ingested. Almost all drugs show up in urine.

Instant urine-test kits, which are often integrated (all-in-one) urine cups, combine detection for several drugs in one test. They are commonly available today.

Analysis of hair will provide a much longer testing window for the presence of drugs and drug metabolites, giving a more complete drug use history that goes back as far as ninety days. Keep in mind that it takes approximately seven to twelve days for the ingested drug to get into the user's hair follicle. Our most popular ten-panel (meaning, it tests for 10 different drugs) drug-test kits detect cocaine, amphetamines, methamphetamine, marijuana, opiates, phencyclidine, barbiturates, benzodiazepines, methadone, and synthetic opiates (Percocet, Percodan). Add the alcohol test, and you have a complete insight into your child's actions and behavior. Testing is key. It prevents, protects, and points out a drug/alcohol problem you may have with your child. Test to save the lives of your loved ones. Our book gives you advice on drugs and how to protect your child, but it also offers vital information on testing.

The Unity Oath is an agreement between you, the parents, and your child. It is like a promissory note, in that the signees vow to *not* do drugs or alcohol and agree to be tested and treated if they are found using or abusing.

Purchasing our drug kits and alcohol swabs, along with this book, gives you reassurance that you have tools to help your child stay off drugs. You'll know when your child experiments with them simply by testing him or her. The fact that you have a testing kit in your home and visible to your child serves as a deterrent to him or her trying drugs. "My parents test me, so I can't try drugs" is a great built-in excuse for children whose parents test them at home. Our SafeBox is perhaps the best gift you can give your family to help keep them free from drugs and alcohol.

Positive results don't always equate to drug use. If your child uses a legal prescription medication (or even some OTC medications), she might test positive for opiates, amphetamines, benzodiazepines, and possibly others.

Testing your children is the best way to maintain control and help you combat drug and alcohol abuse while protecting your children from peer pressure, experimentation, social use, and even addiction.

You can always do a follow-up test later, if you suspect there may be some drug your child is indulging in that wasn't positive in the first test. Users have a drug of choice, but they will substitute if their preferred drug is not obtainable.

Unlike urine testing, hair testing can provide evidence of drug use over approximately the last ninety days. Hair testing can detect marijuana, amphetamines, cocaine, methamphetamine, opiates, and PCP. Hair tests can detect longer than ninety, if required. One and a half inches of hair will give you the ninety-day history. If the hair is long enough, it is possible to go back ninety days for each one and a half inches.

Blood tests are typically used by the police in order to detect immediate drug or alcohol use. Blood testing is not commonly used in the workplace because of its invasiveness and the fact that it has such a short historical look-back period (approximately one and a half days).

For your loved one, it is best to start with in-home testing devices, such as integrated test cups, alcohol swabs, or other types of test kits. If drugs are detected in your child's system by in-home kits or even lab tests, you can then determine what steps you want to take next; generally this means implementing a drug-free program that includes regular testing and treatment.

Children learn self-responsibility and accountability from their parents. You, as parents, must be good role models at all times. Please understand—if you are abusing drugs/alcohol, your children will know. They may not verbalize it, but they notice everything.

Alcohol is the most commonly used and widely abused psychoactive drug in the United States. Alcohol reduces reaction time, slows down the thought process, and lowers inhibitions.

Drug statistics show that most hard-drug users start with using marijuana. Some children are experimenting with drugs as young as eight and nine years old. We suggest a program of random drug testing be implemented by the age of twelve. The transition from grade school to middle school is the time when most kids start using drugs This is usually a result of peer pressure and the need to fit in.

Kids will either learn from their parents or they will learn in the streets. If you talk to your kids about drugs, they are five times less likely to use.

It is never too early to share with your children how you feel about drugs and what your expectations are in terms of zero tolerance. A study showed that 74 percent of fourth graders wished their parents would speak with them about drugs.

The average age for kids to begin experimenting with illegal substances is thirteen. Eighth graders' thirty-day use of an illegal drug was 7.6 percent in 2008;

twelfth graders thirty-day use of an illegal drug was 22.3 percent in 2008. *(Source: University of Michigan "Monitoring the Future" Study)*

Every employee has the right to a drug-free workplace. Alcohol and other drug abuses certainly endanger the safety of the abusing employee, but they also imperil every employee. In a nationwide survey performed for the Institute for a Drug-Free Workplace, the Gallup Organization reported that 28 percent of the full-time employees surveyed identified illicit drug abuse as the greatest threat facing America today. Absenteeism is two to three times higher for drug and alcohol users than for non-using employees. America accounts for approximately 6 percent of the world's population, yet consumes approximately 67 percent of the world's illicit drugs. Every day five thousand people use cocaine or crack for the first time.

Our organization provides tools for drug testing of all types. We also keep abreast of constantly emerging information and technologies regarding new illegal drugs and methods of adulteration.

Gangs are dangerous. They commit terrible crimes and traffic heavily in illegal drugs. If your children become involved with gangs, it is hard to pull them free. Do whatever is necessary to protect your children from being near or getting involved in gangs and drugs.

It is possible to screen an area for drugs without ever testing a single person. We can provide this service as well. But we also supply the devices that can be used in the workplace or home for testing. Additionally, we work with well-known professionals in the drug-prevention sector to implement drug-free testing programs in the workplace and in schools—from providing the needed drug/alcohol policy, to teaching and training staff and supervisors, to doing the actual testing on a one-time or regular basis.

Illegal drugs fund terror groups around the world that wish harm to the United States. Illegal drug sales revenue turns into weapons.

Final Words

We hope this book helps you and provides a better understanding of the drug and alcohol problems in our society and the situations our children face on a daily basis.

Drugs and alcohol are no longer back-alley problems in big-city America. Substance abuse has invaded every aspect of our lives, and it is big business, with crime syndicates, gangs, the Internet, and other countries involved on a global scale. Drugs smuggled into our country are just one example of how illegal drugs become available. Drugs make for huge profits, and our children are the ones who suffer the most from drug trafficking and distribution.

The threat comes from big businesses and street druggies, who deal and do drugs themselves. They think nothing of stealing from others to support their habits, or cutting (diluting) the drugs they sell to include substances that may be lethal. These people and their drugs are the ones most likely to come into contact with our children. Drugs are all around us, and seldom does a day go by at most schools when a dealer doesn't approach a child. These dealers know that if your child tries a substance just once he will likely want more and more, and stronger and stronger, doses. Dealers will often offer a free sample of drugs just to get a nonuser hooked. The second dose in *not free*! In other words, your child is at risk of addiction—and it is the dealer who profits. You may then be pulled into the cycle through worry and fear that your child is doing drugs. If your child *is* doing them, you risk financial ruin and the loss of your child. We urge you to be active in helping your communities and schools beat these problems.

It's not easy being a parent today, nor is it easy being a child in our fast-moving, often impersonal, and stressful world. Much of what we are taught as children holds little bearing on the world we know as adults. We have to keep in tune with life as it stands today, in this high-tech, stressful, confusing, impersonal, and drug-riddled world our children live in. Quite simply, we have to be savvy parents. We have to work on understanding our children and expressing our love for them verbally and through our actions, while making sure we discipline them when they violate our rules. We have to be stern and consistent. And we have to remember that addicted kids grow up to be addicted adults, who will undoubtedly influence others. It is our responsibility as parents to make sure our children grow up as free from the hazards of drugs and alcohol as possible.

Throughout this book we have given suggestions on how you can protect your children from substance abuse. We hope you take our words seriously and go beyond our research and experiences by educating yourself even further on drugs and alcohol. Though we have tried to be as comprehensive as possible with this book, no one text can cover every drug and every situation. But there are plenty of resources here to get you started, and you can visit online sources or local sources to gather more information specific to your location. Many agencies—private, government, public, nonprofit, and Internet-based—exist for the sole purpose of combating substance abuse. It is our hope you take full advantage of them.

We will be updating this book, so we can publish information on the newest trends in substance use. Additionally, we will offer books that target particular sectors of society, such as the workforce.

If we must draw a bottom line, it is that substance abuse can affect anyone, young or old, rich or poor, educated or uneducated, child or adult. Learn as much as possible about drugs and alcohol and abuse, and do whatever you can to help your loved ones avoid addiction. We urge you to act the very instant you suspect a drug and/or alcohol problem exists in your family.

When all the information is stripped down, the fact remains that we need to be parents to our children, not friends. We need to be active participants in their lives, not passive ones. We need to be on top of things, not outside of their circle. We need to stay current, not ignorant, of drug- and alcohol-abuse trends. We need to be communicative with our children.

Your love for your children and your involvement in your children's lives is what will keep them—and you—safe.

Good luck.

Gianni Hayes, Ph.D.
Michael J. Talley Jr.

Appendix

Drug Information Charts

Below are various charts you can photocopy and save for reference.

Drug Classification Charts

These charts show the categorization of drugs. Several of these drugs belong to several different categories. What is offered below is insight on drug effects (i.e., depressant = downers) as well as how they're taken (i.e., inhalants = sniffed).

Depressant Drugs

Alcohol	Diazemuls	Nembutal
Allobarbital	Diazepam	Nitrazepam
Alphenol	Dronabinol	Nobrium
Aprazalom	Efavirenz	Noctamide
Amobarbital	Estazolam	Norbritol
Amobarbital Sodium	Floricet	Oxazepam
Amytal Sodium	Florinal	Ox-Pam
Anxitol	Flurazepam	Pentothal
Ativan	Gamma Hydroxybutyrate	Prazepam
Barbital	Hashish	Primidone
Barbiturates	Klonopin	ProSom
Benzodiazepines	Lerisum	Rivotril
Briantum	Lexotan	Serax
Bromazepam	Lorazepam	Sodium Oxybate
Butabarbital	Lormetazepam	Soma
Butalbital	Marijuana	Somnite
Butisol	Marinol	Soneryl
Carisoprodol	Mebaral	Stesolid
Centrax	Medacepan	Sustiva
Clobazam	Medazepam	Thiopental Sodium
Clonazepam	Mephobarbital	Tranxene
Clonopin	Meprobamate	Tuinal

Clorazepate Dipotassium	Miltown	Valclair
Dalmane	Mogadon	Valium
Delorazepam	Mysoline	Xanax
Demetrin	Nabilone	Xyrem

Stimulant Drugs

Adderall	DOB	Methylphenidate Hydrochloride
Adderall XR	DOM	Modafinil
Adipex-P	Dopram	Pemoline
Afrinol	Dospan	Phendimetrazine Tartrate
Amphetamines	Doxapram Hydrochloride	Phenmetrazine
Benzphetamine Hydrochloride	Ecstasy	Phentermine Hydrochloride
Bontril	Fenflluramine	PMA (Paramethoxyamphetamine)
Cocaine	Focalin	Pondomin
Concerta	I-Methamphetamine HCL	Prelu-2
Crack Cocaine	Ionamin	Preludin
Crystal Meth	KHAT	Provigil
Cylert	MDA	Pseudoephedrine
Desoxyn	MDMA	Pylorid
Dexamphetamine Sulphate	Metadate	Ranitidine
Dexedrine	Methamphetamine Hydrochloride	Ritilan
Dexmethylphenidate Hydrochloride	Methamphetamines	Sudafed

Dextroamphetamine	Methamprex	Tenuate
Didrex	Methedrine	Tylenol Cold
Diethylpropion Hydrochloride	Methylenedioxymethamphetamine	Vick's Inhaler
d-Methamphetamine HCL	Methylin	Zantac

Narcotic Analgesic Drugs

Acetaminophen w/codeine phosphate		
Actiq	Hydrocodone w/ibprofen	Paracetamol
Anexsia	Hydromorphone	Paral
Astramorp PF	Hydrostat	Paraldehyde
Avinza	Infumorph	Paramol
Butorphanol Tartrate	Intensol	Paregoric
Co-codamol	Kadian	Pavacol-D
Codafen	Kapake	Pediatric BP
Codafen Continus	Koalin and Morphine	Pentazocine Hydrochloride
Codeine Linctus	Levo-Dromoran	Percocet
Codeine Phosphate	Levorphanol Tartrate	Percodan
Codeine Sulfate	Loratab	Percolone
Co-dydramol	Lorcet	Pholcodine
Contin	Maxidone	Physetone
Cyclimorph	Meperdine Hydrochloride	Propoxyphene
Darvocet	Meperitab	Propoxyphene Napslate
Darvon	Methadone	Remedeine
Demerol	Methadone Hydrochloride	Remedeine Forte
Dextroproxyphene	Methadone Intensol	Remedine
DHC Continus	Methadose	RMS

Dihydrocodeine	Midazolam Hydrochloride	Roxanol
Dilaudid	Migraleve	Roxicodone
Dilaudid-HP	Morcap	Severedol
Dolophine	Morphine	Solpadol
DTO	MS Contin	Strong BP
Duragesic	MSIR	Sublimaze
Duramorph PF	Norco	Sufenta
Duramorph, Morcap	Norethindrone	Sufentanil Citrate
Entersan	Novocain	Thebacon
Ethylmorphine	Numorphan	Tylenol 3
Fentanyl	Opazimes	Tylenol w/codeine
Fentanyl Citrate	Opium	Tylex
Galcodine	Opium Tincture	Tylox
Galenphol	Oramorph SR	Versed
Heroin	Oxycodone Hydrochloride	Vicodin
Hycomine	OxyContin	Vicodin Tuss
Hydrocodone	OxyDose	Vicoprofen
Hydrocodone w/ acetaminophen	OxyFast	Zydone
Hydrocodone w/ guaifenesin	OxyIR	
Hydrocloride	Oxymorphone	

Hallucinogenic, Steroid, Hypnotic/Sedative Drugs

Hallucinogenic

5-MeO-DIPT	Ketamine	PCP
AMT (Alpha-Methyltryptamin)	LSD	Psilocybin
Amyl Nitrite	Mescaline	Salvia Divinorum
Glyceryl Trinitrate	Nitrites	Zolpidem
Inhalants	Paral	
Ketalar	Paraldehyde	

Steroids

Anadrol	Methenolone	Oxandrolone
Anavar	Methitest	Oxymetholone
Androis	Methyltestosterone	Primobolan
Delatestryl	Nandrolone Decanoate	Stanozolol+F70
Ethylestrenol	Nandrolone Phenpropionate	Testosterone Enanthate
Finaject	Orabolin	Testred
Fluoxymesterone	Oreton	Trenbolone Acetate
Halotestin	Oxandrin	Virilon

Hypnotic/Sedative Drugs

Alurate	Flunitrazepam	Quazepam
Ambien	Glutethimide	Repan
Anolor	Halcion	Restoril
Aprobarbital	Librium	Rohypnol
Aquachloral	Luminal Sodium	Secobarbital
Butabarbital Sodium	Methaqualone	Seconal
Butisol Sodium	Methyprylon	Somnote
Chloral Hydrate	Mogadon	Sonata
Chlordiazepoxide	Nembutal	Supprettes
Doral	Nitrazepam	Temazepam
Esgic	Noctec	Triazolam
Estazolam	Noludar	Valmid
Ethchlorvynol	Pentobarbital Sodium	Zaleplon
Ethinamate	Placidyl	Zebutal
Fioricet	ProDom	Zolpidem

Unity Oath

THIS UNITY OATH IS BETWEEN (PARENT/GUARDIAN) _____
AND CHILD _____

We Agree to Stand by the Following Commitments:

Parents/Guardians Will:

- Calmly listen to our child when he or she is answering our questions.
- If our child calls and needs a ride home, we will pick him up with no questions at that time.
- Get to know all our child's friends and their parents.
- Promise to reproach only the act, and not our child.
- Avow to discuss drug and alcohol use with our child on a regular basis.
- Affirm not to do drugs and drink irresponsibly; we will model good behavior.
- Enforce a non-negotiable, zero tolerance policy for drugs and alcohol.
- Be consistent and fair in disciplining when our child violates our rules.
- Pledge to monitor our child's behavior, his or her activities, and to oversee his or her internet interactions.
- Swear to admit mistakes we may make and to correct them.

Child Will:

- Answer all questions about drug and alcohol use without an attitude.
- Always let my parents know where I am at all times.
- IntroduGe all my friends to my parents/guardians and avoid acquaintances that I know drink and/or use drugs.
- Never drive under the influence of drugs/alcohol or ride with one who is.
- Practice safe habits on the Internet, and allow time for homework.
- Admit when I'm wrong, apologize, and not repeat the same mistakes.
- Abide by the rules my parents layout for me, and accept my punishment.
- Maintain good grades in school.
- Be honest with my parents.
- Commit no crimes, nor help anyone wanting to commit one.
- Watch over my siblings to make sure that they are safe from drugs/alcohol

Signature of Child: _____ Date: _____
Signature of Parent(s) _____

Internet Web Sites

The following Web sites/resources are available to the general public. Since the writing of this book, some of these resources may have been updated or become defunct, so please go online to check. All links were viable at time of printing unless noted otherwise in text.

4-H CARES (Chemical Abuse Resistance Education Series)
http://www.extension.iastate.edu/NR/
rdonlyres/ADE93901-A4F9-48C7-B256-
5EF2F2DB4F68/539/4hcares.docAdolescent

Alcohol and Drug Abuse
http://www.ext.colostate.edu/pubs/consumer/10216.html

Adolescents at Risk: Illicit Drug Use
http://ohioline.osu.edu/flm02/FS15.html

A Prescription for Danger: Teens Using Medicines to Get High
http://www.innovations-report.com/html/reports/medi-
cine_health/report-30840.html

A Prescription for Danger: Use of Painkillers on the Rise
http://www.family.samhsa.gov/talk/painkillers.aspx

A Family Guide to Keeping Youth Mentally Healthy and Drug Free
http://www.family.samhsa.gov

Assessing Substance Use and Abuse among Adolescents: A Guide for Out-
Of-School Time Program Practitioners
http://www.childtrends.org/Files//Child_
Trends-2007_03_14_RB_TeenSubstanceUse.pdf

Publicaciones en español (Spanish version)
https://store.samhsa.gov/espanol

Because I Love You Organization
http://www.becauseiloveyou.org/

Canadian Centre on Substance Abuse
http://www.ccsa.ca/Pages/Splash.htm

CASA Study Finds Alarming Trends in College Substance Abuse
http://www.casacolumbia.org/absolutenm/templates/
PressReleases.aspx?articleid=477&zoneid=65

Certain Parenting Styles Better at Protecting Youth from Marijuana Use
http://www.cyfernet.org/pagelist.php?c=1175

Cocaine Anonymous
http://www.ca.org/

Comparing Drug Testing and Self Report of Drug Use among Youths and
Young Adults in the General Population
http://oas.samhsa.gov/validity/drugtest.cfm

Driving Under the Influence of Alcohol or Drugs
http://family.samhsa.gov/set/driving.aspx

Drug Prevention Lesson Plans
http://www.acde.org/educate/Lessons.htm

Ensuring Solutions to Alcohol Problems
http://www.ensuringsolutions.org/

Fact Sheet on Substance Use: Adolescents and Young Adults
http://nahic.ucsf.edu/downloads/Sub_Use.pdf

Fighting Back
http://www.fightingback.org/

Heads Up: Real News about Drugs and Your Body
http://teacher.scholastic.com/scholasticnews/indepth/
headsup/

Help for Parents
    http://www.drugfree.org/Intervention/HelpingOthers/
    AdultTeen/10_Points_for_Parents_to_Intervene

Helping Youth Succeed: What We All Can Do to Prevent Adolescent
Substance Abuse
    http://collaborate.extension.org/wiki/
    CYFAR_2008_Workshop

High School Success Helps Keep Teens Drug Free
    http://family.samhsa.gov/monitor/highschool.aspx

How Do Kids Get Prescription Drugs?
    http://www.family.samhsa.gov/monitor/howpresdrug.aspx

Illicit Drug Use
    http://www.childtrendsdatabank.org/
    indicators/58IllicitDrugUse.cfm

Illicit Drug Use by Race/Ethnicity in Metropolitan and Non-Metropolitan
Counties: 2004 and 2005
    http://oas.samhsa.gov/2k7/popdensity/popdensity.cfm

Is Your Teen Drug Dependent?
    http://www.yoursocialworker.com/p-articles/teen-drug.
    htm

I Tried Marijuana. What Do I Tell My Teen?
    http://family.samhsa.gov/monitor/triedmarijuana.aspx

Legal but Lethal: The Danger of Abusing Over-the-Counter Drugs
    http://www.family.samhsa.gov/get/otcdrugs.aspx

Marijuana: Facts for Teens
    http://www.nida.nih.gov/MarijBroch/Marijteens.html

Marijuana: Facts Parents Need to Know
    http://www.nida.nih.gov/MarijBroch/MarijparentsN.html

Marijuana: Informacion para los Adolescentes (Marijuana: Facts for Teens)
http://www.safeyouth.org/scripts/display/MatlDisplay.
asp?MatlNbr=419

Marijuana Use
http://www.childtrendsdatabank.org/
indicators/46MarijuanaUse.cfm

Misuse of Prescription Drugs
http://www.samhsa.gov/newsroom/
advisories/061102misuse5701.aspx

Mom, My Friend Is Using Pot
http://www.family.samhsa.gov/monitor/usingpot.aspx

National Alcohol and Addiction Recovery Month
http://www.recoverymonth.gov/

National Alliance for Drug Endangered Children
http://www.nationaldec.org/

National Institute on Drug Abuse (NIDA)
http://www.drugabuse.gov/

National Outcome Measures
http://www.samhsa.gov/SAMHSA_NEWS/
VolumeXV_2/article10.htm

National Registry of Evidence-based Programs and Practices
http://nrepp.samhsa.gov/

National Survey of American Attitudes on Substance Abuse IX: Teen
Dating Practices and Sexual Activity
http://www.casacolumbia.org/absolutenm/templates/
PressReleases.aspx?articleid=366&zoneid=61

National Survey of American Attitudes on Substance Abuse XII: Teens and
Parents
http://www.casacolumbia.org/absolutenm/arti-
clefiles/380-2007%20Teen%20Survey%20XII.pdf

New National Survey Reveals Drug Use Down Among Adolescents in U.S.
http://www.samhsa.gov/newsroom/advisories/0709043102.aspx

NIDA for Teens: The Science behind Drug Abuse
http://teens.drugabuse.gov/

NIDA Goes Back to School
http://www.backtoschool.drugabuse.gov/

NIDA, National Institute on Drug Abuse
http://www.nida.nih.gov/NIDAHome.html

Parent's Prevention Primer—Risk and Protective Factors
http://family.samhsa.gov/get/preventionprimer.aspx

Partnership for a Drug-Free America
http://www.drugfree.org/Portal/

Partners for Substance Abuse Prevention
http://prevention.samhsa.gov/

Predicting Heavy Drug Use: Results of a Longitudinal Study, Youth
Characteristics Describing and Predicting Heavy Drug Use by Adults
http://www.eric.ed.gov/ERICWebPortal/
custom/portlets/recordDetails/detailm-
ini.jsp?_nfpb=true&_&ERICExtSearch_S
earchValue_0=ED503083&ERICExtSearc
h_SearchType_0=no&accno=ED503083

Preventing Drug Abuse among Children and Adolescents
http://www.drugabuse.gov/Prevention/Prevopen.html

Preventing Marijuana Use in Your Family
http://family.samhsa.gov/set/marijuanaseries.aspx

Prevline: Prevention Online
http://ncadi.samhsa.gov/error/updating.aspx

Protecting Your Kids from Substance Abuse and Violence
http://www.youthdevelopment.org/itemdesc.asp?id=25

Rational Recovery Center
http://rational.org/

Risk Factors for Alcohol and Drug Use/Abuse Prevention
http://www.drugabuse.gov/Prevention/risk.html

SAMSHA's Buprenorphine Physician and Treatment Locator
http://buprenorphine.samhsa.gov/bwns_locator/dr_facili-
tylocatordoc.htm

SAMSHA's Partner for Recovery
http://www.pfr.samhsa.gov/

SourceBook of Drug and Violence Prevention Programs for Children and
Adolescents
http://www.umdnj.edu/vinjweb/publications/sourcebook/
about_sourcebook.html

Steroid Abuse
http://www.steroidabuse.org/

Steroid Precursors Can Block Teen Athletes from Their Goals
http://www.family.samhsa.gov/be/athblocked.aspx

Stop Alcohol Abuse
http://www.stopalcoholabuse.gov

Substance Abuse Treatment for Children and Adolescents: Questions to Ask
http://www.aacap.org/cs/root/resources_for_
families/glossary_of_symptoms_and_illnesses/alcohol_
and_drug_abuse

Substance-Free Youth
http://www.tennessee.gov/education/schoolhealth/counsel-
ing/doc/Substance-Free%20Youth%20FS.pdf

Substance Use among Youths Who Had Run Away From Home
http://oas.samhsa.gov/2k4/runAways/runAways.cfm

Substance Use Programs and Resources
http://findtreatment.samhsa.gov/

Teachable Media Moments
    http://family.samhsa.gov/be/media.aspx

Teens and Meth
    http://ncadi.samhsa.gov/govpubs/PHD861/

Tips for Teens about Crack and Cocaine
    http://ncadi.samhsa.gov/govpubs/phd640/

Tips for Teens: The Truth about Club Drugs
    http://ncadi.samhsa.gov/govpubs/phd852/

Tips for Teens: The Truth about Hallucinogens
    http://ncadi.samhsa.gov/govpubs/phd642/

Tips for Teens: The Truth about Heroin
    http://ncadi.samhsa.gov/govpubs/PHD860/

Tips for Teens: The Truth about Methamphetamine
    http://ncadi.samhsa.gov/govpubs/PHD861/

Teens Who Frequently Have Family Dinners Less Likely To Drink, Smoke, or Use Drugs
    http://www.cesar.umd.edu/cesar/cesarfax/vol15/15-39.pdf

The Anti-Drug.Com
    http://www.theantidrug.com/

The George Washington University Medical Center
    http://www.gwumc.edu/

The Higher Education Center for Alcohol and Other Drug Prevention
    http://www.higheredcenter.org/

The NSDUH Report: Substance Use Treatment Need among Adolescents, 2008–2010
    http://oas.samhsa.gov/newpubs.htm#New

The Parent Connection
    http://www.higheredcenter.org/parents/

The Ups and Downs of Adolescence
http://www.ianr.unl.edu/ianr/fcs/upsdowns/

U.S. Department of Human Services and SAMSHA's National Clearing House for Alcohol and Drug Information
https://ncadistore.samhsa.gov/catalog/top.aspx?

Violence and Rural Teens: Teen Violence, Drug Use, and School-based Prevention Services in Rural America
http://rhr.sph.sc.edu/report/SCRHRC_TeenViolence.pdf

U.S. Department of Transportation:
http://www.dot.gov.

United States Department of Health and Human Services Substance Abuse and Mental Health Services Administration
http://www.samhsa.gov/

Wake Up to the Risks of Marijuana: A Guide for Parents
http://ncadistore.samhsa.gov/catalog/productDetails.aspx?ProductID=16412

Web of Addictions
http://www.well.com/user/woa/index.html#return_point

Weed on the Web: Kids Buying Marijuana Online
http://www.family.samhsa.gov/teach/highonline.aspx

What to Know about Teen Alcohol and Other Drug Use: A Publication for Professionals who Work with Adolescents and the Parents of Adolescents
http://www.utextension.utk.edu/publications/spfiles/sp491b.pdf

What Works: Programs that May Influence Binge Drinking
http://www.childtrendsdatabank.org/WhatWorks/2BingeDrinkingww.cfm

What Works: Programs that May Influence Illicit Drug Use
http://www.childrentrendsdatabank.org/WhatWorks/58IllicitDrugUseww.cfm

What You Need to Know about Drug Testing in Schools
http://fl1.findlaw.com/news.findlaw.com/hdocs/docs/
drugs/schldrgtst802whrpt.pdf

When Your Child Needs Substance Abuse Treatment
http://family.samhsa.gov/get/treatment.aspx

Whose Kids? Our Kids! When a Parent Has Used Drugs
http://www.okcareertech.org/cimc/special/nochild/down-
loads/safety/WIteenparentdrugs.pdf

Youth Facts: Drugs and Youth
http://www.youthdevelopment.org/download/drugs.pdf

Youth Illicit Drug Use Prevention: DARE Long-Term Evaluations and
Federal Efforts to Identify Effective Programs
http://www.gao.gov/new.items/d03172r.pdf

Drugs and Their Effects, Reactions, and Symptoms

The following charts detail how drugs affect the body. The higher the dose consumed, the more intense the reaction, in most cases. Many effects may be heightened or lowered depending on what else the person has consumed, how much sleep they've had, how pure the substance is, and the user's physical and mental health. The effects will also depend on the person's metabolism and weight.

Drug Effect on Body

Drug Name	Effect on Body
Alcohol	Depresses central nervous system
Amphetamine	Central nervous system stimulant
Anabolic Steroids	Affects limbic system (impair learning and memory), brain, hypothalamus (interferes with production of testosterone)
Barbiturates	Central nervous system (CNS) depressant
Benzodiazepines	Central nervous system (CNS) depressant
Cocaine	CNS stimulant, halts the reabsorption process of dopamine
Ecstasy	Hallucinogen/stimulant; affects serotonoin (the chemical that allows neurons in the brain to communicate with each other)
GHB	Powerful central nervous system depressant

Inhalants	Affects CNS/brain, can break down myelin and not allow messages to be transmitted, can damage neurons in the hippocampus part of the brain
Ketamine	General anesthetic, dissociative anesthetic
LSD	Hallucinogen, affects interaction of nerve cells and the neurotransmitter called serotonin. Can cause flashbacks without additional use
Marijuana	Mind altering, effects the ability of brain neurons ability to send messages
Methaqualone	Sedative, hypnotic
Methadone	Narcotic analgesic
Methamphetamine	Central nervous system stimulant, effects release of dopamine
Opiates	Narcotic analgesic, effects production of opiate receptors in the limbic system, brainstem and spinal cord
Oxycodone	Narcotic analgesic
Phencyclidine (PCP)	Hallucinogen
Propoxyphene	Narcotic analgesic
Psilocybin mushrooms	Hallucinogen
Rohypnol	Sedative, hypnotic, central nervous system depressant

How Specific Drugs Are Ingested

Drug Name	How ingested
Alcohol	Oral
Amphetamine	Injected, oral, sniffed
Anabolic Steroids	Oral, injected, skin applied
Barbiturates	Oral, injected
Benzodiazepines	Oral, injected
Cocaine	Injected, oral, sniffed
Ecstasy	Oral
GHB	Oral
Inhalants	Inhaled
Keramine	Injected, oral, sniffed, rectally
LSD	Oral
Marijuana	Smoked
Methaqualone	Injected, oral, sniffed
Methadone	Oral, injected
Methamphetamine	Injected, oral, sniffed
Opiates	Injected, oral, sniffed
Oxycodone	Injected, oral, sniffed
Phencyclidine (PCP)	Oral, injected
Propoxyphene	Oral
Psilocybin mushrooms	Oral
Rohypnol	Injected, oral, sniffed

Snorting/Inhaling Drugs

Source: www.dreamstime.com

Injecting Drugs

Source: www.dreamstime.com

Common Street Names for Drugs

Drug Name	Street Names
Alcohol	Beer, wine, liquor, booze, jungle juice, spirits, hooch
Amphetamine	Meth, whites, bennies, crystal, white cross, jelly beans, dexies, uppers, rank, Black beauties, speed, jollies, ups, wake-ups
Anabolic Steroids	Roids, juice, hype, pump, androstendols, dehydroepiandrosterone, designer anabolic steroids, stackers, weight trainers, gym candy
Barbiturates	Dolls, reds, tuinal, yellows, blues, rainbows, downers, goofballs, red devils
Benzodiazepines	Tranqs, downers
Cocaine	Nose candy, crack, white candy, C, flake, toot, blow, rock, coke, freebase, base, big-C, snow, snowbirds, crank, white, zip
Ecstasy	Ecstasy, adam, X, E, XTC, hug drug, love drug, lover's speed, beans, roll, peace, STP, clarity, eve
GHB	Liquid-X, liquid ecstasy, soap, easy lay, goops, everclear, georgia home boy, liquid-E, organic, Quaalude, scoop, sleep, sleep-500, bodily harm, cherry meth
Inhalants	Laughing gas, poppers, rush, snappers, whippets – *Solvents*-industrial or household, paint thinners, degreasers, gasoline, correction fluid, felt markers, electronic contact cleaners, *Gases* – butane lighters, propane tanks, spray paint, hair/deodorant aerosol, ether, chloroform, halothane, nitrous oxide. *Nitrites* – aliphatic nitrides, amyl nitrite, butyl nitrite
Ketamine	Special K, vitamin K, date rape drug, ketaject, new ecstasy, psychedelic heroin, keets, super C, cat valium, lady kay, K, jet, K-hole

LSD	L, blotter, trips, cid, tabs, acid, microdots, sugar cubes, hits, doses, boomers, dots, mellow yello, yellow sunshines
Marijuana (THC)	Pot, joint, reefer, maryjane, dope, smoke, weed, herb, blunt, hash, grass, aunt mary, chronic, gangster, kit, sinsemilla, shunk
Methaqualone	Ludes, mequin, lemon, sopor, Quaalude, quad, quay, mandrex
Methadone	Dolophine, methadose, dolls, done
Methamphetamine	Chalk, croak, crystal, fire, glass, ice, meth, speed, white cross, crank, go fast
Opiates	Heroin (smack, black tar, brown sugar, H, mud, skag, junk, china white, horse), morphine (miss Emma), codeine (school boy), hydrocodone (Vicodin), Hydromorphone (Dilaudid), Oxycodone (Percocet, Percodan, Oxycontin), Oxymorphone (mumorphan), Mexican brown, white lady
Oxycodone	OC's, poor mans heroin, ocycotton, hillbilly heroin, killers, blue, 40/80 dose
Phencyclidine (PCP)	PCP, angel dust, dummy dust, wack, devil stick, embalming fluid, killer weed, super grass, boat, hog, love boat, peace pill
Propoxyphene	Dillies, smack, juice, D, dust
Psilocybin mushroom	Shrooms, musk, purple passion, magic mushrooms
Rohypnol	Rophies, roach, rope, circles, roofies, mexican valium, roofinol, forget-me pill, R2, Roche

Symptoms of Specific Drug Use

Drug Name	Symptoms of use
Alcohol	Confusion, euphoria, false sense of well being, anxiety, restlessness, depression and change in mood
Amphetamine	Severe depression, possible hallucinations, disorientation, paranoia, increase in blood pressure, fatigue
Anabolic Steroids	Females (virilization, sterility, increased sexual desire, beard growth, stoppage of periods, hair loss-these changes are irreversible). Males (enlarged breasts, testicular atrophy, low sperm, hair loss, ED)
Barbiturates	Depression, slowed muscle control, slowed alertness, slurred speech, intoxication and drowsiness
Benzodiazepines	Dilated pupils, weak and rapid pulse, coma, possible death, shallow respiration, old and clammy skin
Cocaine	Dilated pupils, headaches, high body temperature, blurred vision, death, easily agitated, nervousness, highly talkative
Ecstasy (MDMA)	Dizzy, nausea, chills, muscular tightness, teeth and jaw clenching, blurred vision, depression, nervousness, irrationally excited, hallucinations
GHB	Confusion, psychosis, agitation, amnesia, hallucinations, paranoia
Inhalants	Slow down the body functions, intoxication, slight stimulation, fainting. Chronic exposure can lead to brain damage, nerve damage similar to multiple sclerosis, damage to the heart, lungs, liver and kidneys, effected thinking, movement, vision and hearing loss, induce heart failure and death, change in dress/friends,
Ketamine	Visual hallucinations, depression, long term loss of memory, violent behavior, aggressive behavior, delirium anxiety

LSD	Dilated pupils, high body temp, abnormal sweating, low appetite, dry mouth, tremors
Marijuana (THC)	Increased heart rate, impaired short-term memory, lung damage, possible psychosis with chronic use, psychological dependence, anxiety, loss of motivation, impaired learning, slowed thinking and reactions, red eyes, dry mouth, hunger
Methaqualone	Insomnia, confusion, false personal confidence, poor perception and anxiety
Methadone	Anxiety, strange dreams, confusion, abnormal thought process,
Methamphetamine	Anxiety, high energy, heightened alertness, irritable, confusion, rage, violence,
Opiates	Weight loss, hepatitis, lethargy, slow/shallow breathing, possible death
Oxycodone	Anxiety, high energy, heightened alertness, irritable, confusion, rage, violence, aggressiveness
Phencyclidine (PCP)	Elevated heart rate, high pulse, fever and blood pressure, dilated pupils, nausea, rapid eye movement, dizzy, tremors, low coordination, increased salivation, perspiring
Propoxyphene	Blurred vision, depression, nervousness, irrationally excited, hallucinations
Psilocybin mushrooms	Drowsiness, musculature weakness, vomiting and panic attacks
Rohypnol	Amnesia, impaired mental facilities, suicidal tendencies, confusion

Consequences of Drug Abuse

Drug Name	Consequences of Abuse
Alcohol	Slows reaction time, judgment/coordination, possible liver/brain damage, anemia, blood disorders, color blindness, diarrhea, pancreas & stomach lining inflammation
Amphetamine	High depression/blood pressure, hallucinations, disorientation, paranoia, fatigue
Anabolic Steroids	Cardiovascular disease, hypertension, liver dysfunction, infertility liver tumors, liver cysts, weakened immune system, stops bone growth if used when an adolescent
Barbiturates	Rigidity and painful muscle contraction, possible overdose and death, especially when mixed with alcohol, emotional instability
Benzodiazepines	Dilated pupils, weak and rapid pulse, coma, possible death, shallow respiration, sedation, drowsy/dizzy, cold and clammy skin
Cocaine	Fever, anxiety, possible death from convulsions, heart attack or respiratory arrest, shallow breathing, heart attack, seizures, lung damage, brief euphoria, elevated blood pressure/heart rate, restlessness, excitement, feeling of well being followed by depression, stroke, eats holes in nose cartilage
Ecstasy	Hypertension, tachycardia, mydriasis, hyperthermia, diaphoresis, stimulant, visual hallucinations, entactogenic effects, kidney failure
GHB	Respiratory depression, bradycardia, hallucinations, amnesia, anxiety, tremors, tachycardia, delirium, agitation

Inhalants	Decrease body functions, intoxication, slight stimulation, loss of consciousness, chronic exposure can lead to brain damage, nerve damage similar to multiple sclerosis, damage to the heart, lungs, liver and kidneys, effected thinking, movement, vision and hearing loss, induce heart failure and death, damages bone marrow
Ketamine	Hypertension, tachycardia, respiratory depression, hallucinations, cataleptic state
LSD	Hypertension, tachycardia, hyperthermia, lacrimation, mydriasis, visual hallucinations, synthesias ataxia, tremors, hallucinations, mood swings
Marijuana (THC)	Increased heart rate, impaired short-term memory, lung damage, possible psychosis with chronic use, psychological dependence, anxiety, loss of motivation, impaired learning, slowed thinking and reactions, red eyes, dry mouth, hunger
Methaqualone	Decreased coordination, low blood pressure, excessive sleepiness, sexual dysfunction, slowed heart rate/breathing
Methadone	Hypertension, tachycardia, mydriasis, hyperthermia, diaphoresis, stimulant, visual hallucinations, entactogenic effects
Methamphetamine	Diarrhea/dialated pupils/sweating/rigid muscles/rapid breathing/difficulty sleeping/rage/aggression/violence/psychotic behavior/memory loss/decaying of gums & teeth
Opiates	Weight loss, hepatitis, lethargy, slow/shallow breathing, possible death
Oxycodone	Abdominal cramps, euphoria, gastrointestinal inflammation, decreased blood pressure, nausea, difficulty sleeping, loss of appetite
Phencyclidine (PCP)	Unpredictable behavior, possible emotional instability and psychosis, flashbacks, alteration of perception, paranoia, panic attacks

Propoxyphene	Stupor or coma, convulsions, skin rash and other allergic reactions occur occasionally and may be accompanied by drug fever and mucosal lesions, respiratory depression
Psilocybin mushrooms	Dramatic visual and auditory hallucinations, emotional disturbances, panic attacks
Rohypnol	Hypotension, disorientation, dizziness, respiratory depression, visual disturbances, anterograde amnesia

Street Slang (Names)

The charts below give some of the more popular street terms (names) for drugs, along with their definitions. Slang names move in and out of popularity and by location. For a full list of slang and street names, please refer to the following Web site:

http://www.whitehousedrugpolicy.gov/streetterms/ByAlpha.asp?strTerm=A:

(This chart is from the Office of National Drug Control Policy (ONDCP), under "Drug Facts.")

Street Terms for Drugs

Street Term	Definition
007s	Methyleneodioxymethamphetamine (MDMA)
40	OxyContin pill
100s	Lysergic acid diethylamide (LSD)
40-bar	OxyContin pill
A-bomb	Smoke marijuana w/heroin or opium
Bang	Inhalant; to inject a drug
Bender	Drug party
Bennie	Amphetamine
Bibs	MDMA
Black tabs	LSD
Black tar	Heroin
Blue	Crack Cocaine; depressants; OxyContin
Blue microdot	LSD
Golf balls	Depressants
Grass	Marijuana
Hard candy	Heroin
Hillbilly heroin	OxyContin
Hulling	Using others to get drugs
Oxycotton	OxyContin
Pot	Marijuana
Powder	Cocaine HCL; heroin; amphetamine
Quarter bag	$25 worth of drugs
Sextasy	Ecstasy used with Viagra
Snow	Cocaine; heroin; amphetamine
Stackers	Steroids
Super C	Ketamine

Street Terms for Drugs

Street Term	Definition
Bone	Marijuana; $50 piece of crack; high purity heroin
Cancelled stick	Marijuana cigarette
Candy	Cocaine; Crack Cocaine; amphetamine; depressants
Chasing the dragon	Crack mixed with heroin
Chasing the tiger	To smoke heroin
China girl	Fentanyl
Cocktail	Combination of crack and marijuana; cigarette laced with cocaine or crack; partially smoked marijuana cigarette inserted in regular cigarette; to smoke cocaine in a cigarette
Cook down	Process in which users liquefy heroin in order to inhale it
Ecstasy	Methyleneodioxymethamphetamine (MDMA)
Eight ball	1/8 ounce of cocaine
Super grass	PCP; marijuana with PCP; marijuana
Tabs	LSD; MDMA
Tango & Cash	Fentanyl
Tar	Crack and heroin smoked together; heroin; opium
Vita-G	Gamma hydroxybutyrate (GHB)
Vitamin K	Ketamine
Vitamin R	Ritalin (methylphenidate)
Whippets	Nitrous oxide
Whiteout	Inhalants; isobutyl nitrite
Zig Zag man	Marijuana; LSD; marijuana, rolling papers

Our Other Products

Besides the ten-panel instant results drug kit (in several variations), and the alcohol swab, we offer a variety of other products that you may find helpful in your quest to fight the problem of substance abuse.

If you don't see what you need on the following pages, just contact us.

Our Store
We provide many types of drug testing. We work with a number of suppliers and labs, and we maintain strong working relationships with numerous experts in the medical and technical arenas. We monitor technological advancements in the drug/alcohol testing field and represent several forward-looking companies that invent and market new prevention and testing tools.

We ensure that any device, literature, or other related items that we carry and offer to you are safe, accurate, easy-to-use, and viable (up to the expiration date). We also attempt to keep on top of ever-emerging drug advancements and the possible ways in which accurate testing results could be altered or nullified.

Our inventory includes prevention and testing products for families, schools, and the workplace. Our goal is to prevent, protect, detect, and save.

We can ship testing supplies internationally.

Our workplace testing inventory is on the leading edge of available, reliable products and services. We are capable of screening an area for drugs without ever testing a single person. We can also supply devices and services that can be used in the workplace for individual testing. (We suggest that all employers check their state laws regarding testing before implementing drug-testing policies and procedures.) Additionally, we work with well-known professionals in the drug-prevention sector to implement drug-free testing programs in the workplace, from providing the needed drug and alcohol policy, through teaching and training the staff and supervisors, to implementing the actual testing.

For those who want to go to a lab for testing, we can provide lab/clinical forms, referred to as Custody and Control Forms (DOT and non-DOT), after we discuss all the alternatives with you. We work with SAMHSA-approved labs throughout the United States.

We keep our prices as competitive as possible, so that consumers can benefit. Though we are not professional substance-abuse therapists or counselors, we do strive to constantly update our knowledge base in order to answer your questions and to ensure that we understand your needs. If we cannot answer your questions, we will refer you to someone who can. We are good listeners, so please do not be shy about calling us. You would be under no obligation, and we would be happy to be of service.

Available Products

	Home Drug Testing SafeBox **(1 product)** Complete Drug Testing Program with SAFE Book, Ten-Drug Urine Drug Test and Saliva Alcohol Test.
	Instant Integrated Cup Drug Tests **(12 products)** Our Instant Integrated test Cups are 99% accurate (results in minutes). The tester has no contact with the urine. Test for multiple drugs at once!
	DNA / Paternity Tests **(14 products)** Putting your mind at ease has never been more convenient, confidential, affordable or accurate. With our Home DNA Testing Kit you'll collect DNA specimens in the privacy of your home. Results in 7 business bays.
	Hair Follicle Tests **(6 products)** Call to have tests done; we network with collector sites in most areas!
	Instant Saliva Drug Tests **(2 products)** Our Multi-Drug Saliva Tests are on-site, one-step saliva tests that will screen for six drugs of abuse. Accurate results in just 10 minutes!
	Drugs and your Teen Available in paper copy, electronic download and CD
	Alcohol Detection – Swab Test **(DOT and Non-DOT)** Very simple, 1-step, 2 minute test. Our alcohol tests are convenient enough to be used any time, any place. Results - 0.02%, 0.04%, 0.08% and 0.30%
	Nicotine Detection Tests **(2 products)** Our nicotine test is for the detection of residuals of nicotine which remain in the body of habitual tobacco users.
	Dip & Read Drug Tests - By the Case **(36 products)** Buy your Instant On-Site Dip & Read Drug Tests by the case (25/case).
	Home Drug Test Packages **(Multiple product combinations)** Packages of various sizes to meet your home drug testing needs.

Workplace Testing Products

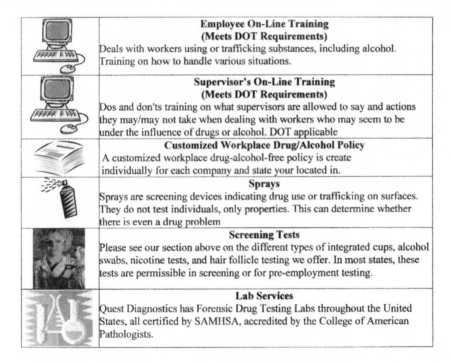

	Employee On-Line Training **(Meets DOT Requirements)** Deals with workers using or trafficking substances, including alcohol. Training on how to handle various situations.
	Supervisor's On-Line Training **(Meets DOT Requirements)** Dos and don'ts training on what supervisors are allowed to say and actions they may/may not take when dealing with workers who may seem to be under the influence of drugs or alcohol. DOT applicable
	Customized Workplace Drug/Alcohol Policy A customized workplace drug-alcohol-free policy is create individually for each company and state your located in.
	Sprays Sprays are screening devices indicating drug use or trafficking on surfaces. They do not test individuals, only properties. This can determine whether there is even a drug problem
	Screening Tests Please see our section above on the different types of integrated cups, alcohol swabs, nicotine tests, and hair follicle testing we offer. In most states, these tests are permissible in screening or for pre-employment testing.
	Lab Services Quest Diagnostics has Forensic Drug Testing Labs throughout the United States, all certified by SAMHSA, accredited by the College of American Pathologists.

For information and pricing, call 888-249-6911
(www.omnidrugscreening.com)

Reader Response Card

Did this book answer your questions?
Comment:

Would you recommend this book to someone else?
Comment:

Were the reference website links useful?
Comment:

Do you have any unanswered questions?
Comment:

If you are a couple owning this book, did both of your read it?
Comment:

As a couple, did you both want to purchase this book?
Comment:

What else should we include in the next edition?
Comment:

Will you keep this book as a reference?
Comment:

Was the book organized to your liking?
Comment:

How would you change the book:

Comment:
Did you share this information with your child?
Comment:
Did this book make you more aware of drug problems?
Comment:
What did you not like about the book?
Comment:
What areas in the book require more clarity or strong/longer explanations?
Comment
Did you feel more comfortable talking to your children after reading this book?
Comment:
Did you share this information with other parent(s)?
Comment

Photocopy or tear out
and
mail to:

Omni Drug Screening
P.O. Box 4405
Salisbury, MD 21803

This book has been made possible through OMNI Drug Screening, LLC, and OMNI Publishing. OMNI Corporation is a joint venture between two drug prevention companies: American Drug Testing Consultants and Drug Test Consultants of PA

To reorder this book; to request duplication, photocopying, or use of quotations; to make suggestions; or to mail your response card, please contact OMNI Corporation accordingly:

OMNI Drug Screening, Inc.
3553 West Chester Pike
PMB 313
Newtown Square, PA 19073
888-249-6911

Endnotes

Bright Futures. Launched by HRSA's Maternal and Child Health Bureau in 1990, the Bright Futures initiative is focused at the American Academy of Pediatrics and is a collaborative of other federally and state-funded Bright Futures projects (click below for select projects). This site has been referred to throughout this book; it is a valuable site. Copyright © 2008, National Center for Education in Maternal and Child Health and Georgetown University. http://www.brightfutures.org/

This is a valuable site with lots of great info: *The Science of Drug Abuse and Addiction.* National Institute on Drug Abuse. The mission of the *National Institute on Drug Abuse (NIDA)* is to lead the nation, bringing the power of science to bear on drug abuse and addiction. http://www.nida.nih.gov

This information came from a White Paper titled: "Submission of the Honorable Rudolph W. Giuliani, Chairman & CEO, Giuliani Partners LLC; Hearing Before The U.S. Senate Permanent Subcommittee on Investigations. *Buyers Beware: The Dangers of Purchasing Pharmaceuticals over the Internet.*" June 17, 2004. Giuliani Partners LLC. Examination and Assessment of Prescription Drug Importation From Foreign Sources to the United States, Interim Findings, May 11, 2004. http://www.pharmamanufacturing.com/Media/MediaManager/061704giuliani2160.pdf

Joseph Califano's information: Califano, Joseph A. Jr., CASA's chairman and president and former U.S. Secretary of Health, Education and Welfare, in Miami to Discuss His New Parenting Book, . Logo: http://www.newscom.com/cgi-bin/prnh/20080814/NYTH004LOGO. Behavioural Health Center. http://behavioralhealthcentral.com/index.php/20100209196273/Patient/Caregiver/joseph-a-califano-jr-casa-chairman-and-president-in-miami-to-discuss-his-new-parenting-book-how-to-raise-a-drug-free-kid-the-straight-dope-for-parents.html

This Web site offers valuable information: *Information Bulletin: Drugs, Youth, and the Internet.* http://www.usdoj.gov/ndic/pubs2/2161/index.htm#Prevalence,%20%20the%20USDOJ

Glossary

We have placed this here so you may familiarize yourself with the terms and meanings used throughout this book. Feel free to bring anything we might have missed to our attention via the response card at the back of this book, or e-mail us at: info@omnidrugscreening.com.

Amphetamines
Amphetamines are central nervous system stimulants with effects similar to those of cocaine. They once were used to fight depression and depress appetite—until adverse side effects were realized. The only medical uses for amphetamines are for the treatment of narcolepsy (sleep disorder) and for children who have hyperactivity disorders. Amphetamines are sold as illegal drugs, as well as in pill form, and on the streets in the form of a white inject-able powder.

Adulterant
Any product or substance added to a drug-test sample to invalidate or change the results.

Barbiturates
A class of drugs used to encourage sleep, eliminate nervousness, and control irritability and tension. They are derived from barbituric acid. Barbiturates produce similar effects to alcohol and are often used with alcohol in order to increase the effect. Personal health risk is greatly increased when barbiturates and alcohol are used together. Pentobarbital (Nembutal) and secobarbital (Seconal) are barbiturates that may also act as sleeping pills.

Buprenorphine
An opiate analgesic with long-lasting qualities, having both opiate agonist and antagonist characteristics. Buprenorphine (Suboxone) is also used to treat opiate addiction.

Benzodiazepines

CNS (central nervous system) depressants, these are minor tranquilizers, prescribed to relieve anxiety and produce sleep. Some examples are diazepam (Valium) and alprazolam (Xanax), which are tranquilizers, and flurazepam (Dalmane) and triazolam (Halcion), which are sleeping pills. This group also includes clonazepam (Klonopin).

Central Nervous System (CNS)

Represents the largest part of the nervous system; includes the brain and the spinal cord. It plays a fundamental role in the control of behavior.

China White

An opiate derivative, sometimes containing a neurotoxin called MPTP, which can kill neurons responsible for making dopamine. This yields symptoms similar to Parkinson's disease. This is a fentanyl analog resembling cocaine. In small amounts, it can be snorted.

Cocaine

A very powerful and addictive stimulant with a direct effect on the brain. It comes as a hydrochloride salt and a "freebase" crack cocaine. The hydrochloride salt can be dissolved in water and taken intravenously or intranasal (injected into a vein or sniffed). The freebase form can be smoked. The typical form of cocaine is a fine white crystalline powder.

Decondition

The unlearning of classically conditioned responses. It is the process of helping drug addicts identify and neutralize the triggers they develop during their addiction. It is similar to detoxification, or detox, which is the process of ridding the body of a specific drug or drugs.

Depressants

Drugs that relieve irritability, tension, and anxiety, they enable sleep to occur. Examples are benzodiazepines, alcohol, methaqualone (Quaaludes), tranquilizers, and chloral hydrate.

Designer Drugs/Club Drugs

Club drugs (including Ecstasy, Rohypnol, Ketamine, GHB, and LSD) are mainly used by young people in raves, dance clubs, and bars. Some of these events run all night. They also have traits of intoxicating highs and increased stamina. Unfortunately, because they are usually tasteless, odorless, and colorless, these drugs can be secretly added to young people's drinks at these events. Examples of designer drugs are DMT, DMA, MDA, MDMA, and DOM.

Dopamine
A chemical produced naturally in the body that functions as a neurotransmitter in the brain and activates dopamine receptors. When released by the brain, it produces feelings of pleasure.

Dronabinol
Synthetic THC, used to counteract nausea caused by certain cancer treatments.

Dynorphins
Opiate-like substances that aid in pain control as well as the regulation of immune response.

Ecstasy (MDMA)
A synthetic psychoactive drug (a stimulant) as well as a psychedelic, it is also neurotoxic. Some withdrawal symptoms are loss of appetite, depression, lack of ability to concentrate, and fatigue. One of the adverse effects of a high dose is an intense increase in body temperature, which can cause muscle breakdown and kidney and/or cardiovascular system failure.

Euphoria
Intense pleasure and/or an extremely elevated mood. This is a drug-induced rush caused by the release of the neurotransmitter dopamine within the brain-reward system.

Halcion
Halcion is a member of the benzodiazepine family. It is a depressant and promotes sleep.

Hallucinogens
Contrary to popular belief, hallucinogens don't cause hallucinations; they alter perception. Some of the drugs considered hallucinogens are MDMA (ecstasy), PCP, LSD, mescaline, and psilocybin (sometimes termed "magic mushrooms" or "shrooms"). They may cause users to see images, hear sounds, and feel sensations that don't exist.

Heroin
An opiate derived from morphine. It can be smoked, injected, or sniffed/snorted. It is extracted from the seedpod of the Asian poppy plant and appears as a white or beige powder or as a black tar. Some of the results of heroin abuse are fatal overdose, spontaneous abortion, collapsed veins, and, particularly in users who inject the drug, contraction of infectious viruses and/or diseases, including HIV and hepatitis.

Inhalants
Any drug administered by breathing its vapors. Includes gases, nitrites, and solvents. The chemical vapors cause psychoactive/mind-altering effects. Inhaling is misuse of legal products, thus is a drug of choice for many young children because of the ease of procurement.

Integrated Test Cup
Instant urine-testing device capable of detecting a number of drugs.

Ketamine
Developed in the 1970s as a medical anesthetic/tranquilizer for humans and animals. It is a CNS depressant, and its use causes a quick dissociative reaction. Some street names are Special K, Vitamin K, K, and Super Acid. It is available in powder, tablet, and liquid form. It can cause extreme physical and mental issues, including amnesia, impaired motor function, delirium, and potentially fatal respiratory problems.

LAAM
Levo-alpha acetylmethadol (LAAM) is one of three existing treatments in the recovery process for those addicted to heroin. The other two are methadone and buprenorphine (Suboxone). LAAM is a synthetic opiate that works by blocking the effects of heroin. Additionally, it works without causing withdrawal symptoms.

Methamphetamine
A powerful and addictive CNS stimulant. It is easy and inexpensive to produce, making it a readily available drug. It works on the brain and spinal cord and interferes with normal neurotransmission. Dopamine is the main neurotransmitter affected by meth. It comes in the form of capsules, pills, powder, and chunks.

PCP

Phencyclidine was first produced as a result in the search for better anesthetics. Deemed unfit for use in anesthetizing humans, because of its psychotropic side effects, it is no longer legally manufactured. It is sometimes called angel dust and is a powerful hallucinogen.

Percodan (oxycodone and aspirin)

A synthetic narcotic pain reliever. It is similar in effects and potency to morphine and heroin.

Percocet (oxycodone and acetaminophen)

A semisynthetic opioid analgesic used to medicate pain.

Psilocybin

Active compounds present in some mushrooms. Psilocybin cause hallucinogenic effects.

Quaaludes

Quaaludes (methaqualone) are prescription drugs used to treat anxiety. They are an anxiolytic and are used to promote sleep. Methaqualone is a CNS (Central Nervous System) depressant, similar to barbiturates. "Ludes" provide a feeling of euphoria.

Rock

A small amount of crack cocaine. It is the solid structure of free-base cocaine.

Rohypnol

Rohypnol (flunitrazepam) has been widely abused as a "date-rape" drug. It can be easily mixed with alcohol and can cause a person to become incapacitated. This could create a situation in which the drugged person could be sexually victimized. It is manufactured primarily in Mexico. It is sometimes used outside of the United States as a short-term treatment for insomnia, but it has the side effect of bringing on amnesia (another condition that makes it possible to be used for sexual abuse). Clonazepam ("roofie") is similar to Rohypnol. It is marketed in the United States as Klonopin and in Mexico as Rivotril.

Seconal

This is a depressant belonging to the barbiturate family, used to promote sleep.

Stimulants
Drugs to increase feelings of general well-being and provide heightened energy and alertness.

Transdermal Absorption
The act of absorbing a drug through the skin via a patch or similar entry method.

Triggers
A reference to how normally stimuli gain the ability to promote the need for the drug of choice. An external stimulus that makes a person feel the need to use by memory association.

Vicodin (Acetaminophen and hydrocodone)
Hydrocodone (a narcotic painkiller) is similar to codeine. The addition of acetaminophen (a less potent pain reliever) increases the effects of hydrocodone.

Xanax (generic name alprazolam)
This is a depressant in the benzodiazepine family. It is used to relieve anxiety.

Index

Symbols

3,4-methylenedioxymethamphetamine 102

A

abstinence 63

abuse xiii, xv, xix, xx, xxiv, 4, 8, 9, 15, 17, 24, 25, 27, 29, 30, 31, 32, 33, 34, 43, 53, 54, 55, 56, 57, 58, 59, 62, 63, 64, 65, 67, 68, 70, 72, 73, 75, 78, 79, 80, 81, 84, 87, 88, 90, 91, 92, 97, 101, 103, 105, 107, 112, 114, 115, 116, 118, 120, 121, 123, 128, 130, 131, 132, 135, 137, 139, 142, 153, 154, 156, 161, 165, 194, 198, 211, 219, 220, 227, 228, 229, 230, 234, 237, 241, 243, 245, 246, 247, 249, 251, 258, 262, 270, 271, 274, 279, 283, 284, 285, 286, 287, 289, 291, 292, 293, 306, 307, 308, 309, 310, 311, 313, 314, 323, 329, 330, 337, 342, 343, 351, 352, 353, 354, 355, 357, 358

Acetylmethadol 342

addiction xix, 3, 5, 12, 19, 20, 24, 29, 30, 33, 54, 57, 58, 60, 61, 62, 67, 68, 69, 70, 73, 80, 84, 88, 92, 97, 98, 101, 105, 106, 108, 113, 117, 118, 119, 130, 131, 135, 151, 154, 218, 219, 229, 230, 240, 245, 246, 247, 248, 249, 252, 253, 254, 256, 257, 258, 285, 286, 289, 292, 293, 309, 337, 339, 340, 351, 354, 355, 358

addicts 19, 21, 32, 54, 55, 67, 80, 91, 97, 106, 117, 118, 146, 229, 230, 234, 243, 246, 247, 248, 340

Alcohol xiii, xix, xx, xxii, xxiii, xxiv, 3, 4, 5, 6, 8, 9, 10, 15, 16, 17, 19, 21, 22, 24, 25, 26, 27, 28, 29, 31, 32, 33, 35, 36, 37, 38, 39, 42, 43, 44, 45, 46, 47, 49, 50, 53, 54, 55, 56, 57, 58, 59, 61, 62, 63, 64, 65, 66, 67, 69, 70, 71, 77, 78, 79, 80, 81, 82, 83, 90, 106, 107, 110, 113, 121, 137, 139, 141, 147, 151, 153, 156, 158, 161, 164, 166, 168, 169, 178, 180, 187, 194, 197, 198, 199, 200, 202, 203, 205, 208, 210, 212, 213, 214, 215, 217, 220, 227, 228, 229, 230, 234, 235, 236, 237, 238, 240, 241, 242, 243, 244, 245, 246, 247, 248, 250, 251, 252, 253, 262, 269, 270, 271, 272, 273, 275, 276, 279, 280, 281, 282, 283, 284, 285, 286, 287, 288, 289, 290, 291, 292, 293, 297, 305, 306, 307, 309, 311, 312, 313, 315, 317, 319, 321, 323, 329, 339, 340, 343, 351, 353, 355

alcoholism 59, 77, 78, 79, 80, 81, 84, 156, 351, 353, 355, 358, 359

Amphetamine 84, 85, 86, 87, 88, 89, 91, 138, 315, 317, 319, 321, 323, 327, 328

Anabolic Steroids 132, 194, 315, 317, 319, 321, 323

antihistamines 113, 130, 131

B

Barbital 297

Barbiturates xxii, 71, 113, 127, 194, 210, 289, 297, 315, 317, 319, 321, 323, 339, 343

Benzodiazepines xxii, 77, 113, 120, 121, 127, 141, 194, 210, 216, 289, 297, 315, 317, 319, 321, 323, 340

Bolasterone Metabolite 133

Boldenone Metabolite 133

Works Cited

About the Institute. The Institute for a Drug-Free Workplace. 2010. http://www. drugfreeworkplace.org/about.html

Alcohol-Related Impairment, Alcohol Alert No. 25, 1994. *National Institute* on *Alcohol* Abuse and *Alcoholism.* New England Journal of Medicine. 1990. http://pubs.niaaa.nih.gov/publications/aa25.htm

America's Mental Health Channel. Addiction Community. http://www.healthyplace.com/Communities/addictions/site/alcohol_substance_abuse. htm; http://www.healthyplace.com/addictions/menu-id-54/

A Parent's Guide to Internet Safety. U.S. Department of Justice. Federal Bureau of Investigations Publications._http://www.fbi.gov/publications/pguide/pguidee.htm

Are You Web Savvy? SAMHSA's "Family Guide To Keeping Youth Mentally Healthy and Drug Free. Know What Your Children Are Doing on the Internet." Referenced December 29, 2006. http://family.samhsa.gov/monitor/internet.aspx

Blakeslee, Sandra. *This Is Your Brain on Meth: A 'Forest Fire' of Damage.* New York Times. July 20, 2004 http://www.loni.ucla.edu/~thompson/MEDIA/METH/nytMETH.htm

Bright Futures. HRSA's Maternal and Child Health Bureau,1990. American Academy of Pediatrics. Copyright © 2008. National Center for Education in Maternal and Child Health and Georgetown University. http://www.brightfutures.org/

Califano, Joseph A. Jr., CASA's chairman and president and former U.S. Secretary of Health, Education, and Welfare (now Health and Human Services). Behavioural Health Center. http://behavioralhealthcentral. com/index.php/20100209196273/Patient/Caregiver/joseph-a-califano-jr-casa-chairman-and-president-in-miami-to-discuss-his-new-parenting-book-how-to-raise-a-drug-free-kid-the-straight-dope-for-parents.html

Chapter 9: Federal Food, Drug, and Cosmetic Act. Title 21*Chapter 9. II / Legal Information Institute, Cornell University Law School. January 5, 2009* http://www.law.cornell.edu/uscode/HowCurrent.php/?tn=21&fr agid=T21F00117&extid=usc_sup_01_21_10_9&sourcedate=2010-07-19&proctime=Tue%20Jul%2020%2007:38:00%202010.

Cockburn, Robert, Paul N. Newton, E. Kyeremateng Agyarko, Dora Akunyili, Nicholas J. White. *The Global Threat of Counterfeit Drugs: Why Industry and Governments Must Communicate the Dangers.* PLoS Medicine. http://www.plosmedicine.org/article/info:doi/10.1371/journal.pmed.0020100

Diagnostic and Statistical Manual of Mental Disorders, Fourth Edition. The American Psychiatric Association. AllPsych Online. http://allpsych.com/disorders/dsm.html

Drugs and the Law. Raising Kids http://www.raisingkids.co.uk/fea/fea113_drugsandthelaw.asp. This Web site has closed and Disney took it over. It is not well organized, but you can find viable info at their site: http://family.go.com/search-familycom/drugs%2520and%2520the%2520law/

Drug Information. Parents—the Anti-Drug. funded in part by the U.S. Department of Health and Human Services Substance Abuse and Mental Health Services Administration Center for Substance Abuse Treatment, the Cardinal Health Foundation, and Endo Pharmaceuticals. http://www.drugstory.org/feature/drug_internet_QR.asp

FDA: Protecting and Promoting Your Health. The U.S. Food and Drug Administration. www.hhs.gov

Ice. Amphetamines and other Psychostimulants. BLTC. Research. http://www.amphetamines.com/ice.html

Information Bulletin: Drugs, Youth, and the Internet. October 2002. Document ID: 2002-L0424-006; Archived: January 1, 2006.

International Classification of Diseases (ICD). WHO (World Health Organization). 2010. http://www.who.int/classifications/icd/en/

Internet Safety: What do I need to know about the Internet and my child? University of Michigan Health System. *Your Child Development and Behavior Resources. A Guide to Information & Support for Parents.* Updated 2007. University of Michigan Health System, Ann Arbor, MI © 2010 Regents of the University of Michigan. http://www.med.umich.edu/yourchild/topics/internet.htm

Jaeger, Paul T., Charles R. McClure. *Potential Legal Challenges to the Application of the Children's Internet Protection Act (CIPA) in Public Libraries,* Strategies & Issues. First Monday. Vol. 9, no. 2, February 2004. Children's Internet Protection Act. Cybertelecom Federal Internet Law & Policy; An Educational Project. http://www.cybertelecom.org/cda/cipa.htm

Kids Health http://www.kidshealth.org/parent/emotions/feelings/kids_stress.html, offers this in their article, "What Kids Say about Handling Stress":

Korenchuk, Keith M. K. *Pharmacy and the Internet: The Challenge and Opportunity of eHealth.* Davis, Wright Tremaine LLP, in the March 2000 article. http://www.dwt.com/

Medical Knowledge that Matters. CMAJ. http://www.cmaj.ca/

Methamphetamine. National Institute on Drug Abuse, InfoFacts: (Rockville, MD. January 9, 2006. US Department of Health and Human Services). http://www.nida.nih.gov/infofacts/methamphetamine.html

Mission Statement. *BLTC Research. http://www.bltc.com*

Modell and Mountz. *Drinking and Flying: The Problem of Alcohol Use by Pilots.* Alcohol-Related Impairment, Alcohol Alert No. 25. the New England Journal of Medicine, 1990. 323(7):455-461, 1990. National Institute on Alcohol Abuse and Alcoholism No. 25 PH 351, July 1994. U.S. Department of Health and Human Services. Public Health Service. National Institutes of Health. Updated October 2000. http://pubs.niaaa.nih.gov/publications/aa25.htm

Modell, J.G., & Mountz, J.M. *Drinking and Flying: The Problem of Alcohol Use by Pilots. New England Journal of Medicine* 323(7):455–461, 1990. pubs.niaaa.nih.gov

Newsroom Best. University of Michigan Health Center. http://www.med.um-ich.edu

NIDA InfoFacts: Treatment Approaches for Drug Addiction. National Institute of Drug Abuse (NIDA). http://www.nida.nih.gov/Infofacts/TreatMeth.html

Nordenberg, Tamar. *The Death of the Party: All the Rave. GHB's Hazards Go Unheeded.* Gold Bamboo. *U.S. Food & Drug Administration* http://www.goldbamboo.com/topic-t1193.html

Parker, Jim. *Crystal Meth; Maximum Speed.* Do It Now Foundation. Catalogue # 101. Nov 2009. http://www.doitnow.org/pages/101.html

Paul T. Jaeger; Charles R. McClure. *First Monday.* Vol. 9, no. 2, February 2004. http://firstmonday.org/issues/issue9_2/jaeger/index.html

Raves worries Edmonton MDs, police. Nouvelles et analyses; 1864 JAMC. June 27, 2000; 162(13). www.cmaj.ca/cgi/reprint/162/13/1864-a.pdf.

Shear, Margaret. *Number of Open FDA Cases.* Chart: Figure 1. The Number of Investigations of Possible Counterfeit Drugs by the FDA Has Been Rising, , Public Library of Science, adapted from [39]). http://www.plosmedicine.org/article/slideshow.action?uri=info:doi/10.1371/journal.pmed.0020100

Stages of Substance Abuse. Amodeo, Mary Ann. Join Together. April 25, 2008. The Partnership for a Drug-Free America. http://www.drugfree.org/Intervention/WhereStart/Stages_of_Substance_Abuse

Stages of Substance Use and Suggested Intervention. Source: Adapted, with permission, from Knight JR, 1997. Adolescent substance use: Screening, assessment, and intervention. *Contemporary Pediatrics* 14(4):45–72: "Info Facts: Treatment for Approaches for Drug Addiction." www.brightfutures.org.

Substance Abuse Facility Locator. SAMHSA. United States Department of Health and Human Services. Substance Abuse and Mental Health Services Administration: "A Life in the Community for Everyone." http://dasis3.samhsa.gov/ and www.findtreatment.samhsa.gov/facilitylocatordoc.htm

Talking to your Child about Drugs. KidsHealth. Nemours Foundation. http://www.kidshealth.org/parent/positive/talk/talk_about_drugs.html, under KidsHealth for Parents.

The Internet Acts as a Megastore where Young People: ... Family Guide http://www.family.samhsa.gov/teach/highonline.aspx

The Science of Drug Abuse and Addiction. National Institute on Drug Abuse. The mission of the *National Institute on Drug Abuse (NIDA)* is to lead the nation, bringing the power of science to bear on drug abuse and addiction. http://www.nida.nih.gov/

Tips for Parents: What To Do and When. Parents: The Anti-Drug http://www.theantidrug.com/ei/advice_parents.asp Call 1-800-662-HELP

Tips for Teens: The Truth About Marijuana. SAMHSA's National Clearinghouse for Alcohol and Drug Information, 2004. Referenced December 29, 2006. SAMHSA Health Information Network. http://ncadi.samhsa.gov/govpubs/phd641/

Title 21, Chapter 9, Federal Food, Drug, and Cosmetic Act. Cornell University Law School. Legal Information Institute. Federal Food, Drug, and Cosmetic Act (21 U.S.C. 301 et seq). http://www.law.cornell.edu/uscode/html/uscode21/usc_sup_01_21_10_9.html

Understanding Addiction. The Partnership for a Drug-Free America. http://www.drugfree.org/Intervention/WhereStart/Understanding_Addiction

Welcome to Child Abuse Prevention Services! National Exchange Club Foundation. http://www.preventchildabuse.com/

Welcome to NetLingo :). NetLingo http://www.netlingo.com/hello/welcome.php

What is Alcoholism? MM (Moderation Management) http://www.moderation.org/faq/alcoholism.shtml

What is SELF-INJURY? Focus Adolescent Services: The Most Comprehensive Information, Resources, Support for Teen and Family Issues on the Internet. http://www.focusas.com/SelfInjury.html. 410-341-4216

You've Got Drugs! Pushers on the Internet Calverton, MD._http://alcoholism.about.com/cs/prescription/a/blcasa040226.htm

Bibliography

We have attempted to include every resource in this book—either cited in the bibliography or referred to in the works cited and endnotes—as a form of documentation. If we missed any, it is entirely a result of oversight, and we beg your forgiveness. Please know that we are grateful to all the Websites and other references we used to help make this book informative.

1   *Tips for Parents. What To Do and When: When you have a suspicion that your teen is experimenting with drugs, what do you do?* www.theantidrug. com/ei/advice_parents.asp

2   *Verbal Abuse Signs and Help. Health Guidance.* Copyright 2010 Healthguidance.org   http://www.healthguidance.org/entry/12798/1/ Verbal-Abuse-Signs-and-Help.html

3   *American Psychiatric Association's Diagnostic and Statistical Manual of Mental Disorders, Fourth Edition* (DSM-IV). Compare to *World Health Organization's International Classification of Diseases,* Tenth Revision, (ICD-10). 1993. http://www.who.int/classifications/icd/en/GRNBOOK. pdf

4   NIDA National Institute on Drug Abuse InfoFacts: Marijuana http://www.nida.nih.gov/infofacts/marijuana.html

5   Ibid

6   NIDA National Institute on Drug Abuse Research Report Series: Marijuana Abuse http://www.nida.nih.gov/ResearchReports/Marijuana/default.html

7   NIDA National Institute on Drug Abuse InfoFacts: Marijuana http://www.nida.nih.gov/infofacts/marijuana.html

8   NIDA National Institute on Drug Abuse Research Report Series: Marijuana Abuse   http://www.nida.nih.gov/ResearchReports/Marijuana/default.html

9   Ibid

10 Ibid

11 Ibid

12 Ibid

13 ProCon.org. "14 Legal Marijuana States and DC" MedicalMarijuana. ProCon.org.   http://medicalmarijuana.procon.org/view.resource.php?resourceID=000881

14 NIDA National Institute of Drug Abuse Research Report Series Marijuana Abuse http://www.drugabuse.gov'ResearchReports/marijuana/marijuana5.html

15 CBS Evening News. States Consider Banning "K2" Imitation Pot http://www.cbsnews.com/stories/2010/02/18/national/main6219210.shtml

16 CBS Evening News. Synthetic Marijuana Gives Users Legal high http://www.cbsnews.com/stories/2010/07.10/eveningnews/main6666078.shtml

17 Drugs Online at Family Guide: The Internet acts as a megastore where young people: ... http://family.samhsa.gov/teach/highonline.aspx

18 Report: CASA (the national Center on Addiction and Substance Abuse at Columbia University). http://www.casacolumbia.org/templates/publications_reports.aspx

19 Beau Dietl & Associates. CASA White Paper Outlines Threat to Children. http://alcoholism.about.com/cs/prescription/a/blcasa040226.htm

20 Prevalence of Drug-Related Information on the Internet.http://www.usdoj.gov/ndic/pubs2/2161/index.htm#Prevalence; http://www.justice.gov/ndic/pubs2/2161/index.htm

21 Guiliani, Rudolph W. *Dangers of Purchasing Pharmaceuticals over the Internet.*. June 17, 2004. U.S. Senate Permanent Subcommittee on Investigation hearing. http://www.pharmamanufacturing.com/Media/MediaManager/061704giuliani2160.pdf

22 Shear, Margaret. *Number of Open FDA Cases.* Chart: Figure 1. *The Number of Investigations of Possible Counterfeit Drugs by the FDA Has Been Rising.* Public Library of Science, adapted from [39]). http://www.plosmedicine.org/article/slideshow.action?uri=info:doi/10.1371/journal.pmed.0020100

23 *Internet Safety: What do I need to know about the Internet and my child?* University of Michigan Health System. *Your Child Development and Behavior Resources. A Guide to Information & Support for Parents.* Updated 2007. University of Michigan Health System, Ann Arbor, MI © 2010 Regents of the University of Michigan.

24 Drugs Online *at Family Guide: The Internet acts as a megastore where young people:* ... http://family.samhsa.gov/teach/highonline.aspx

25 *Information Bulletin: Drugs, Youth, and the Internet.* Beau Dietl, chairman of Beau Dietl & Associates, October 2002; Document ID: 2002-L0424-006; Archived on January 1, 2006. http://alcoholism.about.com/cs/prescription/a/blcasa040226.htm

26 Ibid